THE
FUTURE
OF MANAGEMENT

THE
FUTURE
OF MANAGEMENT

GARY HAMEL

WITH BILL BREEN

HARVARD BUSINESS SCHOOL PRESS

Boston, Massachusetts

Copyright 2007 Gary Hamel
All rights reserved
Printed in the United States of America
11 10 09 08 07 5 4 3 2 1

Library of Congress Cataloging-in-Publication Data
Hamel, Gary.
  The future of management / Gary Hamel.
    p. cm.
  ISBN-13: 978-1-4221-0250-3 (hardcover : alk. paper)
  ISBN-10: 1-4221-0250-5
  1. Management. 2. Technological innovations—Management.
3. Knowledge mangement. I. Title.
  HD31.H25 2007
  658—dc22

                                            2007017286

The paper used in this publication meets the requirements of the American National Standard for Permanence of Paper for Publications and Documents in Libraries and Archives Z39.48-1992.

This book is

dedicated with gratitude to

Eldona Hamel,

Vern Terpstra,

and

John Stopford,

for reasons they know well.

Contents

Preface

On Christmas eve, 1968, the *Apollo 8* command module became the first human-made object to orbit the moon. During its journey back to earth, a ground controller's son asked his dad, "Who's flying the spacecraft?" When the question was relayed up to the homebound crew, astronaut Bill Anders replied, "I think Sir Isaac Newton is doing most of the driving now."

Like that curious lad, I'd like to pose a question: Who's managing your company? You might be tempted to answer, "the CEO," or "the executive team," or "all of us in middle management." And you'd be right, but that wouldn't be the whole truth. To a large extent, your company is being managed right now by a small coterie of long-departed theorists and practitioners who invented the rules and conventions of "modern" management back in the early years of the 20th century. They are the poltergeists who inhabit the musty machinery of management. It is their edicts, echoing across the decades, that invisibly shape the way your company allocates resources, sets budgets, distributes power, rewards people, and makes decisions.

So pervasive is the influence of these patriarchs that the technology of management varies only slightly from firm to firm. Most companies have a roughly similar management hierarchy (a cascade of EVPs, SVPs, and VPs). They have analogous control systems, HR practices, and planning rituals, and rely on comparable reporting structures and review systems. That's why it's so easy for a CEO to jump from one company to another—the levers and dials of management are more or less the same in every corporate cockpit.

Yet unlike the laws of physics, the laws of management are neither foreordained nor eternal—and a good thing, too, for the equipment of management is now groaning under the strain of a load it was never meant to carry. Whiplash change, fleeting advantages, technological disruptions, seditious competitors, fractured markets, omnipotent customers, rebellious shareholders—these 21st-century challenges are testing the design limits of organizations around the world and are exposing the limitations of a management model that has failed to keep pace with the times.

Think about the great product breakthroughs over the last decade or two that have changed the way we live: the personal computer, the mobile phone, digital music, e-mail, and online communities. Now try to think of a breakthrough in the practice of management that has had a similar impact in the realm of business—anything that has dramatically changed the way large companies are run. Not easy, is it? And therein lies the problem.

Management is out of date. Like the combustion engine, it's a technology that has largely stopped evolving, and that's not good. Why? Because management—the capacity to marshal resources, lay out plans, program work, and spur effort—is central to the accomplishment of human purpose. When it's less effective than it could be, or needs to be, we all pay a price.

What ultimately constrains the performance of your organization is not its operating model, nor its business model, but its management model. Hence this book. My goal is to help you become a 21st-century management pioneer; to equip you to reinvent the principles, processes, and practices of management for our postmodern age. I will argue that *management innovation* has a unique capacity to create a long-term advantage for your company, and I will outline the steps you must take to first imagine, and then invent, *the future of management.*

Having said a few words about what this book is about, let me comment briefly on what it's *not* about. While there are plenty of examples and anecdotes in the pages that follow, this is not a compendium of best practices. It's not filled with exhortations to "go thou and do likewise." Frankly, today's best practices aren't good enough. Even the world's "most admired" companies aren't as adaptable as they need to be, as innovative as they could be, or as much fun to work in as they should be. My assumption is that when it comes to the future of management, you'd rather lead than follow. So this is a guide to inventing *tomorrow's* best practices today.

Neither is this book one person's vision for the future of management. While I will point you to what I believe are some of the most promising opportunities for reinventing management, I'm humble enough to know that one person's imagination and foresight are no substitute for those of a multitude. So rather than try to sell you *my* point of view about the future, I want to help you build your own. If you want an analogy, imagine a course in entrepreneurship where the instructor's goal is to teach you how to create a killer business plan. Well, my goal is to give you the thinking tools that will allow you to build your *own* agenda for management innovation, and then execute against it. I can be a coach and a mentor, but in the end, the vision must be yours.

Nevertheless, I do have a dream. I dream of organizations that are capable of spontaneous renewal, where the drama of change is unaccompanied by the wrenching trauma of a turnaround. I dream of businesses where an electric current of innovation pulses through every activity, where the renegades always trump the reactionaries. I dream of companies that actually deserve the passion and creativity of the folks who work there, and naturally elicit the very best that people have to give. Of course, these are more than dreams; they are imperatives. They are do-or-die challenges for any company that hopes to thrive in the tumultuous times ahead—and they can be surmounted only with inspired management innovation.

So this is a book for dreamers *and* doers. It's for everyone who feels hog-tied by bureaucracy, who worries that the "system" is stifling innovation, who secretly believes that the bottleneck is at the top of the bottle, who wonders why corporate life has to be so dispiriting, who thinks that employees really are smart enough to manage themselves, who knows that "management," as currently practiced, is a drag on success—*and wants to do something about it.* If that's you, then welcome.

Acknowledgments

This book reflects the ideas and contributions of many individuals. In particular, I am indebted to my writing partner, Bill Breen, who helped bring to life the stories of management innovation that are sprinkled throughout this volume. Bill's devotion to this task was aided and abetted by the willingness of his colleagues at *Fast Company* to fill in for him during his long absence, and by the unflagging support of his wife, Lise.

I also owe a substantial debt to Liisa Välikangas, who worked with me in beta-testing the methodology for management innovation that is outlined in this book. Likewise, the groundbreaking research of Julian Birkinshaw and Michael Mol on the history of management innovation enriched my thinking in many ways.

A heartfelt thank you is also due Professor Roy Jacques, whose book *Manufacturing the Employee* helped me to better understand how our management orthodoxies came to be, and how they might be overturned. I also drew heavily on the thinking of Stuart Kauffmann, Francis Fukuyama, Richard Florida, and Huston Smith. I am grateful that these individuals were willing to help me translate a bit of their thinking into the world of management.

While the ideas found in this book have been field-tested with many organizations around the world, I owe a special thanks to Brad Anderson, Shari Ballard, Denise La Mere, and Kal Patel of Best Buy. By providing my colleagues and me with a real-world laboratory in which to test some of our more radical ideas, they helped us to better understand the power and the limits of management innovation.

In many places, this book reflects the goodwill of executives who were willing to talk to Bill and me about their unconventional management practices. In this regard, I wish to acknowledge the contributions of the following companies and individuals . . .

At Google: Shona Brown, Marissa Mayer, Eric Schmidt, and Elliott Schrage. At W.L. Gore and Associates: Rich Buckingham, Heidi Cofran, Sonia Dunbar, Donna Frey, Brad Jones, Terri Kelly, Jack Kramer, Tom Moore, Joseph Rowan, Ed Schneider, Matthew Schreiner, Betty Snyder, and Steve Young. At IBM: Rod Adkins, Jeff Benck, Letina Connelly, Mike Giersch, Jan Jackman, Dan McGrath, and Gerry Mooney. At Best Buy: Jeff Severts. At Rite-Solutions: Jim Lavoie.

My long-time colleague Grace Reim spent the better part of a year running interference for me as I researched and wrote this book. More importantly, she project managed the entire process and was, at every juncture, wise, efficient, and unflappable.

Finally, I am grateful to David Goehring and Hollis Heimbouch of the Harvard Business School Press for giving me the chance to work with their magnificent staff. Nowhere else can one find a team of people so dedicated to, and so capable of, bringing new business ideas to life. Jeff Kehoe, my editor, contributed greatly to the quality of the book you now hold in your hands. His enthusiasm, incisive criticism, and numerous suggestions were in every way a boon to my labors. Others who deserve tribute include Stephani Finks, Marcy Barnes-Henrie, and Dino Malvone, as well as the entire Press marketing and publicity team.

If this book has any merit, the credit goes to those mentioned above. Its shortcomings, of course, can be laid at my doorstep.

—Gary Hamel
September 2007

WHY
MANAGEMENT
INNOVATION
MATTERS

PART ONE

One

The End of Management?

WHAT DOES THE FUTURE OF MANAGEMENT LOOK LIKE to you? Cast your mind forward a decade or two and ask yourself: How will tomorrow's most successful companies be organized and managed? What new and unorthodox management practices will distinguish the vanguard from the old guard? What will managers in bellwether organizations be doing, or *not* doing, that would surprise today's business leaders? What will be different about the way companies manage talent, allocate resources, develop strategy, and measure performance?

In other words, can you imagine dramatic changes in the way human effort is mobilized and organized in the years to come? Can you envision radical and far-reaching changes in the way managers manage? Don't be dismayed if the answer is "no." Given how little the practice of management has changed over the past several decades, it's hardly surprising that most people have a hard time imagining how management might be reinvented in the decades to come.

Management—
A Maturing Technology

When compared with the momentous changes we've witnessed over the past half century in technology, lifestyles, and geopolitics, the practice of management seems to have evolved at a snail's pace. While a suddenly resurrected 1960s-era CEO would undoubtedly be amazed by the flexibility of today's real-time supply chains, and the ability to provide 24/7 customer service, he or she would find a great many of today's management rituals little changed from those that governed corporate life a generation or two ago. Hierarchies may have gotten flatter, but they haven't disappeared. Frontline employees may be smarter and better trained, but they're still expected to line up obediently behind executive decisions. Lower-level managers are still appointed by more senior managers. Strategy still gets set at the top. And the big calls are still made by people with big titles and even bigger salaries. There may be fewer middle managers on the payroll, but those that remain are doing what managers have always done—setting budgets, assigning tasks, reviewing performance, and cajoling their subordinates to do better.

Why does management seem stuck in a time warp? Perhaps it's because we've reached the *end* of management—in the sense that Francis Fukuyama argues we've reached the end of history. If liberal democracy is the final answer to humankind's long quest for political self-determination, maybe modern management, as it has evolved over the last century, is the final answer to the age-old question of how to most effectively aggregate human effort. Perhaps we have more or less mastered the science of organizing human beings, allocating resources, defining objectives, laying out plans, and minimizing deviations from best practice. Maybe most of the really tough management problems have already been solved.

Or maybe not. What if modern management *hasn't* reached the apogee of effectiveness and, given the challenges that lie ahead, isn't even climbing the right hill? Stuart Kauffman, the gifted biologist and Santa Fe Institute alumnus, uses the notion of a "fitness landscape" to describe the limits of evolutionary progress.[1] In Kauffman's allegorical mountain range, higher peaks represent higher levels of evolutionary accomplishment. As a species adapts and changes, it climbs ever higher in the fitness landscape. In the beginning, starting from a deep valley, every trail leads upward. But as a species evolves, the percentage of terrain that lies above it steadily dwindles. Over time, there are fewer and fewer routes that lead upward, and ever more that lead downward. As a result, the pace of evolution slows. In an expansive fitness landscape, that is, one with many possible pathways, it is unlikely that a particular species will ever scale the evolutionary equivalent of K2 or Kangchenjunga. Instead, its meandering journey will probably end on the summit of a local peak—a crag that is, by comparison, a mere shadow of the mountains that loom over the horizon.

I believe this may well be the plight of modern-day management. Having evolved rapidly in the first half of the 20th century, the "technology" of management has now reached a local peak. Rather than being perched atop some Everest of accomplishment, it is reclining contentedly on a modest mound in the Appalachians—Mount Love, let's say. While it's possible to see higher peaks from Mt. Love's near-2,000-meter summit, none of them are the 8,000-meter monsters of the Himalayas.

This is not to sell the achievements of management short. If you have two cars in the garage, a television in every room, and a digital device in every pocket, it is thanks to the inventors of modern management. For while institutional innovations such as the joint stock company and patent law paved the way for modern economic progress, and while technology breakthroughs—from the telephone to the microprocessor—provided much of the fuel, it was the invention of industrial management at the dawn of the 20th century that turned enlightened policy and scientific discovery into global prosperity.

Indeed, one could argue that the machinery of modern management—which encompasses variance analysis, capital budgeting, project management, pay-for-performance, strategic planning, and the like—amounts to one of humanity's greatest inventions—right up there with fire, written language, and democracy. Consider the vacation-bound college student who spends less on an airline ticket to Fort Lauderdale than he'll spend on booze over spring break; the twitchy-thumbed gamer who shells out a few hundred bucks for a PC and expects to get a machine that will outperform yesterday's supercomputers; the dedicated foodie who is unimpressed by the fact that her upscale supermarket offers more than twenty varieties of Balsamic vinegar; or the Chinese factory worker who will soon be able to afford his first motorbike—all these souls, and a couple billion more, should prostrate themselves in front of shrines to Daniel McCallum, Frederick Winslow Taylor, Max Weber, Chester Barnard, W. Edwards Deming, Peter Drucker, and all the other apostles and prophets of modern management.

Yet over time, every great invention, management included, travels a road that leads from birth to maturity, and occasionally to senescence. This is the familiar S-curve, and its dynamics mirror those of Kauffman's evolutionary hike. New inventions, like Gottlieb Daimler's gas-powered buggy, which debuted in 1886, typically get off to a slow start. At the beginning, there are dozens of technical challenges that bedevil inventors and curtail progress. As these initial hurdles are surmounted, the pace of improvement accelerates. Knowledge compounds, and soon whole clusters of innovation are redefining what's possible. Inevitably, though, the law of diminishing returns kicks in and at some point the ratio of progress to effort starts to sag. As physical limits are reached, major advances become harder to achieve.

Alas, management's boisterous, inventive adolescence lies nearly a century behind us. In fact, most of the essential tools and techniques of modern management were invented by individuals born in the 19th century, not long after the end of the American Civil War. Those intrepid pioneers developed standardized job descriptions and work methods. They invented protocols for production planning and scheduling. They mastered the intricacies of cost accounting and profit analysis. They instituted exception-based reporting and developed detailed financial controls. They devised incentive-based compensation schemes and set up personnel departments. They created sophisticated tools for capital budgeting and, by 1930, had also designed the basic architecture of the multidivisional organization and enumerated the principles of brand management.

Now think back over the last 20 or 30 years of management history. Can you identify a dozen innovations on the scale of those that laid the foundations of modern management? I can't. Like the gasoline engine, our industrial-age management model is languishing out at the far end of the S-curve, and may be reaching the limits of its improvability.

Of course, this begs the question of whether we actually *need* a new management model, and if so, whether there's one out there waiting to be found. Perhaps we should be celebrating the end of management. Maybe after decades of striving, there are no more towering peaks to climb and no new S-curves to be discovered.

Yet before we break out the champagne, we should ask ourselves whether we're truly satisfied with the status quo. Are our workaday lives so fulfilling, and our organizations so boundlessly capable, that it's now pointless to long for something better? I don't think so. Again, consider democracy. Although it may be, as Winston Churchill famously put it, the worst form of government except for all the others, it contains within its essence contradictions that have yet to be satisfactorily resolved. First among these is the challenge of protecting the rights of minorities while honoring the will of the majority. From America's shameful treatment of its native tribes to current debates over the rights of undocumented workers; from Europe's recurring bouts of anti-Semitism to its recent struggles to integrate a fast-growing Muslim minority; the challenge of protecting the politically disenfranchised is a problem that has long tormented democratic societies around the world. And there are new challenges. How, for example, can democratic societies protect themselves from the threat of terrorism without trampling upon civil liberties? How can they loosen the chains of special-interest gridlock in order to head off the risks of global climate change? Given these and other similarly vexing challenges, we must dare to hope that the practice of democracy will continue to evolve.

If democracy still has mountains to climb, some two-and-a-half thousand years after its birth in ancient Greece, it would be arrogant to assume that after a mere century of progress, modern management has exhausted its own evolutionary potential—just as it would be foolish to assume that a technology that served us so admirably during the 20th century will turn out to be equally well-suited to the demands of the 21st. The fact is, that despite its indisputable accomplishments to date, modern management has bequeathed to us a set of perplexing conundrums, troubling trade-offs that cry out for bold thinking and fresh approaches. And when we look forward, we are confronted by a slew of new problems—predicaments and dilemmas that lay bare the limits of our well-worn management systems and processes.

Transcending Old Trade-offs

Over the course of its development, modern management has wrestled a lot of burly problems to the ground—it has succeeded in breaking complex tasks into small, repeatable steps, in enforcing adherence to standard operating procedures, in measuring costs and profits to the penny, in coordinating the efforts of tens of thousands of employees, and in synchronizing operations on a global scale. Yet these successes have come at a heavy price. The machinery of modern management gets fractious, opinionated, and free-spirited human beings to conform to standards and rules, but in so doing it squanders prodigious quantities of human imagination and initiative. It brings discipline to operations, but imperils organizational adaptability. It multiplies the purchasing power of consumers the world over, but also enslaves millions in quasi-feudal, top-down organizations. And while modern management has helped to make businesses dramatically more efficient, there's little evidence that it has made them more ethical.

Modern management has given much, but it has taken much in return, and it continues to take. Perhaps it's time to renegotiate the bargain. We must learn how to coordinate the efforts of thousands of individuals without creating a burdensome hierarchy of overseers; to keep a tight rein on costs without strangling human imagination; and to build organizations where discipline and freedom aren't mutually exclusive. In this new century, we must strive to transcend the seemingly unavoidable trade-offs that have been the unhappy legacy of modern management.

Surmounting New Challenges

While the practice of management may not be evolving as fast as it once did, the environment that faces 21st-century businesses is more volatile than ever. This new century may still be young, but it has already spawned a sizable brood of daunting management challenges that are markedly different from the ones that taxed our forebears:

- As the pace of change accelerates, more and more companies are finding themselves on the wrong side of the change curve. Recent research by L. G. Thomas and Richard D'Aveni[2] suggests that industry leadership is changing hands more frequently, and competitive advantage is eroding more rapidly, than ever before. Today, it's not just the occasional company that gets caught out by the future, but entire industries—be it traditional airlines, old-line department stores, network television broadcasters, the big drug companies, America's carmakers, or the newspaper and music industries.

- Deregulation, along with the de-scaling effects of new technology, are dramatically reducing the barriers to entry across a wide range of industries, from publishing to telecommunications to banking to airlines. As a result, long-standing oligopolies are fracturing and competitive "anarchy" is on the rise.

- Increasingly, companies are finding themselves enmeshed in "value webs" and "ecosystems" over which they have only partial control. As a result, competitive outcomes are becoming less the product of market power, and more the product of artful negotiation. De-verticalization, disintermediation, and outsourcing, along with the growth of codevelopment projects and industry consortia, are leaving firms with less and less control over their own destinies.

- The digitization of anything not nailed down threatens companies that make their living out of creating and selling intellectual property. Drug companies, film studios, publishers, and fashion designers are all struggling to adapt to a world where information and ideas "want to be free."

- The Internet is rapidly shifting bargaining power from producers to consumers. In the past, customer "loyalty" was often an artifact of high search costs and limited information, and companies frequently profited from customer ignorance. Today, customers are in control as never before—and in a world of near-perfect information, there is less and less room for mediocre products and services.

- Strategy life cycles are shrinking. Thanks to plentiful capital, the power of outsourcing, and the global reach of the Web, it's possible to ramp up a new business faster than ever before. But the more rapidly a business grows, the sooner it fulfills the promise of its original business model, peaks, and enters its dotage. Today, the parabola of success is often a short, sharp spike.

- Plummeting communication costs and globalization are opening up industries to a horde of new, ultra-low-cost competitors. These new entrants are eager to exploit the legacy costs of the old guard. While some veterans will join the "race to the bottom" and move their core activities to the world's lowest-cost locations, many others will find it difficult to reconfigure their global operations. As Indian companies suck in service jobs and China steadily expands its share of global manufacturing, companies everywhere else will struggle to maintain their margins.

These new realities call for new organizational and managerial capabilities. To thrive in an increasingly disruptive world, companies must become as strategically adaptable as they are operationally efficient. To safeguard their margins, they must become gushers of rule-breaking innovation. And if they're going to out-invent and outthink a growing mob of upstarts, they must learn how to inspire their employees to give the very best of themselves every day. These are the challenges that must be addressed by 21st-century management innovators.

Limited by Our DNA

If you've spent any time inside large organizations, you know that expecting them to be strategically nimble, restlessly innovative, or highly engaging places to work—or anything else than merely efficient—is like expecting a dog to do the tango. Dogs are quadrupeds. Dancing isn't in their DNA. So it is with corporations. Their managerial DNA makes some things easy and others virtually impossible. Reengineering, cost-cutting, continuous improvement, outsourcing, and offshoring: these things are entirely consistent with the genetic proclivities of large companies. They're all about better, faster, quicker, and cheaper—the corporate equivalent of dogs chasing cats and peeing on lampposts. Unfortunately, though, resolving some of modern management's more odious trade-offs, and coping with tomorrow's disorienting discontinuities, is going to require something more akin to gene replacement therapy. Let me explain.

Modern management isn't just a suite of useful tools and techniques; it is a *paradigm*, to borrow a sound bite from Thomas Kuhn's overused argot. A paradigm is more than a way of thinking—it's a worldview, a broadly and deeply held belief about what types of problems are worth solving, or are even solvable. Listen to Kuhn on this point: "[A] paradigm is a criterion for choosing problems that . . . can be assumed to have solutions. To a great extent these are the only problems that the community will . . . encourage its members to undertake. Other problems . . . are rejected as metaphysical . . . or sometimes as just too problematic to be worth the time. A paradigm can, for that matter, even insulate the community from those socially important problems that are not reducible to the [familiar] puzzle form because they cannot be stated in terms of the conceptual and instrumental tools which the paradigm provides."[3]

We are all prisoners of our paradigms. And as *managers*, we are captives of a paradigm that places the pursuit of efficiency ahead of every other goal. This is hardly surprising, since modern management was invented to solve the problem of *in*efficiency. A bit of history will help to underline the significance of this point.

While it's impossible to precisely date the genesis of modern management, most historians locate Frederick Winslow Taylor near the beginning of the epic, and regard him as the most influential management innovator of the 20th century. Taylor believed that an empirical, data-driven approach to the design of work would yield big productivity gains. As the father of "scientific management," Taylor battled against wasted motion, poorly designed tasks, lax or unrealistic performance standards, misfits between job requirements and worker capabilities, and incentive systems that discouraged best efforts—adversaries that any 21st-century manager would instantly recognize.

Taylor maintained that efficiency came from "knowing exactly what you want men to do, and then seeing that they do it in the best and cheapest way."[4] He believed that management could be made a "true science, resting upon clearly defined laws, rules and principles as a foundation."[5] For Taylor, as for every economy-minded CEO and efficiency-peddling consultant since, the secret to increased productivity lay in "systematic management."[6] Indeed, one can imagine Taylor looking down from his well-ordered heaven and smiling fondly at the Six Sigma acolytes who continue to spread his gospel. (His only surprise might be that 21st-century managers are still obsessing over the same problems that occupied his inventive mind a hundred years earlier.)

Taylor's contribution to economic progress, and that of management more generally, is evidenced by more than a hundred years of ever-increasing factory productivity. Between 1890 and 1958, for example, U.S. manufacturing output per labor hour grew nearly fivefold; and has continued to rise ever since. Concomitant with this rise in productivity, though, came an increase in bureaucratization. How else could one accomplish Taylor's goal of mechanizing labor but by building up a bureaucracy, with its standardized routines, tightly drawn job descriptions, cascading objectives, and hierarchical reporting structures?

Max Weber, the renowned German sociologist and a contemporary of Taylor, viewed bureaucracy as the pinnacle of social organization: "Experience tends universally to show that the purely bureaucratic type of administrative organization . . . is, from a purely technical point of view, capable of attaining the highest degree of efficiency and is in this sense formally the most rational known means of carrying out imperative control over human beings. It is superior to any other form in precision, in stability, in the stringency of its discipline, and in its reliability. It thus makes possible a particularly high degree of calculability of results for the heads of the organization and for those acting in relation to it."[7]

Weber's ideal organization had several distinguishing features:

- The division of labor and responsibilities were clearly delineated for every member of the organization.

- Positions were organized into a hierarchy resulting in a scale of authority.

- Members were selected for positions based on their technical competence or education.

- Managers worked for the owners of the enterprise, but were not the primary owners themselves.

- Everyone in the organization was subject to strict rules and controls relevant to their particular job. The rules were impersonal and uniformly applied.[8]

There is little here that would surprise a 21st-century manager. And though Max Weber has been dead for nearly 90 years, control, precision, stability, discipline, and reliability—the traits he saluted in his anthem to bureaucracy—are still the canonical virtues of modern management. While we may deplore "bureaucracy," it still constitutes the organizing principle for virtually every commercial and public-sector organization in the world, yours included. And while progressive managers may work hard to ameliorate its stultifying effects, there are few who can imagine a root-and-branch alternative.

So here we are: still working on Taylor-type puzzles and living in Weber-type organizations. To be fair, many of the 21st century's new management challenges have been acknowledged in boardrooms and executive suites, and here and there one finds a truly serious attempt at management innovation (some of which will be described in the chapters that follow). Yet our progress to date has been constrained by our efficiency-centric, bureaucracy-based managerial paradigm. Most of us are still thinking like dogs.

The Revolutionary Imperative

So we improvise and we patch and we retrofit. We create innovation projects and units, instead of organizations that are innovative from top to bottom. We call our employees "associates" and "team members," but don't dramatically enlarge the scope of their discretionary authority. We encourage people to welcome change but resist embracing the principles of grassroots activism. We talk about a meritocracy, but balk at the notion of a 360-degree compensation process.

Truth is, most of us are partisans of the old paradigm. We're members of the *bureaucratic class*. As executives, managers, and supervisors, we've learned how to use the technology of management—the planning conferences, the budget meetings, and the performance measurement systems—to get things done. More importantly, we've learned how to leverage our positional prerogatives, our access to power and our polished professionalism, to get ahead. Talk about revolution—particularly *management* revolution—makes us jittery. Who, one wonders, will come out on top if the rules and roles of management get turned upside down?

Yet despite our reservations, we know that Kuhn's central thesis is incontestable: real progress demands a revolution. You can't shuffle your way onto the next S-curve. You have to leap. You have to vault over your preconceived notions, over everyone else's best practices, over the advice of all the experts, and over your own doubts. As we'll see, you don't have to leap with hundreds of millions of dollars on the line, or with your career dangling precariously out of your pocket. You don't have to leap with no sense of where you're going to land. But you do have to leap—at least with your imagination.

Taylor understood that management breakthroughs require intellectual long jumps. In 1912, 50 years before Kuhn's landmark volume, Taylor appeared in front of a congressional committee and argued that scientific management required nothing less than a mental revolution:

> Now, in its essence, scientific management involves a complete mental revolution on the part of the workingman engaged in any particular establishment or industry—a complete mental revolution on the part of these men as to their duties toward their work, toward their fellow men, and toward their employers. And

it involves the equally complete mental revolution on the part of
those on the management's side—the foreman, the superinten-
dent, the owner of the business, the board of directors—a complete mental revolution on their part as to the duties toward
their fellow workers in the management, toward their workmen,
and toward all of their daily problems. And without this complete mental revolution on both sides scientific management
does not exist.[9]

Like other heralds of the future, Taylor may have gone a bit over-
board with his revolutionary rhetoric, but few of his contemporaries
would have challenged his assertion that scientific management repre-
sented a startling break with precedent.

Consider: in 1890 the average company in the United States had
four employees, and few had more than a couple of hundred workers.
Had you been alive at the time, it would have been hard to imagine
that a company could ever grow to the scale of U.S. Steel, which, after
its acquisition of Carnegie Steel in 1901, became the world's first company with a billion-dollar market value. It would have been nearly impossible to believe that a business founded in 1903—the Ford Motor
Company—would be turning out more than half a million cars per year
a decade later. And it would have been equally hard to foresee all of the
underlying management breakthroughs that would come together to
make all this possible.

Could the practice of management change as radically over the first
two or three decades of *this* century as it did during the early years of
the 20th century? I believe so. More than that, I believe we must *make*
it so. The challenges facing 21st-century business leaders are at least as
intimidating, exciting, and unprecedented as those that confronted the
world's industrial pioneers a hundred years ago. Sure, we're bound by
precedent, and most of us have a vested interest in the management
status quo. But if human beings could invent the modern industrial organization, then they can reinvent it.

Admittedly, there's not much in the average MBA curriculum, management best seller, or leadership development program that would suggest there are radical alternatives to the way we lead, plan, organize, motivate, and manage right now. But true innovators are never bound by what is; instead they dream of what could be. Hence the goal of this book: to help you and your colleagues first imagine, and then invent, the future of management.

Two

The Ultimate Advantage

HY SHOULD YOU AND YOUR COLLEAGUES TAKE ON THE challenge of reinventing management? Because, to put it bluntly, management innovation pays. When compared with other sorts of innovation, it has an unmatched power to create dramatic and enduring shifts in competitive advantage. Before we review the evidence for this claim, let's get our definitions straight. What exactly *is* management innovation? And how is it different from other sorts of innovation?

Management Innovation Defined

For our purposes, management innovation is anything that *substantially alters the way in which the work of management is carried out, or significantly modifies customary organizational forms, and, by so doing, advances organizational goals.* Put simply, management innovation changes the way managers do what they do, and does so in a way that enhances organizational performance.

19

So what is it that managers do? Over the last hundred years, business scholars have pretty much agreed on what constitutes the *work of management*. In 1917, Henri Fayol, an early management theorist, described the work of management as planning, organizing, commanding, coordinating, and controlling[1]—a definition that would provoke little argument from modern-day executives. My own synthesis of a century's worth of management theory suggests that the *practice* of management entails:

- Setting and programming *objective*

- Motivating and aligning *effort*

- Coordinating and controlling *activities*

- Developing and assigning *talent*

- Accumulating and applying *knowledge*

- Amassing and allocating *resources*

- Building and nurturing *relationships*

- Balancing and meeting *stakeholder demands*

These tasks are central to the accomplishment of human purpose, be it mounting a mission to Mars, running a middle school, producing a Hollywood blockbuster, or organizing a church bake sale. Anything that dramatically changes how this work gets done can be labeled as management innovation.

Management innovation also encompasses value-creating changes to organizational structures and roles. Companies consist of business units, departments, work groups, communities of practice, and alliances with suppliers, partners, and lead customers. A new way of connecting these entities can constitute a management innovation. For example, InnoCentive, a spin-off from Eli Lilly and Company, has created a global market for scientific expertise that allows "seeker" companies to bid out tough technical challenges to a network of more than 70,000 scientists around the world. In the three years following its launch,

InnoCentive channeled more than $1 million in "bounty" payments to its community of "solvers," who often succeeded in cracking problems that had stumped internal R&D teams. While the goal of InnoCentive is scientific innovation, the processes and structures that support its global network of seekers and solvers is a first-rate example of management innovation, in that it involves new ways of aligning effort, coordinating activities, and applying knowledge—all components of managerial work.

While operational innovation focuses on a company's *business* processes (procurement, manufacturing, marketing, order fulfillment, customer service, etc.), management innovation targets a company's *management* processes—the recipes and routines that determine how the work of management gets carried out on a day-to-day basis. Typical processes include:

- Strategic planning

- Capital budgeting

- Project management

- Hiring and promotion

- Training and development

- Internal communications

- Knowledge management

- Periodic business reviews

- Employee assessment and compensation

These processes establish standard protocols for common management tasks such as evaluating an employee or reviewing a budget request. They propagate best practice by translating successful techniques into tools and methods that can be broadly applied. They also shape management values by reinforcing certain behaviors and not others.

Put simply, management processes are the "gears" that turn management principles into everyday practice. In even a medium-sized organization, it's impossible to change the *what* and *how* of managing without changing the processes that govern that work.

The Power of
Management Innovation

Over the past few years, I, along with two of my colleagues at the London Business School,* have been examining the history of management innovation. To date, we have studied more than 100 management breakthroughs, stretching across two centuries. One inescapable conclusion: major advances in management practice often lead to significant shifts in competitive position, and often confer long-lasting advantages on pioneering firms.

Consider, for example, a few of the 20th century's most consistently successful companies: General Electric, DuPont, Procter & Gamble, Toyota, and Visa. What is it that propelled these companies to positions of global leadership? Of course, the usual suspects—great products, disciplined execution, and farsighted leaders—played a role. But if you dig deeper, you discover that it was management innovation, first and foremost, that set them on the course to greatness:

- *Managing science.* In the early 1900s, General Electric perfected Thomas Edison's most notable invention, the industrial research laboratory. GE's success in bringing management discipline to the chaotic process of scientific discovery allowed Edison to claim that his labs were capable of producing a minor invention every

---

*Professor Julian Birkinshaw and Dr. Michael Mol.

10 days and a major breakthrough every six months. This was no idle boast. Over the first half of the 20th century, GE won more patents than any other company in America.

- *Allocating capital.* DuPont played a pioneering role in the development of capital-budgeting techniques when it initiated the use of return on investment calculations in 1903. A few years later, the company also developed a standardized way of comparing the performance of its numerous product departments. These advances addressed a pressing problem: How to allocate capital rationally when confronted with a bewildering array of potentially attractive projects? DuPont's new decision tools would help it to become one of America's industrial giants.

- *Managing intangible assets.* Procter & Gamble's preeminence in the packaged goods industry has its roots in the early 1930s, when the company began to formalize its approach to brand management. At the time, the idea of creating value out of intangible assets was a novel idea. In the decades since, P&G has steadily built upon its early lead in building and managing great brands. In 2007, P&G's business portfolio included 16 brands that were delivering more than $1 billion in annual sales.[2]

- *Capturing the wisdom of every employee.* Toyota is the world's most profitable carmaker—by a long margin. Much of its success rests on an unmatched ability to enroll employees in the relentless pursuit of efficiency and quality. For more than 40 years, Toyota's capacity for continuous improvement has been powered by a belief in the ability of "ordinary" employees to solve complex problems. Indeed, people inside Toyota sometimes refer to the Toyota Production System as the "Thinking People System." In 2005, the company received more than 540,000 improvement ideas from its Japanese employees.[3]

- *Building a global consortium.* Visa, the world's first "virtual"
  company, owes its success to organizational innovation. When
  Visa's founding banks formed a consortium in the United States
  in the early 1970s, they laid the groundwork for what would become one of the world's most ubiquitous brands. The key management challenge: building an organization that would allow
  banks to compete for customers while collaborating around infrastructure, standards, and brand-building. Today, Visa is a gos-
  samer web that links more than 21,000 financial institutions and
  1.3 billion cardholders. The Visa network processes more than
  $2 trillion of purchases every year—about 60 percent of all credit
  card transactions.

These cases (as well as more recent ones, which we will explore in
subsequent chapters) highlight the decisive role that management innovation often plays in helping companies build durable advantages.
Indeed, no other factor seems to have been similarly instrumental in
underwriting long-term competitive success.

This assertion, bold as it may seem, is buttressed by the findings of
military theorists who've explored the origins of sustained superiority
in war making. Here, too, management innovation seems to be key. In
battle, as in business, most victories are pyrrhic and temporary. Yet here
and there, in the bloody pages of history, one observes a military regime
that has consistently bested its enemies, often despite a deficit of men
and matériel. As you might imagine, these cases are of great interest to
military scholars who, like business school professors, have an interest
in uncovering the deep roots of competitive advantage. Why is it, these
analysts ask, that some armies and navies have enjoyed prolonged periods of military supremacy?

When confronted with this question, a layperson is likely to credit
superior weaponry. Prime exhibits might include:

- The deadly and much-feared yew-wood longbow, which, in the
  14th century, allowed the archers of King Edward III to deal out
  a series of crushing blows to England's enemies

- The agile and speedy three-masted caravel, a product of 15th-century Iberian ingenuity, which gave European powers a sizable advantage in building their globe-spanning empires

- The breech-loading needle gun, perfected in the mid-19th century, which gave Prussian infantrymen a considerable firepower advantage over their European adversaries

- The laser- and satellite-guided missiles that enabled coalition forces to surgically destroy Saddam Hussein's military installations in both the first and second Gulf Wars

Yet a careful reading of military history, like that offered by MacGregor Knox and Williamson Murray in *The Dynamics of Military Revolution*,[4] suggests that most technology advantages have been short-lived. In battle, one side captures the other's weapons or, better yet, those who manufactured the armaments. Bribes get paid and craftsmen defect. Foreign spies lay their hands on blueprints, or weapons get sold to allies who later become adversaries. Tactical and strategic advantages—the product of inspired wartime leadership—are only slightly less fleeting. Successful battlefield maneuvers and new force formations are usually quickly copied and neutralized. While superior technology, tactical genius, or any of a dozen other factors may explain the outcome of a single battle, they can't account for repeated military success—the ability to emerge triumphant from the chaos of war again and again.

What, then, accounts for *long-term* military advantage—if not advanced armaments and brilliant commanders? Knox and Murray contend that long-lasting leadership is most often the product of fundamental advances in military doctrine and organization.[5] History's most consistently victorious armies and navies have been those that were able to break with the past and imagine new ways of motivating, staffing, training, and deploying warriors. They have been management innovators.

Three short examples will help to underscore this crucial point.

The British army's success in India, from the mid-18th century to its withdrawal from the subcontinent two hundred years later,

owed little to superior firepower. Indian armaments were at least
the equal of English weaponry. Indeed, the Duke of Wellington,
while serving in India in 1800, was so impressed by the quality of
locally made cannon that he incorporated them into his artillery
train.[6] Instead, England's conquest of Southeast Asia relied largely
upon the relative advantages of the regimental structure—an organizational innovation. According to Professor John Lynn:

> The regiment provided the foundation for a permanent British/
> sepoy military establishment in India that defeated the great
> native state of Mysore, the Maratha warrior confederacy, and
> ultimately even the tenacious Sikhs. The regiment turned into
> a highly effective repository for indigenous cultural values that
> tapped native codes of personal and community honor in ways
> that temporary or irregular military units could not.[7]

With the king or queen thousands of miles away, the regiment was
a near-at-hand focal point for a soldier's filial loyalty. Moreover, as a
semipermanent organization, the regiment was an ideal mechanism for transferring hard-won knowledge from one campaign to
another—knowledge that in earlier times had often been lost when
military units were disbanded upon the cessation of hostilities.

Napoleon, whose campaigns are still analyzed in war academies
around the world, owed much of his success to an innovation in
military doctrine. Prior to the French revolution, France's armies
had fought for the monarch—a distant and often uninspiring figure.
But in post-revolutionary France, Napoleon succeeded in fanning
the red-hot embers of nationalism into a firestorm of military zeal.
Citizens, it seemed, could be roused to fight for *la gloire de la France*
with a degree of ferocity that no feudal system could hope to match.
The result: a fighting force that Carl von Clausewitz termed a "jug-
gernaut of war, based on the strength of an entire people."[8]

Having been trounced by Napoleon's forces in 1806, the Prussian
army embraced a series of organizational innovations that would

ultimately be imitated by every large-scale military force in the world. In a wrenching departure from centuries of tradition, the army adopted a rigorously meritocratic approach to the commissioning of officers—no longer would they be promoted on the basis of their aristocratic pedigrees. Another key innovation was the development of the general staff system. Gerhard von Scharnhorst, the Prussian army's great reformer, believed it was dangerous for an army to rely overmuch on the brilliance of one or two generals. What was needed instead was a cadre of technically trained and exceptionally talented junior officers who could provide independent advice to their commanders. Thus was born the concept of line and staff,[9] an organizational principle that has been implemented in virtually every modern company.

Whether one studies industrial history or military history, the lesson is the same: management innovation matters, a lot. But how, exactly, does management innovation create competitive advantage? And what sorts of management innovation are likely to be the most defensible?

From Innovation to Advantage

Management innovation tends to yield a competitive advantage when one or more of three conditions are met: the innovation is based on a *novel management principle* that challenges some long-standing orthodoxy; the innovation is *systemic*, encompassing a range of processes and methods; and/or the innovation is part of an *ongoing program* of rapid-fire invention where progress compounds over time. Let me briefly elaborate on each of these three critical conditions.

Consider first the auto industry. Why, after decades of trying, have America's indigenous automakers so far failed to duplicate Toyota's hyperefficient manufacturing system? This was the question I put to a senior executive group in one of America's big car companies a few years back. We had just finished a sumptuous dinner at an elegant hotel when, over coffee, one of the carmaker's top finance executives mentioned that the company had just completed its 20th annual benchmarking study of Toyota. What, I wondered aloud, had the company learned in year 20 that it hadn't learned in years 19, 18, 17, and so on? The blunt subtext to my question hung in the air like acrid cigar smoke: Why are you still playing catch-up? After a moment of embarrassed silence, a senior staffer spoke up, and offered an explanation that went something like this:

> Twenty years ago we started sending our young people to Japan to study Toyota. They'd come back and tell us how good Toyota was and we simply didn't believe them. We figured they'd dropped a zero somewhere—no one could produce cars with so few defects per vehicle, or with so few labor hours. It was five years before we acknowledged that Toyota really was beating us in a bunch of critical areas. Over the next five years, we told ourselves that Toyota's advantages were all cultural. It was all about *wa* and *nemawashi*—the uniquely Japanese spirit of cooperation and consultation that Toyota had cultivated with its employees. We were sure that American workers would never put up with these paternalistic practices. Then, of course, Toyota started building plants in the United States, and they got the same results here they got in Japan—so our cultural excuse went out the window. For the next five years, we focused on Toyota's manufacturing processes. We studied their use of factory automation, their supplier relationships, just-in-time systems, everything. But despite all our benchmarking, we could never seem to get the same results in our own factories. It's only in the last five years that we've finally admitted to ourselves that Toyota's success is based on a wholly different set of principles— about the capabilities of its employees and the responsibilities of its leaders.[10]

Amazingly, it took nearly 20 years for America's carmakers to decipher Toyota's advantage. Unlike its Western rivals, Toyota believed that first-line employees could be more than cogs in a soulless manufacturing machine. If given the right tools and training, they could be problem solvers, innovators, and change agents. Toyota saw within its workforce the necessary genius for never-ending, fast-paced operational improvement. In contrast, U.S. car companies tended to discount the contributions that could be made by first-line employees, and relied instead on staff experts for improvements in quality and efficiency. Such was the disdain for the intelligence of frontline workers that Henry Ford once wondered querulously, "Why is it that whenever I ask for a pair of hands, a brain comes attached?"

Over the past 40 years, Toyota has gotten more out of its people, day by day and year by year, than its competitors have gotten out of theirs—an advantage that has been reflected in Toyota's ever-rising market share and market value. While U.S. carmakers are now working hard to more fully utilize the brainpower of their employees, they have paid dearly for a management system that was rooted in intellectual feudalism.

As this example illustrates, management dogmas are often so deeply ingrained as to be nearly invisible, and so devoutly held as to be virtually unassailable. When it comes to management innovation, the more unconventional the underlying principle, the longer it will take for competitors to respond. In some cases, the head-scratching can go on for decades.

It's also tough for rivals to replicate advantages that are *systemic*, that encompass a web of individual innovations spanning multiple management processes. In 1999, Dave Whitwam, then chairman of Whirlpool, challenged his colleagues to make innovation a deeply embedded core competence. From the outset, Whitwam made it clear that he didn't want a one-off program, a corporate incubator, or a new ventures division. He wanted something deeper and more systemic. As a first step, he appointed Nancy Snyder, a well-respected corporate vice president, as Whirlpool's innovation czar. Snyder's job: to rally her colleagues around what would become a five-year quest to reinvent the company's management processes. Aided by Strategos, a Chicago-based consulting company, Snyder and her compatriots worked to turn each of Whirlpool's core management processes into a catalyst for innovation. Key changes included:

- Making innovation a central topic in Whirlpool's leadership development programs

- Setting aside a substantial share of capital spending every year for projects that were truly innovative

- Requiring every product-development plan to contain a sizable component of new-to-market innovation

- Training more than 600 innovation mentors charged with supporting innovation throughout the company

- Enrolling every salaried employee in an online course on business innovation

- Establishing innovation as a large component of top management's long-term bonus plan

- Setting aside time in quarterly business review meetings for an in-depth discussion of each unit's innovation performance

- Creating an Innovation Board to review and fast-track the company's most promising ideas

- Building an innovation portal to give employees access to a compendium of innovation tools, data on the company's global innovation pipeline, and the chance to input their ideas

- Developing a set of metrics to track innovation inputs, throughputs, and outputs

These changes were not the product of some highly detailed master plan. Instead, they emerged over the course of Whirlpool's innovation "journey," often in response to roadblocks that would have been diffi-cult to anticipate at the outset.[11]

The payoff? In 2005 Whirlpool derived $760 million of its $14.3 bil-lion in revenues from products that met the company's tough new in-novation standards, up from $10 million in 2001. In addition, it had 568 innovation projects under way, 195 of which were being readied for launch. Jeff Fettig, Whirlpool's current chairman, reckoned that those new initiatives would ultimately add as much as $3 billion annually to the company's top line.[12]

While Whirlpool's innovation efforts have been widely reported, a competitor would find it hard to duplicate what is now a deeply en-grained innovation system—for the same reasons it would be difficult to pick apart Toyota's multifaceted management advantage. A few, fractured insights into a competitor's distinctive management practices are of limited value when one is attempting to replicate the totality of a distinctive management *system*. For an analogy, imagine trying to re-construct a Persian carpet from a few strands of silk.

Finally, a company can sometimes create a management advan-tage simply by being persistent. There is perhaps no company in the world that is better at developing great leaders than General Electric. While many elements of GE's executive development system have been imitated—such as its training facility in Crotonville, New York, its 360-degree evaluation process, the way it encourages managers to collaborate, and its tough and unsentimental culling of underperform-ers—few companies would claim to have matched GE's capacity for growing superlative leaders. GE's prowess is less the product of a sin-gle breakthrough than of a long-running and unflagging commitment to improving the quality of its management stock—a commitment that has spawned repeated management breakthroughs. In 2006, for example, GE announced yet another leadership initiative, this time focused on developing executives who could help the company raise its organic growth rate. Any company hoping to match GE's leadership advantage soon learns that it's not easy to keep a fast-moving quarry in your sights.

Management Innovation in Context

I nnovation comes in many flavors: operational innovation, product innovation, strategy innovation, and, of course, management innovation. Each genre makes its own contribution to success, but if we were to array these various forms of innovation in a hierarchy, where higher tiers denote higher levels of value creation and competitive defensibility, management innovation would come out on top (figure 2-1). Understanding why this is so is an important step in building your company's commitment to management innovation, so let's work our way up from the bottom.

At the base of the pyramid is operational innovation. In a world of hypercompetition, operational excellence is essential, but in the absence of some Toyota-like management innovation or Ikea-style business model breakthrough, operational innovation seldom delivers a decisive, long-term advantage. This is true for several reasons. First, operational preeminence often depends heavily on the quality of a company's IT

FIGURE 2-1

The innovation stack

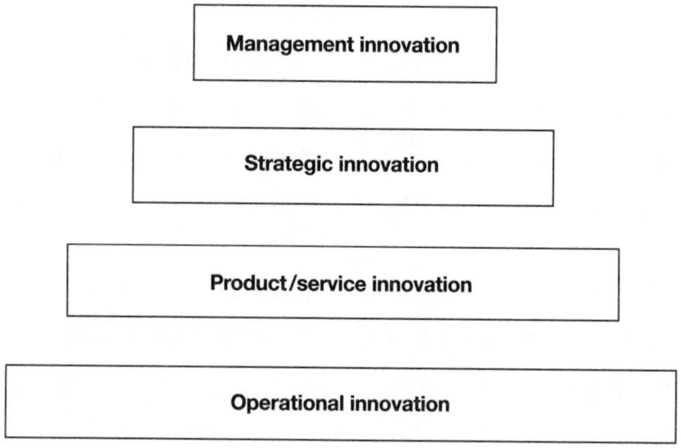

infrastructure. Unfortunately, advances in hardware and software tend to diffuse rapidly, making IT-based advantages notoriously difficult to defend.[13] Secondly, many companies today outsource a wide range of business activities to third parties—vendors who often serve several companies within a single industry, and who typically lack the incentives to help a single customer build a standout advantage. While outsourcing and offshoring can help a company stay even with the competition, they seldom yield a significant proprietary advantage. Finally, there is a growing swarm of consultants who work long days transferring best practices from exceptional companies to mediocre ones. This, too, tends to level out operational advantages.

Next up the food chain is *product innovation*. There's no doubt that an iconic product can lift a company from obscurity to cult status in short order (think, for example, of Dyson's bagless vacuum cleaners). Yet in the absence of enforceable patent protection, most products are quickly knocked off. In addition, an ever-accelerating pace of technological progress often gives upstarts the opportunity to leapfrog yesterday's pioneers. As a result, breakthrough products seldom grant a company long-lasting industry leadership. For example, it only took a few years for Samsung to improve upon Nokia's superslick mobile phone designs, for other golf club makers to match the playability advantages of Callaway's Big Bertha irons, or for Hoover to come up with its own "Cyclonic" vacuum cleaner.

Further up the stack is *strategy innovation*—bold new business models that put incumbents on the defensive. Standout examples include Ryanair, Europe's leading low-cost airline, Apple's iTunes music store, and Zara's chic but cheap couture. A killer business model can generate billions of dollars in market value for the innovator—but on average, a distinctive business model is more easily decoded and counteracted than a heretical management system. Wal-Mart's supposedly invincible lead in discount retailing hasn't prevented other retailers, like Costco and Target, from flourishing. America's crop of low-cost airlines, including Frontier, JetBlue, AirTran, and America West (recently merged with

US Airways), have purloined entire chapters from Southwest Airlines' once-unique playbook. And although India's outsourcing pioneers—companies such as Infosys and Wipro—have become industry giants, they must still scramble every day to defend their lead from a horde of envious and determined wannabes who are equally eager to exploit India's wage advantage.

The point is, not all types of innovation are created equal. When focused on big, chunky problems, management innovation possesses a unique capacity to create difficult-to-duplicate advantages. Why? Because some heresies are more heretical than others. You, for example, would probably find it easier to adjust your fashion preferences than to transpose your religious beliefs. Similarly, most executives find it easier to acknowledge the merits of a disruptive business model than to abandon the core tenets of their bedrock management beliefs.

Caveats

Not every management innovation creates a competitive advantage. Some are incremental. Some are wrongheaded. And many never pay off. Of course, the same can be said for other sorts of innovation. Like its cousins, management innovation follows a power law: for every truly radical idea that forever changes the practice of management there are dozens of others that are less valuable and less influential. But that's no excuse not to innovate. Innovation is always a numbers game: the more of it you do, the better your chances of reaping a fat payoff.

Additionally, no single management breakthrough, no matter how bold or well-executed, will pay competitive dividends forever. In the annals of management innovation, there are many companies that upended conventional thinking once, but never repeated the feat. Though their stars have been waning for decades, Ford and General Motors were once blue-ribbon management innovators. Ford's early leadership was based not only on its development of the moving assembly line, but also on innovation in the management methods needed to run what was, at the time, the world's largest, most vertically integrated firm. And GM, as mentioned earlier, invented the divisionalized organization model. But today, their management models are as undistinguished as their vehicles. It has been nearly a century since either company led a bona fide management revolution.

Management Myopia

Given the power of management innovation to deliver peer-beating performance, it is odd that so few companies possess a well-honed process for continuous management innovation. A stroll through the pages of the world's leading business magazines confirms the steerage-class status of management innovation. Over the last 70 years, the terms "technology innovation" and "technical innovation" have appeared in the title or abstract of more than 52,000 articles. More than 3,000 articles have focused on "product innovation." The comparatively new topic of "strategic innovation" (which includes terms like "business innovation" and "business model innovation") has been covered in more than 600 articles. Yet taken together, articles on "management innovation," "managerial innovation," "organizational innovation," and "administrative innovation" number less than 300, and nearly all of these focus on the *diffusion*, rather than the *invention*, of new management practices—a bias that's understandable only if you believe it's better to follow than to lead.

Today, every CEO claims to be a champion of innovation—so why the barn-sized blind spot when it comes to *management* innovation? I believe there are three likely explanations. First, most managers don't see themselves as inventors. Unlike technologists, marketers, and, more recently, strategists, innovation isn't central to the average manager's role definition. In most companies, managers are selected, trained, and rewarded for their capacity to deliver more of the same, more efficiently. No one *expects* managers to be innovators. Rather, they are expected to turn *other* people's ideas into growth and profits.

Second, many executives doubt that bold management innovation is actually possible. R&D staffers and product-development specialists are sustained by the belief that the next big thing is just around the corner. How many executives, by contrast, are buoyed up by the hope that they might get the chance to lead the next great management revolution? Strangely, managers are unsurprised when science advances by leaps and bounds, yet seem unperturbed when the practice of management fails to do the same.

When confronted with this discrepancy, many executives claim that the immutable laws of human nature constrain the range of feasible options for mobilizing and organizing human effort. There are limits, they argue, to the number of people that one person can effectively supervise, to the degree to which accountability can be distributed, to the extent to which employees can be trusted, to the willingness of individuals to subordinate their self-interests to the interests of the corporation as a whole. Whether these limits are real or imagined (mostly the latter, I will argue), they offer managers a soothing alternative to the premise that it is a lack of imagination that constrains management innovation.

Most managers see themselves as pragmatic doers, not starry-eyed dreamers. In their experience, management progress is accretive rather than revolutionary—and they have little reason to believe it could ever be otherwise. But as we'll see, it *can* be otherwise, and it *must* be—the future demands it.

Three

An Agenda for Management Innovation

S HUMAN BEINGS, WE ARE DEFINED BY THE CAUSES WE serve and the problems we struggle to surmount. Whether it's Nelson Mandela battling the scourge of apartheid, Craig Venter unraveling the human genome, or Larry Page and Sergey Brin bringing order to the vastness of cyberspace, it is a passion for solving *extra*ordinary problems that creates the potential for *extra*ordinary accomplishment. Thus to invent the future of management you're going to need more than an intellectual faith in the value of management innovation. You're going to need a passion for some very specific, very noble challenge.

Be Bold

If management innovation has been mostly incremental in recent years, it may be due to a lack of daring in the choice of problems to tackle. Ask yourself, has your company ever taken on a management challenge that was truly unprecedented, where you couldn't rely on another company's experience as a guide? General Electric has. In 2006, chairman Jeff Immelt set his colleagues the goal of growing GE's top line at twice the rate of global GDP growth—net of acquisitions. No company of GE's size has ever managed to sustain this sort of growth, yet that didn't deter Immelt from taking on the challenge. There's no guarantee that GE will achieve its growth goals, but if it fails, it won't be for a lack of moxie.

While big problems don't always yield big advances, small ones never do. As the Nobel Prize–winning zoologist Sir Peter Medawar once put it: "Dull or piffling problems yield dull or piffling answers."[1] So you're going to need to think big.

If you are worried about biting off more than you can chew, keep two things in mind. First, you don't always have to take big risks to solve big problems. Innovation is usually an iterative process where solutions emerge through trial and error. In the early years of the U.S. space program, scientists sent more than ten monkeys into space before strapping a human being to a rocket. As we'll see in subsequent chapters, you don't have to take a big gamble to test out a bold new management idea.

Second, if the problem is big enough, progress of any sort will be valuable, even if you never find a "solution." I once heard former U.S. Secretary of State George Shultz draw a distinction between "problems you can solve" and "problems you can only work at." As a seasoned diplomat, Shultz knows that some problems, like ethnic strife, global poverty, and terrorism, defy once-and-for-all solutions. Yet he also understands that when you're up against problems of this scale and significance, even modest advances can yield big dividends. It may turn out that many of the 21st century's most perplexing management problems are ones we can only work at—they will resist attempts at a quick fix, but will reward persistent, imaginative effort.

It takes ingenuity, pluck, and perseverance to solve big problems. These human qualities are most abundant when the problem to be addressed is not only weighty but soul-stirring as well. As a devout Quaker, Frederick Taylor's single-minded devotion to efficiency stemmed from a conviction that it was iniquitous to waste even an hour of human labor when a task could be redesigned to be performed more efficiently. That Taylor could spend days studying the most productive ways to shovel coal was evidence not only of an obsessive mind, but of a missionary zeal for multiplying the value of human effort. This passion shines through in the introduction to his 1911 opus, *Principles of Scientific Management*: "We can see and feel the waste of material things. Awkward, inefficient, or ill-directed movements of men, however, leave nothing visible or tangible behind them. Their appreciation calls for an act of memory, an effort of the imagination. And for this reason, even though our daily loss from this source is greater than from our waste of material things, the one has stirred us deeply, while the other has moved us but little."[2]

Given Taylor's singularly influential role in the history of management, we would do well to heed his example: to maximize the chances for precedent-breaking management innovation, devote yourself to a problem that is consequential *and* inspiring, essential *and* laudable.

If you don't already have such a challenge in mind, here are a few leading questions that will help you focus your search:

- First, what are the new challenges the future has in store for your company? What are the emerging discontinuities that will stretch its management processes and practices to the breaking point? *What's the "tomorrow problem" that you* need *to start working on right now?*

- Second, what are the tough balancing acts your company never seems to get right? Is there a critical trade-off where one side always seems to prevail at the expense of the other? *What's the frustrating "either/or" you'd like to turn into an "and"?*

- Third, what are the biggest gaps between rhetoric and reality in your company? What are the values it has the hardest time living up to, or finds the most difficult to institutionalize? *What's the espoused ideal you'd like to turn into an embedded capability?*

- Finally, what are you indignant about? What are the frustrating *in*competencies that plague your company and other organizations like it? *What's the "can't do" that needs to become a "can do"?*

Having zeroed in on a big-league challenge, you'll need to break it into smaller, more tractable components. This will allow you to focus your energies on high-impact subproblems, and will help to maximize the returns on your innovation efforts.

Because the technology of management varies only modestly from company to company, you'll find that most of the failings you need to address are endemic rather than idiosyncratic. This will make the diagnostic process easier. Much has been written, for example, on why companies are slow to change, and how bureaucracies stifle new thinking.[3] The real challenge, though, is not diagnostic but therapeutic. We know a lot about *why* large companies are incompetent at certain things (like proactively reinventing their strategies or growing new businesses), yet despite a mountain of advice and admonition, few companies seem to have overcome these limitations. What's lacking is not insightful analysis, but truly bold and imaginative alternatives to the management status quo—and an army of innovators who have the stamina to reinvent management from the ground up.

Calibrating Your Agenda for Management Innovation

In the remainder of this chapter, I'll outline three of the most formidable challenges that confront companies in this new century.

1. Dramatically accelerating the pace of strategic renewal in organizations large and small

2. Making innovation everyone's job, every day

3. Creating a highly engaging work environment that inspires employees to give the very best of themselves

I'll explain why these challenges deserve to be at the top of *your* agenda for management innovation, and will then break them down into a number of more focused subsidiary challenges.

My goal here is twofold. First, I want to help you become passionate about some big 21st-century management challenge. Each of the problems discussed below is meaty and righteous. Taken together, they are to 21st-century organizations what efficiency, scale, and control were to early 20th-century businesses—and I have no doubt that the most successful companies in the years ahead will be the ones that take the lead in tackling these capstone challenges.

Second, I want to illustrate the sort of argument you'll need to make if you hope to recruit others to your cause. Potential coconspirators are going to ask: Why is it important that we address this problem *now*? Why does it require *radical* innovation? And what, *exactly*, needs fixing? You will need convincing answers to these questions.

The purpose of this chapter, then, is not to propose specific solutions to our trio of make-or-break problems—that will come later. Rather, the goal is to give you some benchmarks that will help you calibrate your own management innovation agenda: Am I thinking big enough? Can I make a compelling case? And am I digging deeply enough into the root causes?

Building a Company That Is as Nimble as Change Itself

There's little that can be said with certainty about the future except this: sometime over the next decade your company will be challenged to change in a way for which it has no precedent.[4] It will

either adapt or falter, reinvent itself or struggle through a painful restruc-
turing. Given the recent performance of industry incumbents around
the world, the latter is more likely than the former. Few companies, it
seems, are able to change ahead of the curve.

There have always been dinosaurs—companies like Kodak, Sony,
Sears, General Motors, Toys "R" Us, and Sun Microsystems—that have
failed to reinvent themselves on a timely basis and have paid the price.
Yet in recent years, entire industries have been caught behind the change
curve. Television broadcasters and newspaper publishers, record companies and French vintners, traditional airlines and giant drug companies,
American carmakers and European purveyors of haute couture—all have
been struggling to rejuvenate seriously out-of-date business models.
Sure, many of the companies in these industries will regain their footing—eventually. But in the meantime, billions of dollars and millions of
customers will be lost. Such is the price of maladaptation.

What accounts for this epidemic of senescence? Is it that executives
around the world have suddenly become dull-witted? Unlikely. If once-
immortal business models are abruptly going toes-up, it's because the
environment has changed—and what has changed most remarkably is
change itself. What distinguishes our age from every other is not the
world-flattening impact of communications, not the economic ascen-
dance of China and India, not the degradation of our climate, and not
the resurgence of ancient religious animosities. Rather, it is a franti-
cally accelerating pace of change.

Over the coming decades the adaptability of every society, organization, and individual will be tested as never before. Luckily, perturba-
tions create opportunities as well as challenges. But the balance of
promise and peril for any particular organization depends on its capacity for adaptation. Hence the most critical question for every 21st-century
company is this: Are we changing as fast as the world around us? As
we've already seen, the answer for many companies is "no."

While executives readily acknowledge that products and services
need to be periodically refreshed, they often assume that strategies,

business models, competencies, and core values are more-or-less immortal. Such an assumption is increasingly foolhardy. Companies miss the future when they mistake the temporary for the timeless; and today, just about everything is temporary.

A review of the extensive library on managing change reveals a disturbing fact. Nearly all the accounts of *deep* change—entailing big shifts in a company's business model or core mission—are stories of turnarounds, with a new CEO typically cast as the hero. It seems that deep change is nearly always crisis-led, episodic, and programmatic—accomplished through a top-to-bottom cascade of tightly scripted messages, events, goals, and actions. Sadly, it is rarely opportunity-led, continuous, and a product of the organization's intrinsic capacity to learn and adapt. While one can celebrate Lou Gerstner's turnaround at IBM, Carlos Ghosn's Lazarus-like resurrection of Nissan, or Rosemary Bravo's revitalization of the Burberry fashion brand, a turnaround is transformation tragically delayed—an expensive substitute for well-timed adaptation.

The goal, then, is to build organizations that are capable of continual, trauma-free renewal. An apt analogy is found in the body's autonomic systems. When you step on a treadmill and start to jog, your heart automatically increases the blood supply to your muscles. When you stand up in front of an audience to speak, your adrenal gland spontaneously pumps out a hormone that accelerates your heart rate and heightens your faculties. And when you glance at someone who is physically attractive to you, your pupils dilate reflexively, drinking in the agreeable visage. Automatic. Spontaneous. Reflexive. These aren't the words we typically use to describe deep change in large organizations. And therein lies the challenge: to make deep change more of an autonomic process—to build organizations that are capable of continuous self-renewal in the absence of a crisis.

Many factors contribute to strategic inertia, but three pose a particularly grave threat to timely renewal. The first is the tendency of management teams to deny or ignore the need for a strategy reboot. The second is a dearth of compelling alternatives to the status quo, which often leads to strategic paralysis. And the third: allocational rigidities that make it difficult to redeploy talent and capital behind new initiatives. Each of these barriers stands in the way of zero-trauma change; hence each deserves to be a focal point for management innovation.

Denial

Every business is successful until it's not. What's disconcerting, though, is how often top management is surprised when "not" happens. This astonishment, this belated recognition of dramatically changed circumstances, virtually guarantees that the work of renewal will be significantly, if not dangerously, delayed.

Denial follows a familiar pattern. Disquieting developments are at first *dismissed* as implausible or inconsequential, then *rationalized* away as aberrant or irremediable, then grudgingly *mitigated* through defensive action, and then finally, though not always, honestly *confronted*.

The recent travails of the music industry provide us with a typical case. Record companies were initially contemptuous of downloaded music. MP3 files were sonically inferior to CDs, and downloading music was a clumsy and time-consuming process. Who'd want to listen to music on a PC anyway? Yet despite this self-soothing disdain, the downloading snowball started to roll down the hill. Still, executives in New York and London discounted the trend, complaining loudly that the new distribution model was based entirely on theft. If people had to *pay* for their music, they argued, the torrent of downloads would slow to a trickle. Acting on this logic, the industry embraced a draconian strategy: it would threaten to sue all those morally defective college students who would rather download Coldplay than spend their 15 bucks at Tower Records. When the industry finally began experimenting with its own online distribution model, its Fort Knox approach to digital rights management made the nascent services virtually unusable. With the door to the future left wide open, Apple sauntered in and quickly became the world's leading online music retailer. Such is the price of denial.

As you might expect, the propensity to disclaim disconcerting facts increases as one moves up the hierarchy. One reason: corporate leaders are often not close enough to the bleeding edge of change to sense for themselves the growing risks to a long-venerated business model. In the absence of their own corroborating evidence, they are unlikely to give much credence to the distant echo of alarm bells rung by individuals out in the corporate hinterlands.

A Dearth of New Strategic Options

To escape the gravitational pull of an economically challenged business model, a company needs a compelling array of *new* strategic options—exciting alternatives to the status quo. Problem is, few companies have a disciplined process for generating hundreds of new strategic options, yet that's what it takes to fuel renewal.

Innovation follows a power law: for every 1,000 oddball ideas, only 100 will be worth experimenting with; out of those, no more than 10 will merit a significant investment, and only two or three will ultimately produce a bonanza. Venture capitalists understand this arithmetic. In a given year, a typical VC firm will review thousands of business plans, meet with hundreds of would-be entrepreneurs, invest in a dozen or so companies, and then hope that one or two of them will become the next Google, Cisco, or Amgen. Few managers, though, seem eager to acknowledge the inescapable arithmetic of innovation.

The majestic oak tree provides a good analogy. Walk through a forest in Northern California and you'll find that the ground is covered with acorns. Nature isn't wasteful, so how does one explain this extravagance? Simple: the oak doesn't know which patches of ground are fertile and which aren't. The profusion of acorns is a "search strategy" aimed at finding the most felicitous combination of soil, light, and moisture. As with the tender seeds of innovation in a corporate setting, it's almost impossible to know in advance which acorns will germinate and which won't. (For example, in 1996, who would have guessed that eBay, then a fledgling start-up, would one day have a market value in excess of $35 billion?) This is why innovation suffers when senior executives demand ironclad assurances of future success before investing even small amounts of capital and talent in nascent ideas.

This doesn't mean that every new idea, however loopy, deserves to be funded. Just as it's possible for a hiker to distinguish between acorns and rabbit pellets, it's possible to differentiate between ideas that are inherently promising and those that are patently stupid. It does mean, though, that executives, like VCs, must invest in a portfolio of strategic options, and must resist the temptation to prematurely focus their resources on one or two "surefire" ideas. Again, it's a numbers game. While the median return on a VC's portfolio may be close to zero (many, if not most, ventures will ultimately fail), the average return can be eye-popping—thanks to the disproportionate effect of one or two runaway successes. The lesson is clear: to build an adaptable company, managers need to worry less about weeding out low-probability ideas, and more about building a diverse portfolio of nonincremental strategic options.

Allocational Rigidities

Sometimes the real hurdle to renewal is not a lack of options, but a lack of flexibility in resource allocation. All too often, legacy programs get richly funded year after year while new initiatives go begging. This, more than anything, is why companies regularly forfeit the future— they overinvest in "what is" at the expense of "what could be." There are several things that typically frustrate the timely redeployment of resources in medium- and large-scale organizations.

In most companies, a manager's power correlates directly with the resources he or she controls—to lose resources is to lose status and influence. Moreover, personal success often turns solely on the performance of one's own unit or project. As a result, program managers resist attempts to reallocate "their" capital and talent to new initiatives—regardless of how attractive those new projects may be. Of course it's unseemly to appear too parochial, so executives often hide their motives behind the façade of an ostensibly prudent business argument. New projects are deemed "untested," "risky," or a "diversion of resources." Thus while senior execs may happily fund a billion-dollar acquisition, someone a few levels down who attempts to "borrow" a half dozen talented individuals for a new project, or carve a few thousand dollars out of a legacy budget, is likely to find the task on par with a dental extraction.

The tendency to overfund the status quo is aggravated by two additional factors. First, in most companies there is a monopsony on new ideas (a monopsony implies one buyer; a monopoly, one seller). Typically, a lower- or midlevel employee with a new idea has only one place to go for funding—up the chain of command. If the nascent project doesn't jibe with the boss's near-term priorities, it won't get funded. For an analogy, try to imagine Silicon Valley with a single venture capital company. Given that scenario, how many great ideas would never see the light of day? Keep in mind that most entrepreneurs get turned down by seven or eight VCs before finding a willing investor.

Second, the resource-allocation process is typically biased against new ideas, since it demands a level of certainty about volumes, costs, timelines, and profits that simply can't be satisfied when an idea is truly novel. While it's easy to predict the returns on a project that is a linear extension of an existing business, the payback on an unconventional idea will always be harder to calculate. That's why VCs spread their risk by investing in a number of companies, rather than in a single start-up. Large companies, by contrast, tend to view every new idea as a stand-alone investment, and consequently require a degree of certitude that can be met only by projects that are modest extensions of existing activities. In contrast, managers running established businesses seldom have to defend the strategic risk they take when they pour good money into a slowly decaying business model, or overfund an activity that is already producing diminishing returns.

This brief examination of the barriers to strategic adaptability highlights several critical management innovation challenges:

1. How do you ensure that discomforting information isn't ignored or simply "explained away" as it moves up the hierarchy?

2. How do you build a management process that continually generates hundreds of new strategic options?

3. How do you accelerate the redeployment of resources from legacy programs to future-focused initiatives?

We'll add to this list as we dig into our next two future-focused management problems.

Making Innovation Everyone's Job

In a world where strategy life cycles are shrinking, innovation is the only way a company can renew its lease on success. It's also the only way it can survive in a world of bare-knuckle competition.

In decades past, many companies were insulated from the fierce winds of Schumpeterian competition. Regulatory barriers, patent protection, distribution monopolies, disempowered customers, proprietary standards, scale advantages, import protection, and capital hurdles were bulwarks that protected industry incumbents from the margin-crushing impact of Darwinian competition. Today, many of these fortifications are collapsing.

*   Deregulation and trade liberalization are reducing the barriers to entry in industries as diverse as banking, air transport, and telecommunications.

- The power of the Web means upstarts no longer have to build a global infrastructure to reach a worldwide market. This has allowed companies like Google, eBay, and MySpace to scale their businesses freakishly fast.

- The disintegration of large companies, via de-verticalization and outsourcing, has also helped new entrants. In turning over more and more of their activities to third-party contractors, incumbents have created thousands of "arms suppliers" that are willing to sell their services to anyone. By tapping into this global supplier base of designers, brand consultants, and contract manufacturers, new entrants can emerge from the womb nearly full-grown.

- Incumbents must also contend with a growing horde of ultra-low-cost competitors—companies like Huawei, the Chinese telecom equipment maker that pays its engineers a starting salary of just $8,500 per year. Not all cut-price competition comes from China and India. Ikea, Zara, Ryanair, and AirAsia are just a few of the companies that have radically reinvented industry cost structures.

- Web-empowered customers are also hammering down margins. Before the Internet, most consumers couldn't be sure whether they were getting the best deal on their home mortgage, credit card debt, or auto loan. This lack of enlightenment buttressed margins. But consumers are becoming less ignorant by the day. One U.K. Web site encourages customers to enter the details of their most-used credit cards, including current balances, and then shows them exactly how much they will save by switching to a card with better payment terms.

- In addition, the Internet is zeroing-out transaction costs. The commissions earned by market makers of all kinds—dealers, brokers, and agents—are falling off a cliff, or soon will be.

- Distribution monopolies—another source of friction—are under attack. Unlike the publishers of newspapers and magazines, bloggers don't need a physical distribution network to reach their readers. Similarly, new bands don't have to kiss up to record company reps when they can build a fan base via social networking sites like MySpace.

Collapsing entry barriers, hyperefficient competitors, customer power —these forces will be squeezing margins for years to come. In this harsh new world, every company will be faced with a stark choice: either set the fires of innovation ablaze, or be ready to scrape out a mean existence in a world where seabed labor costs (Chinese prisoners, anyone?) are the only difference between making money and going bust.

Given this, it's surprising that so few companies have made innovation everyone's job. For the most part, innovation is still relegated to organizational ghettos—it is still the responsibility of dedicated units like new product development and R&D, where creative types are kept safely out of the way of those who have to "run the business."

Today innovation is the buzz word du jour, but there's still a yawning chasm between rhetoric and reality. If you doubt this, seek out a few entry-level employees and ask them the following questions:

1. How have you been equipped to be a business innovator? What training have you received? What tools have you been supplied with?

2. Do you have access to an innovation coach or mentor? Is there an innovation expert in your unit who will help you develop your breakout idea?

3. How easy is it for you to get access to experimental funding? How long would it take you to get a few thousand dollars in seed money? How many levels of bureaucracy would you have to go through?

4. Is innovation a formal part of your job description? Does your compensation depend in part on your innovation performance?

5. Do your company's management processes—budgeting, planning, staffing, etc.—support your work as an innovator or hinder it?

Don't be surprised if these questions provoke little more than furrowed brows and quizzical looks. Truth is, there are not more than a handful of companies on the planet that have, like Whirlpool, built an all-encompassing, corporatewide innovation *system*.

While there are many impediments to innovation in large companies, there are three barriers that are particularly pernicious, and therefore essential to surmount.

Creative Apartheid

There are many folks, CEOs included, who believe that creativity is narrowly distributed in the human population. In this view, there is a tiny minority of individuals who are highly inventive and a big majority who are not. In my experience, this prejudice is particularly strong among those who have "creative" careers—filmmakers, designers, entrepreneurs, and the like. While these individuals may be innately creative, they often fail to adequately credit the myriad of environmental factors—inspiring teachers, iconoclastic parents, and lucky job breaks—that fueled their passions and afforded them the opportunity to develop their talents. Most human beings are creative in some sphere of their lives. Stephen Fry, the English actor who, like all actors, makes his living by parroting lines that other people have written, is an accomplished author and poet. Other folks paint, compose music, garden, or figure out new ways to entertain their bored toddlers. If folks don't appear to be creative at work, it's not because they lack imagination, it's because they lack the opportunity.

Fifty years ago, most CEOs believed that "ordinary" employees were incapable of tackling complicated operational problems like quality and efficiency. To a modern executive familiar with the benefits of *kaizen*, total quality management, and Six Sigma, such a belief seems like simple bigotry. Yet today many CEOs seem unwilling to acknowledge that the next billion-dollar idea in their company might come from an hourly employee or a road-weary sales rep. Nevertheless, history shows that innovation almost always comes from unexpected quarters, often from individuals who appeared quite ordinary to their friends and family. Sir Godfrey Hounsfield, the Nobel Prize–winning inventor of the CAT scanner, never earned a university degree. Neither did Richard Branson, who got his start in the music business selling records from the trunk of his car. Andreas Pavel, who invented the idea of a personal music player, was a Brazilian-educated philosophy student living in Switzerland. (His pioneering patent would eventually earn him millions of dollars in royalties from Sony.)[5] Despite these and thousands of similar examples, few executives seem to believe that "ordinary" employees can be extraordinary innovators. Yet in a world where innovation is more essential than ever, this sort of chauvinism is not only wrongheaded, it's potentially suicidal.

In the midst of writing this chapter, I was interviewed by CNBC on the topic of innovation. During the discussion, I commented on the fact that Whirlpool had trained more than 35,000 of its employees in the principles of business innovation. At that point, one of my fellow panelists butted in: "You can't teach people how to be creative," he declared. "You're either creative or you're not." Now if this were true, art institutes, design schools, and architectural programs wouldn't exist, and courses in creative writing would be pointless. The fact is, creativity is a human aptitude, like intelligence, musical ability, or eye-hand coordination. Like any other aptitude, it can be strengthened through instruction and practice.

Sure, some people are more creative than others, but in the colorless corridors of corporate-dom, hardly anyone lives up to their creative potential. Why? Because they haven't been given the tools and the time to exercise their gifts, and aren't held accountable for doing so. As a result, companies regularly waste prodigious quantities of human imagination—a profligacy that's hard to defend when the winds of creative destruction are blowing at gale force. R&D departments and new venture units have their place, but a small conclave of ingenious souls is no match for an entire company filled with employees who are giving full expression to their creative urges. If Toyota became one of the world's most renowned companies by harnessing the problem-solving abilities of its employees, just think of what your company could accomplish if it fully utilized the creative capabilities of each and every one of its employees.

The Drag of Old Mental Models

Innovators are, by nature, contrarians. Trouble is, yesterday's heresies often become tomorrow's dogmas, and when they do, innovation stalls and the growth curve flattens out.

Take the case of Dell Inc. Dell's business model—indirect channels, generic product designs, and Web-based customer support—made it the world's largest maker of PCs, and made Michael Dell, the company's founder, a multibillionaire. Given that, how tough do you think it would be for Michael Dell to admit that his profusely praised business model might have reached its sell-by date? How hard would it be for him to admit that Hewlett-Packard had closed its cost gap with Dell? Or that Apple's slick products and high-concept stores were making customers swoon? In the end, it seems to have been very hard, and very costly: as I write this, Dell has lost its leadership position to HP, has suffered a precipitous drop in its share price, and has been rocked by the forced resignation of its once highly regarded CEO, Kevin Rollins.

In this case and many others, the real barrier to strategic innovation is more than denial—it's a matrix of deeply held beliefs about the inherent superiority of a business model, beliefs that have been validated by millions of customers; beliefs that have been enshrined in physical infrastructure and operating handbooks; beliefs that have hardened into religious convictions; beliefs that are held so strongly, that nonconforming ideas seldom get considered, and when they do, rarely get more than grudging support.

Contrary to popular mythology, the thing that most impedes innovation in large companies is not a lack of risk taking. Big companies take big, and often imprudent, risks every day. The real brake on innovation is the drag of old mental models. Long-serving executives often have a big chunk of their emotional capital invested in the existing strategy. This is particularly true for company founders. While many start out as contrarians, success often turns them into cardinals who feel compelled to defend the one true faith. It's hard for founders to credit ideas that threaten the foundations of the business models they invented. Understanding this, employees lower down self-edit their ideas, knowing that anything too far adrift from conventional thinking won't win support from the top. As a result, the scope of innovation narrows, the risk of getting blindsided goes up, and the company's young contrarians start looking for opportunities elsewhere.

When it comes to innovation, a company's legacy beliefs are a much bigger liability than its legacy costs. Yet in my experience, few companies have a systematic process for challenging deeply held strategic assumptions. Few have taken bold steps to open up their strategy process to contrarian points of view. Few explicitly encourage disruptive innovation. Worse, it's usually senior executives, with their doctrinaire views, who get to decide which ideas go forward and which get spiked. This must change.

No Slack

In the pursuit of efficiency, companies have wrung a lot of slack out of their operations. That's a good thing. No one can argue with the goal of cutting inventory levels, reducing working capital, and slashing overhead. The problem, though, is that if you wring *all* the slack out of a company, you'll wring out all of the innovation as well. Innovation takes time—time to dream, time to reflect, time to learn, time to invent, and time to experiment. And it takes *uninterrupted* time—time when you can put your feet up and stare off into space. As Pekka Himanen put it in his affectionate tribute to hackers, "... the information economy's most important source of productivity is creativity, and it is not possible to create interesting things in a constant hurry or in a regulated way from nine to five."[6]

While the folks in R&D and new product development are given time to innovate, most employees don't enjoy this luxury. Every day brings a barrage of e-mails, voice mails, and back-to-back meetings. In this world, where the need to be "responsive" fragments human attention into a thousand tiny shards, there is no "thinking time." And therein lies the problem. However creative your colleagues may be, if they don't have the right to occasionally abandon their posts and work on something that's *not* mission critical, most of their creativity will remain dormant.

OK, you already know that—but how is that knowledge reflected in your company's management processes? How hard is it for a frontline employee to get permission to spend 20 percent of her time working on a project that has nothing to do with her day job, nor your company's "core business"? And how often does this happen? Does your company track the number of hours employees spend working on ideas that are incidental to their core responsibilities? Is "slack" institutionalized in the same way that cost efficiency is? Probably not. There are plenty of incentives in your company for people to stay busy. ("Maybe if I look like I'm working flat out, they won't send my job offshore.") But where are the incentives that encourage people to spend time quietly dreaming up the future?

So here's another clutch of challenges for the intrepid management innovator:

1. How can you enroll every individual within your company in the work of innovation, and equip each one with creativity-boosting tools?

2. How can you ensure that top management's hallowed beliefs don't straitjacket innovation, and that heretical ideas are given the chance to prove their worth?

3. How can you create the time and space for grassroots innovation in an organization that is running flat out to deliver today's results?

Make progress on these challenges and your company will set new benchmarks in innovation.

Now let's move on to our last meta-challenge.

Creating a Company Where Everyone Gives Their Best

Ask a group of your colleagues to describe the distinguishing characteristics of your company, and few are likely to mention adaptability and inventiveness. Yet if you ask them to make a list of the traits that differentiate human beings from other species, resilience and creativity will be near the top of the list. We see evidence of these qualities every day—in ourselves and in those around us. All of us know folks who've switched careers in search of new challenges or a more balanced life. We know people who've changed their consumption habits for the sake of the planet. We have friends and relatives who've undergone a spiritual transformation, or risen to the demands of parenthood, or overcome tragedy. Every day we meet people who write blogs, experiment with new recipes, mix up dance tunes, or customize their cars. As human beings, we are *amazingly* adaptable and creative, yet most of us work for companies that are *not*. In other words, we work for organizations that aren't very human.

There seems to be something in modern organizations that depletes the natural resilience and creativity of human beings, something that literally leaches these qualities out of employees during daylight hours. The culprit? Management principles and processes that foster discipline, punctuality, economy, rationality, and order, yet place little value on artistry, nonconformity, originality, audacity, and élan. To put it simply, most companies are only fractionally human because they make room for only a fraction of the qualities and capabilities that *make* us human. Billions of people show up for work every day, but way too many of them are sleepwalking. The result: organizations that systematically underperform their potential.

In 2005, Towers Perrin, a consulting company, conducted a survey of 86,000 employees working for large and medium-sized companies in 16 countries.[7] The researchers used a nine-item index to measure the extent to which employees felt engaged in their work. Respondents were asked how strongly they agreed with the following statements:

- I really care about the future of my organization.

- I am proud to tell others I work for my organization.

- My job provides me with a sense of personal accomplishment.

- I would recommend my organization to a friend as a good place to work.

- My organization inspires me to do my best.

- I understand how my unit/department contributes to the success of the organization.

- I understand how my role in my organization is related to my organization's overall goals, objectives, and direction.

- I am willing to put in a great deal of effort beyond what is normally expected to help my organization succeed.

- I am personally motivated to help my organization be successful.

An aggregate score was calculated for each respondent measuring the extent to which that individual was "highly engaged," "moderately engaged," or "disengaged" at work. Once all the data had been tabulated, the researchers had no choice but to conclude that: *"The vast majority of employees across all levels in an organization are less than fully engaged in their work.*"[8] [Emphasis in the original.] According to the study, a mere 14 percent of employees around the world are highly engaged in their work, while 24 percent are disengaged. Everyone else is somewhere in the tepid middle.

In other words, roughly 85 percent of those at work around the world—from Montreal to Munich, from Pittsburgh to Paris, and from Dublin to Delhi—are giving less of themselves than they could. This is a scandalous waste of human capability, and it helps to explain why so many organizations are less capable than the people who work there.

Weirdly, many of those who labor in the corporate world—from lowly admins to high powered CEOs—seem resigned to this state of affairs. They seem unperturbed by the confounding contrast between the essential nature of human beings and the essential nature of the organizations in which they work. In years past, it might have been possible to ignore this incongruity, but no longer—not in a world where adaptability and innovation have become the sine qua non of competitive success. The challenge: to reinvent our management systems so they inspire human beings to bring all of their capabilities to work every day.

The human capabilities that contribute to competitive success can be arrayed in a hierarchy. At the bottom is obedience—an ability to take direction and follow rules. This is the baseline. Next up the ladder is diligence. Diligent employees are accountable. They don't take shortcuts. They are conscientious and well-organized. Knowledge and intellect are on the next step. Most companies work hard to hire intellectually gifted employees. They value smart people who are eager to improve their skills and willing to borrow best practices from others. Beyond intellect lies initiative. People with initiative don't wait to be asked and don't need to be told. They seek out new challenges and are always searching for new ways to add value. Higher still lies the gift of creativity. Creative people are inquisitive and irrepressible. They're not afraid of saying stupid things. They start a lot of conversations with, "Wouldn't it be cool if . . ." And finally, at the top, lies passion.

Passion can make people do stupid things, but it's the secret sauce that turns intent into accomplishment. People with passion climb over obstacles and refuse to give up. Passion is contagious and turns one-person crusades into mass movements. As the English novelist E. M. Forster put it, "One person with passion is better than forty people merely interested."

If we were to measure the relative contribution that each of these human capabilities makes to value creation, recognizing we now live in a world where efficiency and discipline are table stakes, the scale would look something like this:

Passion	35%
Creativity	25%
Initiative	20%
Intellect	15%
Diligence	5%
Obedience	0%
	100%

I'm not suggesting that obedience is literally worth *nothing*. A company where no one followed *any* rules would soon descend into anarchy. Instead, I'm arguing that rule-following employees are worth zip in terms of the competitive advantage they generate. In a world with 4 billion nearly destitute souls, all eager to climb the ladder of economic progress, it's not hard to find biddable, hardworking employees. And what about intelligence? For years we've been told we're living in the knowledge economy; but as knowledge itself becomes commoditized, it will lose much of its power to create competitive advantage.

Today, obedience, diligence, and expertise can be bought for next to nothing. From Bangalore to Guangzhou, they have become global commodities. A simple example: turn over your iPod, and you'll find six words engraved on the back that foretell the future of competition: "Designed in California. Made in China." Despite the equal billing, the remarkable success of Apple's music business owes relatively little to the company's network of Asian subcontractors. It is a credit instead to the imagination of Apple's designers, marketers, and lawyers. Obviously, not every iconic product is going to be designed in California, nor manufactured in China. The point, though, is this: if you want to capture the economic high ground in the *creative economy*, you need employees who are more than acquiescent, attentive, and astute—they must also be zestful, zany, and zealous. So we must ask: what are the obstacles that stand in the way of achieving this state of organizational bliss?

Too Much Management, Too Little Freedom

While most executives would willingly attest to the value of initiative, creativity, and passion, they face a troubling conundrum. They are, by training and temperament, *managers*. They are paid to oversee, control, and administer. Yet today the most valuable human capabilities are precisely those that are the least manage*able*. While the tools of management can compel people to be obedient and diligent, they can't make them creative and committed.

Anyone who has ever run a university, a film studio, or an open source software project will tell you that getting the most out of people seldom means managing them more, and usually means managing them less. It means giving fewer orders, worrying less about alignment, and spending less time checking up on folks. Managing less implies more than having fewer managers. Powerful new communication tools have allowed companies to thin the ranks of middle management— but this doesn't mean that employees are any less fettered than they were in the past; it just means that it's easier for managers to manage more people. Management has become more efficient, but I doubt that most employees feel like there's less of it about.

Asking a manager to manage less is a bit like asking a carpenter to pound fewer nails, or imploring a high school principal to hand out fewer detention slips—this is what these people *do*. Yet the oversight, the rigid plans, the comprehensive assessments, the strict policies, the mandatory procedures—in short, the whole "father knows best" premise of management—is antithetical to building companies that are filled with energetic, slightly rebellious, votaries. If you want unbounded contributions from your employees, you're going to have to bind the hand of management—or at least a few fingers.

In recent years there's been a lot of rhetoric about involvement, empowerment, and self-direction. In many companies, employees are now referred to as "associates" or "team members" in an attempt to disguise their powerlessness. But ask yourself, have the liberties and prerogatives of first- and second-level employees in your company expanded dramatically over the past decade? Do they have more freedom to design their own jobs? Do they have greater discretion in choosing what to work on, or in deciding how to execute their responsibilities? These are important questions. Most of us are unlikely to get excited about a task that has been *assigned* to us. We bristle when we're bridled. In a sense, it's a zero-sum game: the more meddlesome the managerial oversight and the more constricting the shackles of policy and process, the less passionate people are going to be about their work. You can't expect automatons to be zealots.

Too Much Hierarchy, Too Little Community

When in your life have *you* felt the most joyful and the most energized by work? Maybe you were leading a skunk works project populated with brilliantly inventive coworkers. Maybe you were building a new company with a small, entrepreneurial team. Maybe you were plastering walls at a Habitat for Humanity build, along with other bighearted volunteers. Whatever the particulars of that episode in your life, I bet it involved a group of people who were bound by their devotion to a

common cause, who were undeterred by a lack of resources and un-
daunted by a lack of expertise, and who cared more about what they
could accomplish together than how credit would be apportioned. In
short, you were part of a community.

Hierarchies are very good at *aggregating* effort, at coordinating the activities of many people with widely varying roles. But they're not very
good at *mobilizing* effort, at inspiring people to go above and beyond.
When it comes to mobilizing human capability, communities outperform bureaucracies. This is true for several reasons. In a bureaucracy, the
basis for exchange is contractual—you get paid for doing what is assigned to you. In a community, exchange is voluntary—you give your
labor in return for the chance to make a difference, or exercise your talents. In a bureaucracy you are a factor of production. In a community you
are a partner in a cause. In a bureaucracy, "loyalty" is a product of economic dependency. In a community, dedication and commitment are
based on one's affiliation with the group's aims and goals. When it
comes to supervision and control, bureaucracies rely on multiple layers
of management and a web of policies and rules. Communities, by contrast, depend on norms, values, and the gentle prodding of one's peers.
Individual contributions tend to be circumscribed in a bureaucracy—
marketing people work on marketing plans, finance people run the numbers. In a community, capability and disposition are more important than
credentials and job descriptions in determining who does what. And
where the rewards offered by a bureaucracy are mostly financial, in a
community they're mostly emotional. When compared with bureaucracies, communities tend to be undermanaged. That, more than anything
else, is why they are amplifiers of human capability.

Before you accuse me of being a starry-eyed idealist, or just plain
goofy, let me be clear: I'm not arguing that we should turn every organization into some version of the Boy Scouts. I'm not naïve. I know
it would be impossible to keep people coming to work every day without the inducement of a paycheck—warm and fuzzy feelings won't put
food on the table and gas in the car. But here's an interesting thought

experiment: suppose you knew that in 12 months' time, a looming financial crisis would force you to cut the salary of every employee in your company by a third. Assume further that your company is running very lean and that every associate is making an indispensable contribution. Now, if the goal is to minimize the risk of a mass exodus when the financial crunch finally hits, what changes would you make over the next few months to keep your colleagues from jumping ship? Take some time with this question, be creative. My guess is that the changes you ultimately envision will be precisely those that would make your company feel less like a hierarchy and more like a community.

Too Much Exhortation, Too Little Purpose

Initiative, creativity, and passion are gifts. They are benefactions that employees choose, day by day and moment by moment, to give or withhold. They cannot be commanded. If you're a CEO, you won't get these gifts by exhorting people to work harder, or by ordering them to love their customers and kill their competitors. You'll only elicit these capabilities when you start asking yourself and your colleagues: What kind of purpose would *merit* the best of everyone who works here? What lofty cause would inspire folks to give generously of their talents?

Over the years, I've sat through a lot of rah-rah pep talks in big companies. I've seen CEOs pound the lectern, have had my eardrums pummeled by upbeat rock anthems, and have watched thousands of pumped up employees cheer and stomp. Trouble is, an adrenaline rush is transient. It can produce a thunderclap of emotion, but it can't produce a long, nourishing rain of inspired contribution—that takes more than breathless exhortation, it takes a moral imperative. That imperative could be producing impossibly beautiful products—a goal which motivates many at Apple. It could be curing diseases that were once thought incurable—a mission that inspires the folks at Genentech. It could be harnessing the world's wisdom and making it available to everyone, for nothing—the majestic notion behind Wikipedia.

A moral imperative can't be manufactured by speech writers or ginned up by consultants. It can't be cobbled together in a two-day offsite. Rather, it must grow out of some genuine sense of mission, possibility, or outrage. A moral imperative is not something one invents to wring more out of people. To be regarded as authentic, it must be an end, not a means.

Think about the management processes in your company. How much time and priority do these rituals give to conversations around purpose and destiny? Not much, I warrant. Sit in on a typical management meeting—to discuss strategy, budgets, employees, or anything else—and not only will you observe a distinct lack of right-brain thinking, you'll also hear virtually nothing that suggests the participants have *hearts*. Beauty. Truth. Love. Service. Wisdom. Justice. Freedom. Compassion. These are the moral imperatives that have aroused human beings to extraordinary accomplishment down through the ages. It is sad, then, that the vernacular of management has so little room for these virtues. Put simply, you are unlikely to get bighearted contributions from your employees unless they feel they are working toward some goal that encompasses bighearted ideals.

As a management innovator, you may not be in a position to singlehandedly craft a sense of purpose for your company, but you can look for ways of weaving discussions of purpose and principle into the fabric of your company's management conversations. For example, the next time you're in a meeting and folks are discussing how to wring another increment of performance out of your workforce, you might ask: "To what end, and to whose benefit, are our employees being asked to give of themselves? Have we committed ourselves to a purpose that is truly deserving of their initiative, imagination, and passion?"

There are a few more tasks, then, that we must add to our management innovation agenda:

1. How can you broaden the scope of employee freedom by managing less, without sacrificing focus, discipline, and order?

2. How can you create a company where the spirit of community, rather than the machinery of bureaucracy, binds people together?

3. How can you enlarge the sense of mission that people feel throughout your organization in a way that justifies extraordinary contribution?

I hope the problems discussed in this chapter will inspire you, and will help you to benchmark your own aspirations as a management innovator. At this point, you may be wondering whether it's really possible to make progress on problems this big. Are they tractable? Can you actually manage less without ending up in chaos? Is it really feasible to let employees choose what they'd like to work on? Can you build slack into an otherwise highly disciplined company? Can you make a profit-making enterprise feel like a community? If you're skeptical, then it's time to meet three modern-day management pioneers. These companies have been wrestling with the seemingly intractable challenges that I've laid out in this chapter—and they've been making real progress.

Whole Foods has some of the most amped-up and engaged employees of any big retailer. W.L. Gore has been labeled the world's most innovative company, and has one of the weirdest, most effective organizations on the planet. And then there's Google. Though young and still untested, it has been honing a management system that values adaptability above all else. While these companies aren't perfect, or invincible, they are heralds of a new management order—ongoing experiments in management innovation from which we can learn lessons both salutary and cautionary. So if you're still not sure it's possible to spit in the face of management orthodoxy and live to tell about it, read on. Let this trio of management renegades inspire you. Then keep on reading, and I'll lay out the building blocks for turning aspiration and inspiration into bona fide management innovation.

MANAGEMENT INNOVATION IN ACTION

PART TWO

Four

Creating a Community of Purpose

Whole Foods Market

IMAGINE A RETAILER WHERE FRONTLINE EMPLOYEES decide what to stock; where the pressure to perform comes from peers rather than from bosses; where teams, not managers, have veto power over new hires; and where virtually every employee feels like he or she is running a small business.[1] Try to envision a company where everyone knows what everyone else gets paid, and where senior execs limit their pay to 19 times the average wage. Picture, if you can, a company that doesn't think of itself as a company, but as a community of people working to make a difference in the world, where the mission matters as much as the bottom line. Conjure up all of this, and you'll have a portrait of Whole Foods Market, a company whose game-changing business model is wrapped inside an even more iconoclastic management model.

An Industry Revolutionary

The U.S. supermarket industry would seem to be an unlikely place to look for a breakthrough business model, much less for inspired management innovation. For more than 50 years, major supermarkets have competed with the same basic recipe: load up the shelves with "factory food," lure shoppers in with cut-price promotions and the promise of pint-sized rebates from coupons and "loyalty" cards, rely on suppliers to stoke demand with national TV advertising, and grow by gobbling up competing chains. Today, that stale old strategy is well past its sell date. In recent years, America's grocery chains have seen their growth rates flatten and their profits shrink as they have been forced by Wal-Mart to slash prices and pare costs to the bone. Their reward: anorexic margins, steadily declining market share, and chronic labor strife.

If you've ever shopped at Whole Foods, you know it's not your grandma's supermarket. Stuffed full of organic and natural products, a Whole Foods store is a commodious, eye-popping, mouthwatering temple to guilt-free gastronomy.

Whole Foods' business model is built around a simple but powerful premise: people will pay a premium for food that's good for them, good-tasting, and good for the environment. Ever since cofounder, chairman, and CEO John Mackey opened the original Whole Foods Natural Market, one of the country's first supermarket-style natural-food stores, in Austin, Texas, the company has focused its attentions on health-minded shoppers. In the beginning, the typical Whole Foods' customer was a Birkenstock-wearing, Volvo-driving tree hugger who refused to buy products made from ingredients that sounded more like chemical compounds than food.

Mackey, though, never intended to run a "holy-foods market," as he once put it.[2] From the beginning, his ambition was to offer a full-service, natural-food alternative for mainstream shoppers. Even in the early 1980s, one could sense big changes afoot in America's increasingly industrialized food business. These included mounting worries over pesticides and chemicals in the food supply; a fast-growing population of food-aware customers eager to buy out-of-the-ordinary comestibles; and an increasing desire among many to live in more ecologically sustainable ways. It would take the better part of a generation for America's big supermarkets to cotton on to these trends. In the mean time, their dithering allowed Mackey to build a new kind of supermarket that satisfied customers in new kinds of ways.

At every turn, this inventive company has taken the road less traveled. Whole Foods' commitment to organic produce and sustainable agriculture is unmatched by any competitor. Its stores are laid out to make shopping feel less like a chore and more like a culinary adventure. And unlike its hidebound rivals, which compete with a promotion-driven, loss-leader pricing model, Whole Foods charges a premium for its superfresh, environmentally friendly products, a fact that has led some critics to rebrand the store "Whole Paycheck." Nevertheless, Whole Foods has become the grocery store of choice for the hip and the health-conscious—the supermarket equivalent of Starbucks.

Today, Whole Foods operates 194 stores and generates nearly $6 billion a year in sales. It is also America's most profitable food retailer when measured by profit per square foot. Whole Foods has also done well by its investors. In the 15 years following its IPO in 1992, the company's stock price rose by nearly 3,000 percent, dramatically outperforming its grocery-sector rivals. Between 2002 and 2007, its same-store sales growth averaged 11 percent per annum, nearly triple the industry average. Just as impressive, Whole Foods' revenue per square foot was $900 in 2006, double that of any traditional competitor. Even after a major correction to Whole Foods' soaring share price in 2006, the company still had a market value of nearly $7 billion. And while Kroger, America's second-largest grocery retailer (after Wal-Mart), was worth nearly three times that amount, it operated more than 2,500 stores, or roughly 12 times as many as Whole Foods.

A Contrarian Management Model

Anyone can walk into a Whole Foods store and inspect the layout, peruse the shelves, and squeeze the produce, but it takes a lot more effort to decode the company's peculiar, if not exotic, management model. Whole Foods' approach to management twines democracy with discipline, trust with accountability, and community with fierce internal competition. It is the skillful juxtaposition of these counterpoised values that makes the company's management system both uniquely effective and hard to duplicate.

Freedom and Accountability

At Whole Foods, the basic organizational unit is not the store, but the team. Small, empowered work groups are granted a degree of autonomy nearly unprecedented in retailing. Each store consists of roughly eight teams that oversee departments ranging from seafood to produce to checkout. Every new associate is provisionally assigned to a team. After a four-week work trial, teammates vote on the applicant's fate; a newbie needs a two-thirds majority vote to win a full-time spot on the team. This peer-based selection process is used for all new employees, including those hoping to join teams at Whole Foods' headquarters, such as the national IT or finance squads. The underlying logic is powerful, if unconventional: Whole Foods believes that critical decisions, such as whom to hire, should be made by those who will be most directly impacted by the consequences of those decisions.

One observes this spirit of radical decentralization in every component of the Whole Foods' management model. Small teams are responsible for all key operating decisions, including pricing, ordering, staffing, and in-store promotion. Consider product selection. Team leaders, in consultation with their store manager, are free to stock whatever products they feel will appeal to local customers. This is a marked departure from standard supermarket practice, in which national buyers dictate what each store will carry, and big food manufacturers pay thousands of dollars in slotting fees to get their products on the shelf. At Whole Foods, no executive sitting in Austin decides which products will appear on what shelves. Stores are encouraged to buy locally as long as the items meet Whole Foods' stringent standards. As a result, every store carries a unique mix of products. Teams also control staffing levels within their departments, a prerogative that is elsewhere usually reserved for the store manager.

In essence, each team operates like a profit center and is measured on its labor productivity. While associates are highly empowered, they are also highly accountable. Every four weeks, Whole Foods calculates the profit per labor hour for every team in every store. Teams that exceed a certain threshold get a bonus in their next paycheck. Each team has access to performance data for every other team within its store, and for similar teams in other stores. The fact that no team wants to end up as a laggard adds to the motivation to do well. All this explains why the hiring vote is such a big deal at Whole Foods. Vote in a slacker, and your paycheck may take a beating. Indeed, CEO Mackey argues that department members really don't take ownership of their performance until they've stood up to a team leader and voted down a new hire.

This exceptional degree of autonomy conveys a simple but invigorating message: it is you, rather than some distant manager, who controls your success. The fact that this freedom is matched by a high level of accountability ensures that associates use their discretionary decision-making power in ways that drive the business forward. Unlike so many other companies, frontline employees at Whole Foods have both the *freedom* to do the right thing for customers, and the *incentive* to do the right thing for profits.

In a more hierarchical company, top management only sees problems once they've become pervasive and, therefore, expensive to fix. At Whole Foods, tight linkage between business intelligence and decision-making authority ensures that little problems don't have to compound into big problems before action is taken. Couple this localized decision-making model with a system that gives employees the incentive to borrow best practices from better-performing stores, and you have the foundation for an operationally resilient company.

The tight link between autonomy and accountability also diminishes the need for motivation-sapping, bureaucratic controls. Says Mackey, "We don't have lots of rules that are handed down from headquarters in Austin. We have lots of self-examination going on. Peer pressure substitutes for bureaucracy. Peer pressure enlists loyalty in ways that bureaucracy doesn't."[3]

Trust

Putting so much authority in the hands of associates requires that top management trusts them to do the right thing for the business. Conversely, team members will stay motivated over the long term only if they trust top management to let them share in the bounty of their own productivity. Whole Foods builds that trust in a variety of ways. For example, each associate has access to the compensation data for every other store employee. This transparency makes it difficult for managers to play favorites or be idiosyncratic in their compensation decisions, since disgruntled associates can challenge the logic of salary discrepancies. The ability to compare salaries also spurs employees to develop their skills and take on new responsibilities, since they can easily see which sorts of jobs, and people, get most generously compensated.

Whole Foods' transparency extends far beyond salary data. Much of the company's sensitive operating and financial data—daily store sales, team sales, product costs, profits for each store, and more—are available to any staffer who wants to see them. Store teams need detailed financial data to make decisions on issues like ordering and pricing, but Whole Foods' "no-secrets" management philosophy, has a larger purpose: open books are the only way to build a company that is bound by trust. It's standard practice at many companies to conceal information as a way of controlling employees—a formula that's toxic to trust. By contrast, the top team at Whole Foods believes you can't have secrets and have a high-trust organization.[4]

Equity

In a myriad of ways, the folks at Whole Foods have worked to build a company that feels more like a community than a hierarchy. The company's mission statement is titled a "Declaration of Interdependence" and describes Whole Foods as "a community working together to create value for other people." To an outsider, such a sentiment sounds sloppy and disingenuous. All too often, business leaders blithely tell employees that "we're-all-in-this-together," while simultaneously tolerating Switzerland-Somalia disparities in CEO-associate pay. The result: a cynical workforce. In contrast, the top team at Whole Foods puts its money where its mouth is. Believing that 100-to-1 salary differentials are incompatible with the ethos of a community, and more likely to inspire resentment than trust, Whole Foods' leaders have set a salary cap that limits any individual's compensation to no more than 19 times the company average. (In the average *Fortune* 500 company, the ratio is more than 400 to 1.) In the same spirit, 93 percent of the company's stock options have been granted to nonexecutives. (In most companies, 75 percent of the stock options are distributed to five or fewer senior executives.[5]) To further reinforce the notions of community and interdependence, every Whole Foods meeting ends with a round of "appreciations," where each participant acknowledges the contributions of his or her peers.

The national leadership team at Whole Foods understands that the company's success depends critically on getting employees to bring more than their bodies and brains to work each day. Senior executives often include a slide of Maslow's hierarchy in their presentations. They know that employees will find fulfillment only if they've been given the chance to exercise their higher order capabilities—initiative, imagination, and passion.

Purpose

What ultimately binds Whole Foods' 30,000-plus associates into a community is a common cause—to reverse the industrialization of the world's food supply and give people better things to eat. This is capitalism with a conscience. A few rubber-meets-the-road examples:

- Whole Foods has used its buying power to change modern factory farming, so that animals are treated humanely before slaughter.

- It has created "Take Action" centers in its stores where customers can learn about PCB levels in salmon and living conditions for farm-raised ducks.

- Whole Foods is the only U.S. supermarket that owns and operates its own seafood-processing plants, and the company's salmon-sourcing policies have been deemed sustainable by the Marine Stewardship Council.

- In January 2006, Whole Foods made the largest-ever purchase of renewable energy credits from wind farms—enough, in fact, to cover all of the company's electric energy consumption.

In the same way Mackey sees no conflict between food that's healthy and food that's delectable, he sees no inconsistency between a passion for sustainability and a passion for profitability. "Our customers want us to act in an environmentally responsible way," he says. "To maximize shareholder value, you'd better be a positive force in the community."[6]

Communities are usually built around a shared sense of purpose, and so it is with Whole Foods. For many associates, working at Whole Foods is an expression of their own lifestyle choices and values: they get to sell nutritious food, contribute to sustainable farming, and support pesticide-free agriculture. All this is summed up in the company's oft-repeated mantra: "Whole Foods. Whole People. Whole Planet." Says one senior leader, "We don't think about growing the brand—that's MBA talk. We're about fulfilling our mission."

It is a sense of shared fate, and faith in a shared mission that makes the Whole Foods community whole. Shared fate is seen in team-based rewards, in the transparency of financial information, and in the limits of top management's compensation. Shared mission emanates from a calling to change the way the world farms and eats. But you won't find team members sitting around holding hands and singing "Kum Bay Yah." Whole Foods is a formidable competitor because it competes relentlessly against itself. Teams compete against their own historic benchmarks, against other teams within their store and similar teams across Whole Foods. Success translates directly into recognition, bonuses, and promotions. Ten times a year, each store is assessed by a head office executive and a regional leader who rate the store on 300 different performance measures. Each store's "customer snapshot" scores are distributed to every other store—another way that Whole Foods fuels the competitive instincts of its associates.

Mackey sees profits as a means to the end of realizing Whole Foods' social goals. "We want to improve the health and well-being of everyone on the planet through higher quality foods and better nutrition," Mackey wrote in a September 2005 entry to his blog. "We can't fulfill this mission unless we are highly profitable."[7] At Whole Foods, profits are the score, not the game. This ordering often gets reversed in companies that lack any greater purpose than making sure top management's stock options stay in the money.

Of course, there's no guarantee that Whole Foods' smooth-running escalator of success will keep climbing upward. Like every company in the 21st century, Whole Foods is challenged on all sides. Some of its most loyal customers, those who've been shopping at Whole Foods for far longer than the Range Rover set, worry that the company will compromise its values as it expands. Small organic farmers complain that a move to consolidate suppliers has made it tougher to sell locally grown produce to Whole Foods. And then there are those massive, wallowing competitors. They may be slow, but Whole Foods is now too big and too prosperous to ignore. With Wal-Mart committed to offering a full line of organic produce, Whole Foods is bound to face stiffer competition in the years to come. In this environment, the company will need the imagination of every employee to maintain its class-leading margins.

Yet the industry's veterans are competing with much more than a novel business concept. They're competing with a community, a mission, and a dramatically different management philosophy. Despite having had a quarter of a century to unravel the secrets of Whole Foods' success, the old guard is still playing catch-up to this irrepressible and sometimes sanctimonious "upstart"—a fact that testifies to one of the cardinal axioms of management innovation: it's usually harder for competitors to imitate an unconventional management model than it is for them to decode an unconventional business model.

Lessons for Management Innovators

What should you take away from the experience of this modern management pioneer? Let me suggest three essential lessons, each of which will be reinforced when we delve into W. L. Gore and Google.

One: Principles matter.

In 1992, one year after Whole Foods went public, Mackey reiterated his intention of "creating an organization based on love instead of fear."[8] It is difficult to imagine many CEOs embracing such a view, let alone articulating it publicly. Given the sorry state of industrial relations in America's grocery industry, where screwing down wages and benefits has often seemed to be management's top priority, it's hardly surprising that supermarket employees are generally disinclined to deliver outstanding service or to bring their very best to work each day. Loving your employees may seem sensible, but it's a mandate that's more often ignored than honored.

Whole Foods' unique management *system* is based on a nexus of distinctive management *principles*: Love. Community. Autonomy. Egalitarianism. Transparency. Mission. Over the past 25 years Whole Foods has turned these contrarian principles into an interlocking set of management processes and practices that energize and shape the day-to-day actions of its team members. A management system this comprehensive, this evolved, and this different doesn't emerge fully born. And it certainly doesn't come from benchmarking industry incumbents. It comes instead from a fundamentally different philosophical starting point.

Translating high-sounding principles into day-to-day management practices is hard, painstaking work. It requires an unshakeable faith in your tenets, even though their application confounds traditional management theory and seems sure to undermine productivity and unleash chaos. Whole Foods took the risk and so far, anyway, it has paid off.

Two: The biggest obstacle to management innovation may be what you already believe about management.

"One of the keys to understanding this company," says Mackey, "is that the people who started it did not know how they were supposed to do it."[9] Although he majored in philosophy at the University of Texas, Mackey never earned a college degree, an MBA. Having sidestepped a formal business education, Mackey didn't start his career with a head stuffed full of stale business clichés and conventional management nostrums. He was able to invent an unorthodox management model because he wasn't a prisoner of orthodox training. Of course, Whole Foods is not *entirely* different from your company, nor do its executives reject time-tested management practices out of hand. But before borrowing any bit of conventional management wisdom, they first ask, is this consistent with our unique values and our sense of mission? Mackey's near-fanatical zeal and his on-the-job management education have allowed him to challenge and overturn management dogma that would be regarded as near sacred by better-trained, less mission-driven executives. Indeed, says one former Whole Foods executive: "Mackey is hardly a manager at all. He's an anarchist."[10]

Three: Inspired management innovation can help to resolve intractable trade-offs.

In many ways, Whole Foods is a study in contrasts: freedom and responsibility, community and competition, social mission and fat profits. But it is these carefully managed tensions that account for much of the company's success. Accountability ensures that autonomy doesn't produce chaos. Internal competition ensures that a strong sense of community doesn't degenerate into complacency. Outstanding financial results allow the company to make a difference on a scale that most non-profits would find hard to match.

Too often, companies try to sidestep difficult trade-offs. To them, paradoxes are a pain. So they adopt metrics, processes, and decision rules that give one operational objective or performance goal an almost permanent advantage over its opposite number. Typically, the short-term beats the long-term, discipline trounces innovation, and internal competition drives out collaboration. Successful management innovators like John Mackey find ways of reconciling irreconcilable trade-offs and capturing the benefits of two-sided advantages.

Revisiting Our Management Innovation Agenda

Whole Foods' innovative management model has allowed the company to successfully address several of the next-generation challenges laid out in chapter 3.

Management Innovation Challenge	*Whole Foods' Distinctive Management Practices*
How do you empower people by managing less while retaining discipline and focus?	Give employees a large dose of discretion; provide them with the information they need to make wise decisions; and then hold them accountable for results.
How do you create a company where the spirit of community binds people together?	Manage as if you really believe that the interests of stakeholders are interdependent; create a high degree of financial transparency; and limit compensation disparities.
How do you build an enlarged sense of purpose that merits extraordinary contributions?	Make the pursuit "Whole Foods, Whole People, Whole Planet" as real and tangible to employees as the pursuit of profits.

Given all of this, it's hardly surprising that Whole Foods has been ranked as one of *Fortune* magazine's "100 Best Companies to Work For" every year since 1998, when the list was first published. In 2007, Whole Foods was voted as the fifth most rewarding place to work in America. Turns out that management innovation really *can* help a company overcome the disengagement and malaise that is endemic in traditionally managed workplaces.

Looking forward, no one knows whether Whole Foods will soar or sink. But if it's the latter, it won't be for lack of ambition. In one of the company's annual reports, as one senior executive boldly put it "We intend to be the best grocery store, bar none, while still upholding the high quality standards that our customers have come to expect." If Whole Foods evolves its management model as rapidly over the next 25 years as it has over the past quarter century, it may have a shot at achieving this lofty goal; if not, it may get overtaken. For now, one can simply say, this is a community that *performs*.

Five

Building an Innovation Democracy

W.L. Gore

IMAGINE THAT YOU'VE JUST QUIT YOUR JOB WITH A widely admired industry leader. The decision to leave wasn't easy. Your career was on an upward swing and you were working on an exciting new technology. But after a near-20-year stint, you've decided you've had enough—enough of the politicking, enough of the pokey decision making, and enough of the endless wrangling over budgets and priorities. Over the years you saw a lot of great ideas get flushed down the toilet of management indifference—or languish while some upstart seized the lead. So you're leaving to start a new company, one where inventors like you won't get bogged down in a swamp of bureaucracy; one where associates will spend a lot more time innovating and a lot less time brownnosing the boss. You hope your company will grow big, but you also want it to feel intimate and stay entrepreneurial.[1]

Given this goal, where would you begin? What core principles would you start with? How would your company be organized? How would decisions get made? Who would be in control? As you look around for answers, you quickly conclude that no one has a blueprint for building an innovators' paradise. It isn't just your company—every big organization is inhospitable to innovation. If you want to build an innovation-friendly management system, you're going to have to invent it.

Bill Gore:
Management Innovator

This was the challenge that faced Wilbert ("Bill") L. Gore in 1958 when, after a 17-year career, he left DuPont to strike out on his own. Gore dreamed of building a company devoted to innovation, a company where imagination and initiative would flourish, where chronically curious engineers would be free to invent, invest, and succeed. Over the next several decades, Gore's vision took shape in the form of W. L. Gore & Associates, a company built around a set of management principles diametrically opposed to much of modern business orthodoxy. Bill's legacy is an organization that today generates $2.1 billion in annual sales and employs more than 8,000 employees in 45 plants around the world.

You've probably gotten up-close and personal with Gore's best-known product, Gore-Tex fabric, the laminate that helped usher in a revolution in breathable, waterproof outdoor-wear. With its headquarters tucked away in the leafy suburbs outside of Newark, Delaware, Gore has operations in the United States, Scotland, Germany, Japan, and China. A privately held company, Gore is ignored by Wall Street. Yet over the past five decades, it has conducted a bold, and so far successful, experiment in radical management innovation.

Compared with Gore-Tex, the rest of the company's product lineup may seem unheralded, but it is so extensive and varied that at times it seems nearly unquantifiable. Gore's pioneering fabrics, which are found in boots, shoes, headwear, gloves, and sleeping bags, have been worn on expeditions to the North and South Poles and to the top of Mt. Everest. Its medical products, which include synthetic vascular grafts and surgical meshes, have been implanted in more than 13 million patients. Gore fibers are woven into the space suits worn by NASA astronauts. Its membrane technology is used in hydrogen-powered fuel cells. Time and again, Gore has jumped into new, untested markets and seized the lead, as it did with its Elixir guitar strings and Glide dental floss, a product line it sold to Procter & Gamble for an undisclosed sum in 2003. At any one time, there are hundreds of nascent projects under development at Gore. This is a big company that really does behave like a start-up—and makes money doing so. While Gore doesn't break out its annual financial data, it has reportedly produced a profit every year since its founding.

The seeds of what would become Gore's revolutionary management model were planted while Bill Gore was still at DuPont. Over the course of his career, Gore had several times been assigned to small R&D task groups. These freewheeling teams, with their outsized objectives and operational autonomy, energized Gore—and he knew they invigorated his colleagues as well. Initiative, passion, and courage seemed to flourish in the hothouse of a small, focused team, even when that team was part of a much bigger organization. Why, wondered Gore, couldn't an entire company be designed as a bureaucracy-free zone?

Gore's entrepreneurial zeal was further fueled by a belief that DuPont was grossly underestimating the potential of polytetrafluoroethylene (PTFE), the slick, waxy fluoropolymer known more commonly by the brand name Teflon. Gore felt that DuPont's allegiance to its traditional business model—large-scale production of basic industrial materials—was preventing the company from imagining new uses for quirky but exciting materials like PTFE.

So it was that Gore and his wife, Genevieve ("Vieve"), both 45 years old, dumped their life savings into the newly christened company and started ramping up production in the basement of their home. With five children to support, and as many college educations to fund, they had no option but to make the new venture a success. Yet at every step, the Gores stayed true to their goal of creating a company that would be a multiplier of human imagination.

Bill Gore's embryonic management philosophy was deeply influenced by Douglas McGregor's best seller, *The Human Side of Enterprise*, which was published in 1960.[2] McGregor, as you'll recall, boldly challenged the management dogma that prevailed at the time. Conventional wisdom, which McGregor termed "Theory X," viewed employees as lazy, disinterested in their work, and motivated only by money. "Theory Y," by contrast, assumed that human beings were self-motivating problem solvers who found meaning in their work.

Gore knew that executives would often slop a little Theory Y varnish onto their Theory X management practices, but he didn't know of any company that had been built from the ground up on Theory Y principles. Yet this was precisely the challenge that he was itching to take on. Still, there were a lot of questions to answer: Could you build a company with no hierarchy—where everyone was free to talk with everyone else? How about a company where there were no bosses, no supervisors, and no vice presidents? Could you let people choose what they wanted to work on, rather than assigning them tasks? Could you create a company with no "core" business, where people would put as much energy into finding the next big thing as they did into milking the last big thing? And could you do all of this while still delivering consistent growth and profitability?

In each case, the answer turned out be "yes"—but only because Gore and his colleagues were willing to defy a host of sacrosanct management principles. To see the results of their contrarian thinking, you'll need to visit W.L. Gore's head office, or step into one of its plants. When you do, here's what you'll find.

A Lattice,
Not a Hierarchy

At first glance, Gore seems to bear some of the same structural trappings of other big organizations. There's a CEO, Terri Kelly, who earned a degree in mechanical engineering at the University of Delaware and has spent her entire 23-year career at Gore. There are four major divisions, a broad array of product-focused business units, and the usual gamut of companywide support functions. Each of these organizations has a recognized leader at the helm.

Dig a little deeper, though, and you'll quickly discover that Gore is as flat as the proverbial pancake. There are no management layers and there is no organizational chart. Few people have titles and no one has a boss. As is true at Whole Foods Market, the core operating units at Gore are small, self-managing teams, all of which share two common goals: "to make money and have fun."

Bill Gore conceived of the company as a "lattice" rather than a ladderlike hierarchy. In theory, a lattice-based architecture connects every individual in the organization to everyone else. Lines of communication are direct—person to person and team to team. In a hierarchy, responsibilities are more up and down than they are lateral. A lattice, on the other hand, implies multiple nodes on the same level; a dense network of interpersonal connections where information can flow in all directions, unfiltered by an intermediary. In a lattice, you serve your peers, rather than a boss, and you don't have to work "through channels" to collaborate with your colleagues.

No doubt recalling his own experience at DuPont, Gore once observed, "Most of us delight in going around the formal procedures and doing things the straightforward and easy way,"[3] which in his view begged the obvious question: Why have a formal, authoritarian structure in the first place? Gore believed that in every organization there was an informal matrix of relationships underlying what he called, "the façade of authoritarian hierarchy." His goal: get rid of the façade.

Gore understood the potential pitfalls in abandoning a hierarchical organization. Could a lattice respond nimbly to a fast-moving market? Where would discipline and direction come from, if not from a cascade of goals passed down through a chain of command? Would a bunch of free spirits taking direction from no one descend into operational anarchy? Gore recognized that the "simplicity and order of an authoritarian organization" made hierarchy "an almost irresistible temptation." But an organization that by design stifled creativity and individual freedom repelled him. For all of its potential shortcomings, he felt a lattice was preferable to the alternative.

No Bosses,
but Plenty of Leaders

Walk around the halls at Gore, or sit in on meetings, and you won't hear anyone use words like "boss," "executive," "manager," or "vice president." These terms are so contrary to Gore's egalitarian ideals that they are effectively banned from conversation.

Although there are no ranks or titles at Gore, some associates have earned the simple appellation "leader." At Gore, senior leaders do not appoint junior leaders. Rather, associates become leaders when their peers judge them to be such. A leader garners influence by demonstrating a capacity to get things done and excelling as a team builder. At Gore, those who make a disproportionate contribution to team success, and do it more than once, attract followers. "We vote with our feet," says Rich Buckingham, a manufacturing leader in Gore's technical-fabrics group. "If you call a meeting, and people show up, you're a leader."[4] Individuals who've been repeatedly asked to serve as tribal chiefs are free to put the word "leader" on their business card. About 10 percent of Gore's associates carry such a designation.

The way Terri Kelly earned her CEO stripes is typical of Gore's approach. When Chuck Carroll, Gore's previous CEO, retired, the board of directors supplemented its discussions by polling a wide cross-section of Gore associates. They were asked to pick someone they'd be willing to follow. "We weren't given a list of names—we were free to choose anyone in the company," Kelly recalls. "To my surprise, it was me."

Through its embrace of what it terms "natural leadership," Gore has created a system in which executive power can never be taken for granted. Since a team is free to fire its chief, peer-chosen leaders must continually re-earn the allegiance of their colleagues to retain their authority. This ensures that a leader's primary accountability is always to the led. It also means that leaders can't abuse their positional power, since they have none.

Sponsors Instead of Bosses

At Gore, newcomers are confronted with some perplexing questions: Who do I work for? Who can make a decision? What's the next rung on the career ladder? In most companies, the answers to these questions are straightforward. Not so at Gore.

New recruits are hired into broad roles—as HR generalists, business-development leaders, or R&D engineers—rather than into narrowly defined jobs. To help newcomers navigate the organization and find their niche, each is assigned a starting "sponsor"—a veteran who decodes the jargon, makes introductions, and guides the tyro through the lattice. In their first few months, new hires are likely to circulate among several teams. At each stop they are, in effect, auditioning for a part. It's the sponsor's job to help a new associate find a good fit between his or her skills and the needs of a particular team. In true Gore fashion, an associate is free to seek out a new sponsor if he or she so desires. Likewise, teams are free to adopt a new associate or not, as they choose.

Associates are responsible to their teams, rather than to a boss. The absence of formally chartered supervisors may seem like a demented omission, but it reflects one of Gore's core principles: in a high-trust, low-fear organization, employees don't need a lot of oversight—they need to be mentored and supported, rather than bossed around.

Free to Experiment

The primary fuel for Gore's innovation machine is the discretionary time of its associates. All employees are granted a half day a week of "dabble time," which they can devote to an initiative of their own choosing—so long as they are fulfilling their primary commitments.

Every associate knows that most of Gore's product breakthroughs started as dabble-time projects. After all, the seminal moment in the company's history came in 1969, when Bill Gore's son, Robert ("Bob") W. Gore (the company's current chairman), stumbled upon a way of stretching PTFE. The resulting polymer—expanded PTFE—proved to be simultaneously durable and porous. Trademarked as Gore-Tex, PTFE became the springboard for hundreds of products, including the family of fabrics that make up the company's biggest business. It's hardly surprising, then, that Gore's recipe for product innovation starts with a deeply held belief that serendipity can strike at any time, and that anyone can be an innovator.

As a case in point, consider Gore's guitar-string business, which got its start when Dave Myers, an engineer based in Flagstaff, Arizona, coated his mountain-bike cables with the same polymer that comprises Gore-Tex fabric. Pleased with the result, Myers suspected that the cables' grit-repelling coating might be ideal for guitar strings, which lose some of their tonal qualities when skin oils build up in their steel coils. Although Myers was principally engaged in developing cardiac implants, he decided to spend his dabble time pursuing the guitar-string project, despite the fact that Gore had no presence in the music industry.

Based in a grouping of ten plants, Myers quickly tracked down R&D help and soon had a small team of volunteers working on his bootstrap project. After three years of on-and-off experimentation—and without ever seeking a formal endorsement for his initiative—Myers's team finally hit the bull's-eye with a string that held its tone three times longer than the industry standard. Today, Elixir acoustic guitar strings outsell their closest U.S. competitor by a two-to-one margin. It's hard to imagine the medical products division of any other company spawning a line of best-selling guitar strings, yet this is par for the course at Gore.

At its core, Gore is a marketplace for ideas, where product champions like Myers compete for the discretionary time of the company's most talented individuals, and where associates eager to work on something new vie for the chance to join a promising project. Recruiting people to a new initiative is, says CEO Kelly, a "process of giving away ownership of the idea to people who want to contribute. The project won't go anywhere if you don't let people run with it."[5] In this sense, Gore is a "gift economy." Would-be entrepreneurs give the gift of a new opportunity and in return, peers donate their talent, experience, and commitment. As one engineer put it: "If you can't find enough people to work on your project, maybe it's not a good idea."[6] The result is that ideas at Gore compete on a level playing field. Since there are no EVPs or business heads, no one's pet project gets a free pass, but neither can any one person abort an embryonic project.

Commitments, Not Assignments

During his years at DuPont, Bill Gore developed a keen appreciation for the difference between commitment and compliance. As he often put it, "Authoritarians cannot impose commitments, only commands." Gore believed deeply that willing commitment is many times more valuable to an organization than resigned compliance. This belief lies at the heart of another Gore tenet: "All commitments are self-commitments." In practice, this means that associates negotiate job assignments and responsibilities with their peers. At Gore, tasks can't be assigned, they can only be accepted; but since associates are measured and rewarded on the basis of their contribution to team success, they have an incentive to commit to more rather than less. While associates are free to say "no" to any request, a commitment once made is regarded as a near-sacred oath. New associates are regularly admonished not to overextend themselves, since a bungled commitment will impact their compensation. While the process of negotiating commitments can be time-consuming, the payoff in terms of morale is substantial. At Gore, virtually every associate can truthfully say, "I'm doing exactly what I signed up to do."

Seasoned executives who join Gore from other companies are initially bewildered by the ethos of voluntary commitment. Those who survive must adapt to life in the lattice. As Steve Young, a consumer-marketing expert hired from Vlasic Foods, quickly discovered, "If you tell anybody what to do here, they'll never work for you again."

Energizing and Demanding

Within Gore, the pressure to contribute can be both exhilarating and exhausting. Within a few months of signing up with their first team, newcomers at Gore will be encouraged to add a second or third project to their portfolio. Since people are assumed to be multifaceted, with a wide range of interests, no one is expected to devote 100 percent of his or her time to a single task.

Despite the unprecedented freedom granted to associates, Gore isn't a company for slackers. Once a year, every associate receives a comprehensive peer review. Typically, data is collected from at least 20 colleagues. This information is shared with a compensation committee comprising individuals from the employee's work area. Each associate is then ranked against every other member of the business unit in terms of overall contribution. This rank ordering determines relative compensation. While the list isn't published, people are told in which quartile they rank. Seniority yields no dividends in Gore's compensation system. For example, an experienced business leader might be paid less than a PhD scientist. The formula is unblinking: the more you contribute, the more highly regarded and rewarded you will be. Consequently, most associates feel pressured to take on more rather than less. Critically, though, this pressure doesn't come from a whip-cracking boss, but from one's own teammates.

While Gore's compensation system clearly differentiates between those who add more value and those who add less, the company also works hard to create a deep sense of shared destiny. Every associate is a shareholder. After their first year at Gore, new associates are awarded 12 percent of their salary in the form of stock. The shares vest over time, and employees can cash out when they leave the company. For most associates, this allotment of Gore stock is their single biggest financial asset, and the ticket to a comfortable retirement. Gore also features an annual profit-sharing program that enables employees to share in the short-term success of the enterprise. Not surprisingly, most associates feel they have a big stake in helping the company to grow.

Big Yet Personal

There are few $2 billion-a-year companies that feel as intimate as Gore. In a small company, most meetings take place face-to-face, and Gore has worked hard to maximize opportunities for personal interaction. R&D specialists, salespeople, engineers, chemists, and machinists typically work in the same building. The proximity of different disciplines helps cut time to market and keeps everyone focused on the goal of satisfying customers. Associates are encouraged to talk to their colleagues face-to-face, rather than relying on e-mail.

To better mobilize people and ideas, the company organizes its plants into clusters, like the 10 factories located in Flagstaff, or the 15 that sit near the Delaware-Maryland border. The fact that most of Gore's plants are located near sister sites is a boon to associates scouting for a new team to join, and to new product champions looking for expert advice and volunteers. While it might be cheaper to locate new facilities in lower-cost locations, Gore believes the benefits of dense, cross-functional, and cross-team communication more than outweigh the economic penalty of its cluster model.

With few exceptions, no facility or manufacturing site is allowed to grow to more than 200 people. Bill Gore believed that as the number of people in a business increased, associates inevitably felt less connected with one another and with the ultimate product. Moreover, the bigger the unit, the smaller the stake people would have in key decisions, and hence the less motivated they would be to carry them out. To borrow Gore's simple phrasing, once a unit reaches a particular size, "'we decided' becomes 'they decided.'" Gore realized that while bigger units can bring greater efficiency, they also bring more bureaucracy, since that's the only way to keep poorly motivated, disconnected employees on track.

Focused, but No Core Business

Though Gore is organized into four divisions—fabrics, electronics, medical, and industrial—leaders at Gore don't spend much time trying to define the boundaries of the company's "core business." With more than 1,000 products in its portfolio, Gore is a classic example of a company that has leveraged a small number of world-beating competencies into a dizzying array of product markets. While leaders encourage innovation that extends Gore's presence in existing markets, such as surgical supplies, anything that exploits Gore's expertise in PTFE and other polymers is considered in scope. This provides associates with a remarkably broad canvas for innovation.

Given the freedom that associates have to pursue their own interests and their ability to recruit talent from across the company, Gore is able to maintain a healthy balance between investments that extend today's businesses and those that open gateways to new markets.

Tenacious, and Risk Averse

Tenacity is another ingredient in Gore's recipe for relentless innovation. This is coupled with a deeply embedded management process for identifying and minimizing unnecessary investment risks. Gore is patient—a promising project can bubble along for as long as it continues to hold the interest of a few associates. In many companies, "patience" is equated with a willingness to endure losses over a long time frame, rather than with the sort of tenacity that keeps folks chipping away at big, important problems. At Gore, though, determination and perseverance don't come at the expense of prudence. The company never bets big until all of a project's key uncertainties have been resolved.

Every new product champion knows the drill: clearly identify critical hypotheses and develop low-cost ways of testing important assumptions. Once a project moves beyond the dabble stage, there is a cross-functional review process that periodically puts the development team through an exercise called "Real, Win, Worth." To attract resources, a product champion must first demonstrate that the opportunity is *real.* Colleagues will ask, "Does this product solve a bona fide customer problem? How many customers have this need and how much will they pay for a better solution?" As development proceeds, the question becomes whether or not Gore can win in the marketplace. Questions at this stage include: "Do we have a defensible technology advantage?" "Do we have skill gaps that will require us to find partners?" "Are there any regulatory hurdles that must be overcome?" Once these questions have been addressed, the focus turns to profitability: "Can we price the product high enough to get a good margin?" "Can we build a business system that makes money?" "How quickly will we hit our breakeven point?" There is no predetermined timetable that drives a product from concept to reality, no calendar-driven stage gates. While the early conversation around customer value helps to weed out truly loopy ideas, intriguing product concepts are given plenty of time to make the journey from "Real" to "Worth"—as long as they're not burning through too much cash. Along the way, everyone pays close attention to "waterline" scenarios—missteps that could seriously harm the company's financial position or reputation. Gore wins big not by betting big, but by betting often—and by staying at the table long enough to collect its winnings.

Eccentric as they are, all of the various elements of Gore's unique management system serve one overriding objective: continuous, rule-breaking innovation. While Gore's leaders understand that it's tough to *plan* for innovation, they have no doubt that it's possible to *organize* for innovation. Not surprisingly, most associates love working at Gore. Like Whole Foods, Gore has been included in every one of *Fortune*'s annual rankings of the "100 Best Companies to Work For." Just as importantly, Gore has delivered nearly 50 years of steady earnings growth without a single annual loss. It seems unlikely that Bill Gore, who died in 1986, would be surprised by his company's continuing success. He always believed that the conventional way of managing a big company wasn't the only way, and that when it comes to management innovation, radical doesn't have to mean screwball.

Essential Lessons

So what can prospective management innovators learn from Gore's success?

> One: Management innovation
> often redistributes power.
> (So don't expect everyone
> to be enthusiastic.)

Over the decades, thousands of executives have visited Gore hoping to learn from its inspiring example. So it's worth asking: Why does Gore's management model seem as weird and unprecedented today as it did nearly five decades ago? Maybe it's because Gore continues to take innovation more seriously than just about any other company in the world. Maybe it's because Gore is a privately held company and can get away with exotic management practices that wouldn't fly with public shareholders. Or maybe it's because Bill Gore had a clean sheet of paper and never had to battle the barons of bureaucracy. All of these are plausible explanations, yet none provides an entirely adequate answer to our question: Why, after 50 years, is Gore's management model still more studied than emulated?

I believe it's because Gore's eccentric management system is deeply disturbing to executives who've grown comfortable with the power and perquisites of life in more hierarchical companies. While executives often talk glibly of "inverting the pyramid," they are undoubtedly unnerved when they discover it can actually be done! How, a power-wielding executive is bound to ask, could I ever succeed in an organization like *this*?

Leaders who have learned to rely on their titles to get things done are likely to view Gore's model with as much trepidation as envy. A traditionally minded manager is understandably disconcerted when confronted by the reality of an organization where power is disconnected from position—where you can't push decisions through just because you're perched higher up the ladder; where you don't have "direct reports" to command; where your power erodes rapidly if no one wants to follow you; and where your credentials and intellectual superiority aren't acknowledged with the laurel wreath of a grand title.

For most executives, the synchronization of power with a precisely calibrated scale of management titles and grades is one of the defining, and comforting, realities of managerial life. It should hardly be surprising then, that radical *management* innovation often fractures this central pillar of organizational design. Whether it's the power granted to first-level employees at Toyota, the discretion given to team members at Whole Foods, or the lack of status differentiators at Gore, management innovation almost always delegates power downward and outward. In my experience, most managers support the *idea* of empowerment, but become noticeably less enthusiastic when confronted with the necessary corollary—to enfranchise employees you must *dis*enfranchise managers. Yet as we'll see in subsequent chapters, the redistribution of power is one of the primary means for making organizations more adaptable, more innovative, and more highly engaging.

Two: In the short run,
the costs of management innovation
may be more visible than the benefits.

Even when management innovation doesn't entail a wholesale reallotment of power, it can be a hard sell when the costs seem more tangible than the benefits. For example, any half-decent accountant could easily calculate the economies Gore would reap if it sited a new plant in one of the world's ultra-cheap offshore manufacturing centers rather than near a cluster of existing plants. But how would one calculate the lost opportunity for cross-business learning? How would you price the reduction in the opportunities for employees to enhance their skills through lateral career moves? Likewise, anyone with a sharp pencil could tell Gore what it would save by consolidating its small-scale facilities. But how would one compare the savings of bigger, more integrated factories, with the loss of intimacy and *esprit de corps*?

Sally Gore is Bob Gore's wife, and a former HR leader at Gore. She recognizes the difficulty of putting a price tag on some of the hard-to-quantify benefits of the company's management system: "I often compare our organizational structure to a democracy to explain the trade-offs. A democratic government might not be the most time- or cost-effective way to run a country. In the end, however, the quality of life is far better than what you'll find in a dictatorship."[7]

The fact that an accountant's yardstick can't easily measure the value of adjacency, autonomy, and amity doesn't mean these things are valueless. Intangible doesn't mean inconsequential. Even Terri Kelly can't tell you just how much Gore's egalitarian management principles are worth, nor how much would be lost if any one of them was abandoned. Yet internal surveys reveal that Gore's associates regard the company's seemingly perverse management practices as a major source of competitive advantage.

As we move toward a world in which economic value is increasingly the product of inspiration, mission, and the joy that people find in their work, the sorts of management innovation that will be most essential are precisely those whose benefits will be most difficult to measure—an important fact for every management innovator, and every CEO, to keep in mind.

Three: Don't be timid.

Like Frederick Winslow Taylor, Bill Gore wasn't intimated by a big challenge. Nor was he afraid to upset the applecart of management orthodoxy. His rebellious pronouncements—"No [person] can commit another," is one rabble-rousing example—weren't empty slogans but resolute statements of intent. While others were happy to make margin notes in the annals of conventional wisdom, Bill Gore rewrote entire chapters. Take Gore's approach to bureaucracy, for example.

Every executive is in favor of reducing bureaucratic waste, unless, of course, he or she is one of the bureaucrats getting pruned. In truth, though, most executives don't want to vanquish bureaucracy, they just want to kick it in the shins: take out a couple of organizational layers, trim corporate staff groups, simplify decision making, and eliminate some paperwork. As commendable as these things are, there's a big difference between reducing overheads and actually giving people control over their work lives, as Gore has done. The distinction is akin to the difference between shrinking a tumor and cutting it out.

Revisiting Our Management Innovation Agenda

Let's return once again to some of the gnarly problems I outlined in chapter 3—and summarize briefly the radical management practices that have helped Gore address these challenges.

Management Innovation Challenge	*W.L. Gore's Distinctive Management Practices*
How do you enroll everyone in your company as an innovator?	Do away with heirarchy; continually reinforce the belief that innovation can come from anyone; colocate employees with diverse skills to facilitate the creative process.
How do you make sure that management's hallowed beliefs don't strangle innovation?	Don't make "management" approval a prerequisite for initiating new projects; minimize the influence of hierarchy; use a peer-based process for allocating resources.
How do you create time and space for innovation when everyone's working flat out?	Carve out 10 percent of staff time for projects that would otherwise be "off budget" or "out of scope"; allow plenty of percolation time for new ideas.

Bill Gore was a 40-something chemical engineer when he laid the foundations for his innovation democracy. I don't know about you, but a middle-aged polytetrafluoroethylene-loving chemist isn't my mental image of a wild-eyed management innovator. Yet think about how radical Gore's vision must have seemed back in 1958. Fifty years later, postmodern management hipsters throw around terms like *complex adaptive systems* and *self-organizing teams*. Well, they're only a half century behind the curve. So ask yourself, am I dreaming big enough yet? Would my management innovation agenda make Bill Gore proud?

Aiming for an Evolutionary Advantage

Google

NYONE WHO'S EVER BOOTED UP A PC KNOWS ABOUT Google, the Mountain View, California–based company whose brightly-hued logo is a universal welcome mat to the World Wide Web.[1] As the heavyweight of online search, Google is one of the world's most ubiquitous brands and an indispensable tool for anyone navigating cyberspace. In May 2007, Google handled 65.2 percent of all U.S. Internet searches, compared with 20.7 percent for Yahoo! and 7.7 percent for Microsoft.[2] Globally, Google conducts more than two-thirds of the world's Web searches.

Google's breakneck growth is already part of Silicon Valley lore. In 1996, two Stanford University doctoral students in computer science, Sergey Brin and Larry Page, churned out an algorithm that delivered a quantum leap in Web-search performance. Their insight: rank pages based on how many links they have to other pages—in essence, an index of popularity. Google's search service debuted in 1998 and was soon fielding over 500,000 queries a day. Over the next few years, Google's eponymous service would grow as fast as the Web itself, but unlike the dot-com flameouts of the late 1990s, Google found a magic elixir that turned all those clicks into cash—search-based advertising. In the three years following Google's 2004 IPO, its revenues more than tripled, from $3.2 billion to $10.6 billion, and its market value soared to more than $140 billion.

As an industry revolutionary, Google has profoundly changed the software business. Unlike Microsoft, Google delivers its software over the Web in the form of online services, rather than as a suite of physical products sold through traditional retail channels. While Microsoft's revenues come largely from licensing fees, Google makes most of its money by selling "click-through" ads that are appended to various forms of Web-based content. And where Microsoft's applications are designed to work seamlessly with one another and integrate tightly with the Windows operating system, most of Google's various services, like search, Gmail, and Google Maps, are stand-alone products. As a result, Google doesn't face the development complexities that Microsoft must confront when it seeks to upgrade a major component of its interlaced product line.

A New Management Model

What makes Google unique, though, is less its Web-centric business model than its brink-of-chaos management model. Key components include a wafer-thin hierarchy, a dense network of lateral communication, a policy of giving outsized rewards to people who come up with outsized ideas, a team-focused approach to product development, and a corporate credo that challenges every employee to put the user first.

Google's one-of-a-kind management system owes much to the way in which Brin and Page have chosen to interpret the company's early success. Both founders are quick to admit that luck played a nontrivial role in Google's rocketlike takeoff. Having built their company in Silicon Valley, where for every meteoric success there are dozens of companies that crash and burn, Brin and Page know well that entrepreneurial success is the product of Darwinian selection—and that like an organism favored by genetic good fortune, Google's success owes much to serendipity. So rather than assume they're the smartest people on the planet, and should, therefore, be the sole architects of Google's long-term strategy, the founders have sought to recreate in Google the same fertile innovation climate that is found within Silicon Valley itself.

Brin and Page understand that in a discontinuous world, what matters most is not a company's competitive advantage at a single point in time, but its evolutionary advantage *over* time. Hence their desire to build a company that is capable of evolving as fast as the Web itself.

With this goal in mind, Google's engineers have worked hard to push the company beyond its search engine roots. Google Apps, a suite of personal productivity tools that targets Microsoft's Office franchise, exemplifies this commitment to developing new business models. Designed primarily for enterprise use, Google Apps encompasses a wide range of essential business applications, such as e-mail, online calendaring, and document production. Rather than give these "hosted services" away for free, Google levies an annual fee for each registered user—a charge that is a small fraction of what customers must pay to license a similar package of applications from Microsoft. Nevertheless, the jury is still out on whether Google's founders will succeed in their quest to build a company that can outrun the future. As of this writing, Google still derives nearly 100 percent of its revenues from ad-supported search. While a few nonsearch products have made strong showings—Gmail, Google News, and Google Maps, for instance—many others have received a lukewarm reception from users. Marissa Mayer, Google's Stanford-educated head of search products, defends the company's performance: "We anticipate that we're going to throw out a lot of products. But [people] will remember the ones that really matter and the ones that have a lot of user potential."[3] Mayer, employee number 20 and Google's first female engineer, estimates that as many as 80 percent of Google's new products will ultimately fail. That's lousy by the standards of most companies, where conservative product-evaluation criteria tend to weed out everything that's not a sure bet, but it's about average by the standards of a venture capitalist. And with a research budget that now tops $1 billion annually, Google can afford to place a lot of bets.

Google's executives are quick to point out that growth in non-search revenues is but one way to measure the company's evolutionary progress. In their view, Google's capacity to rapidly evolve its core business is an equally critical barometer of success. After all, they argue, online search and Web-based advertising are still in their infancy—and the only way for Google to protect its early lead is to innovate relentlessly. It is telling, therefore, that despite well-financed efforts by Microsoft and others, Google's lead in search has widened rather than narrowed in recent years. Much of the credit for this accomplishment rests with the company's unique product-development process, which is built around a swarm of small, autonomous teams. Each of these teams hopes to invent the next big breakthrough in search, or to dream up another new, and indispensable, Web service. At Microsoft, hundreds of developers are often assigned to a single software project. At one point, for example, there were 4,000 Microsofties working on Vista, the long-delayed Windows update that was finally launched in late 2006. The logic behind Google's loosely linked and multifaceted development approach is simple: a host of nimble, independent teams increases the company's odds of stumbling upon "the next big thing." Says Eric Schmidt, who in 2001 resigned as the chairman of Novell to become CEO of Google: "The fact that Google is a Web-based service makes all the difference in the world."[4]

Given his preoccupation with Google's adaptability, it's not surprising that one of Schmidt's favorite metaphors is basketball. Unlike

American football, which proceeds in a series of carefully staged maneuvers, basketball is played on the fly, with little chance to pause and regroup. On the basketball court, strategy is dynamic and improvisational. Players must react instinctively to a competitor's shifting tactics and have enough stamina to keep up with the game's frantic pace of play. Like Schmidt, most people you meet at Google seem to understand that tomorrow's profitability depends on today's *evolvability*.

Thus far, Google certainly *seems* to be adaptable. In less than a decade its business model has gone through five major iterations:

- *Google 1.0:* Brin and Page invent a search engine that crawls the Web and wins millions of eyeballs but generates no real revenue.

- *Google 2.0:* Google sells its search capacity to AOL, Yahoo!, and other major portals. These partnerships generate revenue and spark a surge in search requests. Suddenly, Google is starting to look like a business.

- *Google 3.0:* Google crafts a clever model for selling ads alongside search results. Unlike Yahoo! and others, it eschews banner ads, and takes a newspaper's church-and-state view of advertising and content by clearly differentiating between ads and search results. Moreover, advertisers pay only when users actually click on a link. Google is now on its way to becoming the Internet's leading retailer of ad space.

- *Google 4.0:* Google's initially controversial Gmail service, which serves up ads based on a computer analysis of each incoming message, provokes a serendipitous bit of learning that leads to the creation of AdSense. This breakthrough gives Google the ability to link its ads to virtually any sort of Web content, not just its own search results. AdSense gives webmasters a new way of monetizing their content and vastly expands the scope of Google's business model.

- *Google 5.0:* Google uses its windfall from advertising to fund a flock of new services, including Google Desktop (a cluster of information utilities accessible directly from a user's PC screen), Google Book Search (an ambitious plan to digitize the books from the world's greatest libraries), and Google Scholar (a tool for searching academic papers).

Whether Google continues to evolve at this pace will depend largely on whether its unique management model ultimately delivers the adaptability advantage its founders yearn for. Key components of that model include:

A Formula for Innovation

Schmidt recalls that, while at Novell, he spent 90 percent of his time fighting for small increments of market share in the company's core business. Time is a nonrenewable resource, and he rarely felt he had enough of it to devote to new products and services. Yet when he arrived at Google, Schmidt found the company had developed an explicit formula for ensuring that innovation didn't get shortchanged, known internally as "70-20-10." The policy stipulates that Google will devote 70 percent of its engineering resources to enhancements of its base business. Twenty percent will get focused on services that significantly extend the core—products like Google Checkout (which simplifies online shopping), Images (a search tool for photos on the Web), Directory (for browsing the Web by topic), and Translate (for viewing Web pages in foreign languages). The remaining 10 percent is to be allocated to fringe ideas like helping municipalities set up public Wi-Fi networks.

So central is this formula for innovation that when asked how she would summarize Google's strategy for a new hire, Mayer says she'd start by describing the logic of 70-20-10. Does this heuristic actually help make Google an innovative company? It would appear so. In early 2006, an internal Google Web site listed 370 development projects that were under way—230 were extensions of Google's core business, "70 percent" offerings, and 140 were "30 percent" initiatives.

A Company That Feels Like Grad School

From the beginning, Page and Brin set out to create a company where they'd like to hang out—a place filled with clever overachievers energized by the chance to work on some of the world's most beguiling problems. Given this goal, it's not surprising that the founders have modeled Google, in part, on a top-flight university. Like an elite engineering school, Google's management model is built around small work units, lots of experimentation, vigorous peer feedback, and a mission to improve the world. The company's intellectual climate also mirrors academic values, in that it is both disputatious and meritocratic. At Google, position and hierarchy seldom win an argument, and the founders want to keep it that way.

The Chance to Change the World

In their letter to prospective shareholders, Page and Brin claimed that "talented people are attracted to Google because we empower them to change the world." Talk to just about anyone in Google's developer ranks and this bold assertion is quickly validated. Anurag Acharya, a veteran computer science professor, says he joined the company for one simple reason: "I was looking for a problem that would last me a very long time—10 years, 15 years."[5] He scarcely needs to add that Google's bold ambition to organize the world's information is just such a problem.

If, as has often been claimed, Googlers are an arrogant lot, they are also surprisingly idealistic. Sit down with anyone from Google and before long you'll be involved in a conversation about how to democratize knowledge or change the way the world learns. Says Mayer, "We're doing things that make people better educated and smarter—that improve the world's intelligence."

In many companies, employees pursue no higher purpose than "making the quarter," a paltry incentive for the kind of imagination and courage that are required to drive continuous strategic renewal. If Google attracts more than its share of top-drawer talent, it's because the company's bold mission is an irresistible come-on to brainiacs who get off on solving problems that are as important as they are seemingly intractable.

A Bozo-free Zone

Google's leaders believe that one exceptional technologist is many times more valuable than one average engineer; hence they insist on hiring only the brightest of the bright—folks out on the right-hand end of the bell-shaped curve. They also believe that if you let one "bozo" in, more will surely follow. Their logic is simple: A-level people want to work with A-level people—fellow savants who will spark their thinking and accelerate their learning. Trouble is, B-level people are threatened by A-class talent, so once they get in the door, they tend to hire colleagues who are as unremarkable as they are. Worse, a B-class staffer with a bit of an insecurity problem may opt to hire C-grade employees who lack the self-confidence to challenge *anyone's* point of view. As the ranks of the mediocre expand, it becomes harder to attract and retain the truly exceptional. And before you know it, the process of dumbing-down has become irreversible.

Not surprisingly, Google's hiring process is grueling. Candidates submit to a series of interviews that often extends over several weeks. Computer scientists are given Mensa-level problems and are expected to crack them on the spot. A final decision is rarely made without a thorough vetting from a hiring committee comprising veteran associates and executives. It's an admittedly brutal process, but it weeds out anyone who's merely average.

Dramatically Flat, Radically Decentralized

In many ways, Google is organized like the Internet itself: it's highly democratic, tightly connected, and flat. Like so much of Google's culture, the source of the company's radical decentralization can be traced back to Brin and Page, both of whom attended Montessori schools and credit much of their intellectual independence to that experience. Says Mayer: "They don't like authority and they don't like being told what to do." Brin and Page understand that breakthroughs come from questioning assumptions and smashing paradigms. Mayer recalls how the pair once challenged Dean Kamen, the world-famous inventor who spawned the Segway scooter, on some arcane principle of mechanical engineering. A bystander might have thought them impertinent but, contends Mayer, "Larry and Sergey simply wanted to understand Dean's thought process." She goes on: "That atmosphere permeates Google—don't do something just because someone said to do it." To Google's engineers, "Question Authority" is not an anarchist's bumper sticker, it's an innovator's imperative.

Googlers expect to have the right to opine, intelligently, about anything to anyone—and be taken seriously. After all, that's how the Net works. Eric Schmidt saw this firsthand during his inaugural meeting at the Googleplex, the company's rambling corporate campus. Sure, Page and Brin had plenty to say in the meeting, but so did everyone else. As a flurry of points and counterpoints bounced around the room, Schmidt felt as if he were watching three or four simultaneous tennis matches. Normally, in meetings like this, he could quickly calibrate the relative status of the participants. But at Google, the freedom with which people expressed themselves, and their near-total lack of deference, yielded few clues as to the rank of those present. Schmidt left the meeting wondering who, exactly, was in charge. Reflecting on this experience, Schmidt realized that if he was going to succeed as CEO, he'd have to adapt his management style to Google's, rather than the other way around. While his title might impress an external audience, it wouldn't guarantee his credibility with the company's strong-minded employees. Instead, like everyone else, he'd have to earn his "share of voice" by adding value to the free-flowing conversations that were continually shaping, and reshaping, Google's strategy.

In the typical corporate model, CEOs are expected to drive strategy top-down—but not at Google, where Schmidt is more inclined to provoke than proclaim. In practice, that means playing host to a company-wide soirée. "If you run the company as a set of extended conversations," he says, "you get a lot of buy-in, and buy-in drives execution." One avenue for influence is the company's Product Strategy meeting. Each week, Schmidt and his staff spend up to six hours in dialogue with team members from across Google, every one of whom believes that he or she is working on a mother-lode project. This substantial allocation of time keeps Schmidt and his senior associates closely connected to Google's frontline innovators.

Only recently has Google experimented with a formal planning process—but true to the company's culture, it was a lot more bottom-up than top-down. Schmidt got the conversation started by posing a broad set of questions: How could Google take downloadable video and make it truly usable? How could the company get its services on hundreds of millions of mobile phones? How could it build a scalable software infrastructure? Fourteen teams were formed to answer these questions and others. Says Schmidt, "They all came back and said that the questions weren't very interesting but the group interactions were terrific. In the process, they developed some really intriguing ideas." That, presumably, was the point of the exercise: to get people thinking creatively about how to evolve the company's business model.

As you might expect, decision making at Google is highly consultative. Command and control isn't an option when your "employees" are some of the smartest people on the planet. One core management principle requires that all interested parties be in the room when a key decision is reached. The logic: those who are impacted by executive decisions have a right to participate directly in the decision process—

and to disagree. Schmidt reverts to the university analogy in character-izing Google's approach to decision making. While there's a lot of dis-sent in universities, there's often no one with enough clout to force a deadline—so debates drag on for months or years. As CEO, Schmidt believes it's his job to make sure contentious issues get resolved in a timely manner, but he doesn't regard himself as decision-maker-in-chief. Says Schmidt, "I'm usually okay with the outcome, but I want to get us to a decision."

When highly motivated and eminently capable people share a com-mon vision, they don't need to be micromanaged. This is a lesson Google learned early on. As the company grew, an attempt was made to layer on the kind of supervisory structure found in traditional software com-panies, where engineering managers have a relatively narrow span of control. It soon became obvious that an excess of oversight was putting a damper on innovation. Google's "I think I can" culture was in danger of becoming a "No you can't" bureaucracy. Within weeks, the new layer was ripped out and the recently appointed middle managers were reabsorbed into the engineering ranks. Today, the average manager in Google's product-development group has more than 50 direct reports, and for some leaders the number tops 100.

It's not that Google's mission-driven innovators don't need a bit of supervision, or a counterbalance to the centrifugal force of all their un-bounded creativity. But instead of relying on midlevel bureaucrats to ride herd on its engineers, Google depends on the frank and voluble feedback its associates provide one another within and across the com-pany's hundreds of small, mostly autonomous teams. As is true in aca-demic life or on the Net, control at Google is more peer-to-peer than manager-to-minion.

Small, Self-Managing Teams

Roughly half of Google's 10,000 employees—all those involved in product development—work in small teams, with an average of three engineers per team. Even a large project such as Gmail, which might occupy 30 people, is broken into teams of three or four, each of which works on a specific service enhancement, such as building spam filters or improving the forwarding feature. Each team has an "über-tech leader," a responsibility that rotates among team members depending on shifting project requirements. Most engineers work on more than one team, and no one needs the HR department's permission to switch teams. "If at all possible, we want people to commit to things, rather than be assigned to things," says Shona Brown, Google's VP for operations. "If you see an opportunity, go for it."

Google believes that small teams confer a number of advantages. When projects are parceled into small pieces, new initiatives can take off more quickly, since there are fewer people to convince and fewer interdependencies to manage. By keeping the teams small and every project slightly under-resourced, Google prevents the "excessive prettying-up," as Mayer puts it, that adds time and cost without adding much value. "That's why a lot of Google's projects stay in beta for a while and are rough around the edges," she says. "Solving 80 percent of a big new problem creates a lot more value than noodling out the last 20 percent." The downside: some users complain that Google has been too slow to upgrade some of its "rough-and-ready" products.

Small teams also help Google to feel like an intimate company—more like a start-up than a bloated bureaucracy. Within a large team, outstanding personal contributions are often expropriated by superiors or neutralized by dim-witted colleagues. At Google, small teams help to maintain a close coupling between individual effort and personal accomplishment.

The Freedom to Follow Your Nose

For Google's software engineers, the company's 70-20-10 policy amounts to a non-revocable license to pursue their passions. Every developer is free to devote up to 20 percent of his or her time to noncore initiatives. In this way, Google sanctions the unsanctioned. While this policy helps Google to continually refresh its portfolio of strategic options, it also helps the company to retain its best people. Google hires curious people with wide-ranging interests. The 20 percent policy ensures that no one has to leave Google to pursue a personal passion.

In practice, few people spend 20 percent of each day or every week tinkering on a pet project. More typical is the engineer who, after working flat out for six months on a critical project, decides to take six weeks off to experiment with a new idea. This freedom, says Schmidt, helps to "avoid the problem of the petty dictator—the tank commander who won't allow any deviations from the plan." The payoff? In one recent period, more than half the company's new product launches traced their roots back to a 20 percent project.

How does Google keep people from using their 20 percent time to simply fool around? It doesn't try. The company figures that the cost of closely supervising *everyone's* 20 percent time, measured in terms of the bureaucratic drag it would impose on all the Googlers who *aren't* wasting their time, would far outweigh any benefit.

The 20 percent rule has several important consequences: It ensures that short-term pressures don't consume 100 percent of the company's energies. It makes it clear that innovation is everyone's responsibility. It also means that at any one time, a certain number of people are "out of control." So be it, says Schmidt: "If you want complete order, join the Marines."

Rapid, Low-Cost Experimentation

Evolutionary adaptation isn't the product of a grand plan, but of relentless experimentation. Google gets this. As Schmidt puts it, "Our goal is to have more at bats per unit of time and effort than anyone else in the world." That's why Googlers are encouraged to spawn a lot of little "Googlettes." Put simply, if you can experiment more cheaply and rapidly than your competitors, you can test more ideas and improve your odds of getting to the future first.

Google estimates it needs to launch from 10 to 12 new service offerings or major service enhancements every quarter to stay on its growth curve. Across Google there is an almost palpable pressure to "launch early, launch often, and launch fast." Every would-be entrepreneur at Google knows that the surest way to attract the attention of one's peers, and to get more financial support for a pet project, is to actually throw something onto the Web that garners positive customer feedback. This is where Google Labs come in. The Labs' public access Web site allows curious users to test-drive Google services that aren't ready for a full roll-out. In return, Google gets a load of customer feedback. If a product is too buggy to try out on customers, or too competitively sensitive, team leaders will sign up internal users. For example, Paul Buchheit first tested Gmail's automated ad insertion algorithm on the internal e-mail traffic of Page and Brin.

As in science, Google's experiments often produce unexpected results. For example, the idea behind AdSense—context-appropriate ads—had its start in the Gmail project. Having figured out how to attach relevant ads to e-mails, Buchheit wondered whether it might be possible to insert context-relevant ad into Web pages. While Gmail may never make a lot of money for Google, the fortuitous learning it provoked already has.

Google's "just-try-it" philosophy is applied to even the company's most daunting projects, like digitizing the world's libraries. Like every new initiative, Google Book Search began with a makeshift experiment aimed at answering a critical question; in this case: how long does it take to digitize a book? To find out, Page and Mayer rigged up a piece of plywood with a couple of clamps and proceeded to photograph each page of a 300-page book, using a metronome to keep pace. With Mayer flipping pages, and one half of Google's founding team taking digital snapshots, it took 40 minutes to turn the ink into pixels. An optical character recognition program soon turned the digital photos into digital text, and within five days the pair had ginned up a piece of software that could search the book. That kind of step-wise, learn-as-you-go approach has repeatedly helped Google to test critical assumptions and avoid making bet-the-farm mistakes.

Differential Rewards

No one expects Google's share price to rise as dramatically over the next few years as it did immediately following the IPO. Hence Google faces a challenge that confronts every successful start-up: How do you keep on attracting superstars who hunger for the chance to get rich, even as the stock price levels out? In Google's case, the answer lies in a compensation system that discriminates crisply between those who add a lot of value and those who don't.

Generally, Google employees earn a base salary that's on par with, or slightly lower than the industry average—but the standard deviation around that average is higher at Google than it is at most other companies. At Google, annual bonuses amount to 30 percent to 60 percent of base salary, but the financial upside can be much, much bigger than that for those who dream up a profit-pumping idea.

In 2004, Google introduced its quarterly "Founders Awards," which grant millions of dollars worth of restricted stock to teams that have made remarkable contributions to the firm's success. Thus far, the largest such award has gone to a team led by Eric Veach, an ultra-smart engineer who thinks like a classic entrepreneur. From the moment he joined the company, Veach was obsessed with a single question: How can I add millions of dollars to Google's bottom line? The answer ultimately came in the form of a new advertising algorithm, dubbed "SmartAds." In Google's cost-per-click advertising model, the company makes money only when end-users click on an ad. Although an advertiser might outbid its rivals for some key search term, that doesn't guarantee users will ultimately click on the ad—so a bad ad isn't good for the advertiser and it isn't good for Google. SmartAds' clever algorithm helps predict the "click-through" rate for every ad, allowing Google to preemptively weed out those that are unlikely to be productive. Known internally as

"Smart Ass," the new program quickly produced a 20 percent jump in click-throughs, and won Veach and his team a $10 million Founders Award.

Google knows you can't expect people to act like entrepreneurs without the prospect of entrepreneurial rewards. The Founders Awards are based on the premise that an employee shouldn't have to join a start-up to get rich.

A Continuous, Companywide Conversation

In hierarchical companies, communication pathways are primarily vertical rather than horizontal, and information systems are built first and foremost to move data from the front lines to top-level decision makers. Google's executives certainly don't lack for data. Yet the lateral flow of communication within the company is even denser than the vertical flow. This is no accident. Google has invested heavily in building a highly networked organization that makes it easy for employees to share ideas, poll peers, recruit volunteers, and build constituencies for change—all of which requires a lot more than a good e-mail system.

At Google, there are several mechanisms that knit together all those independent teams and lightly supervised engineers. First is "Misc List," an ever-changing smorgasbord of ideas and comments that's open to every team member. Subjects range from Google's controversial strategy in China to the menu in the company's dining rooms. Second is Google's intranet, "MOMA," the IT acronym for "Message Oriented Middleware Application." MOMA includes a Web page and threaded conversation for each of the company's several hundred internal projects, making it easy for teams to communicate their progress, garner feedback, and solicit help. Third is "Snippets," a site where every Google engineer posts a weekly summary of personal actions and accomplishments. Any Googler can search the Snippets list to locate individuals working on similar projects, or to simply stay abreast of what's happening. Fourth is "TGIF," a weekly all-hands meeting at the Googleplex café, where Brin and Page introduce new hires, summarize the week's milestones, and lead an open-mike Q&A session.

It is Google's internal transparency and continuous peer-to-peer feedback, rather than a large cadre of middle managers, that keeps the company's disparate initiatives on track. Sure, Google's engineering managers and senior executives are in the loop when decisions have to be made that involve big resource commitments or could impact Google's brand or user experience, but before senior management weighs in on a new initiative, it's likely that dozens of Googlers and hundreds or thousands of customers will have already made their views known.

Google's executives understand that it's easy to run a flat organization when everyone's doing the same thing. How many supervisors, after all, do you need to run a giant call center where everyone is following the same carefully scripted routine? But it's not so easy to run a company filled with iconoclasts who aren't easily corralled and answer mostly to their own curiosity. Indeed, the only way to "manage" in this context is to bring the collective genius of the organization to bear on decisions large and small—and this demands openness, transparency, and a lot of lateral communication.

An Expansive Business Definition

The breadth of Google's ambition, and the scope of its innovation efforts are an insurance policy against the kind of conservatism and incrementalism that so often causes companies to miss the future. Indeed, the founders made it clear in their IPO letter that Google would not be constrained by anyone else's definition of its core business. "Do not be surprised," they warned, "if we place smaller bets in areas that seem speculative or even strange." When asked what business Google is in, Schmidt replies grandly that the company "wants to help people find anything." While there are many reasons Google might fail, a blinkered business model is unlikely to be one of them.

Some (Tentative) Lessons

Few tech companies ever get a second act. Despite its innovation-friendly management model, Google's fortunes are still tied to one business: search-driven advertising. Odds are, Google will never find another Google, since truly revolutionary, global-scale business models don't come along every day, or even every decade. Alternately, the company may fall victim to imperial overstretch, as it takes on Microsoft, Yahoo!, eBay, and pretty much everyone else online. Yet whatever the future holds for Google, its success to date offers some worthwhile lessons for would-be management innovators.

One: The Internet itself may be the best metaphor for 21st-century management.

When it comes to its business model, Google is a second-generation Internet company—unlike its predecessors, it makes money. Yet when it comes to its management model, Google is a first-generation pioneer—the first sizable, publicly listed company to build its management system around Web-centric principles. While other Web companies have opted for more traditional management structures, Google has used the Web's *social architecture*—open, flat, malleable, nonhierarchical—as the model for its *management architecture*. This is Google's biggest experiment of all, and the world will keep learning from it whether the King of Search soars or sputters.

Two: Experienced managers may not make the best management innovators.

Did you notice? John Mackey, Bill Gore, Sergey Brin, and Larry Page—none of these management innovators went to business school. This is a bit humbling for someone like me who's been a b-school professor for a quarter of a century, but there's no way around it. When you go to business school, you get a lot of wisdom, but you get a lot of dogma, too.

On the other hand, anyone can learn how to challenge conventional wisdom, and I'll show you how in the next chapter. For now, it's enough to note that management innovators should take a lot of advice from people who've never learned what they're *not* supposed to do. My own experience suggests that the people with the boldest and most useful ideas about how to reinvent your company's core management process are probably *not* the folks who are managing those processes right now.

Three: Management innovations that humanize work are irresistible.

The Internet took off fast because it was a multiplier of human capability—it made it easier to do the things that human beings love to do: connect, chat, brag, schmooze, opine, share, flirt, create, laugh, and learn. Similarly, management innovations that humanize work are the ones most likely to succeed—and they'll help your company recruit the best of the best.

Marissa Mayer gets to meet many of Google's new hires. When she asks them what convinced them to sign on, they invariably mention the company's highly empowering environment. This is hardly surprising. If you create a management system that encourages people to speak up, that lets them pursue their passions, that substitutes the wisdom of peers for the wisdom of the elite, and is mostly free of bureaucratic quicksand, there are a lot of people who are going to thank you. Another thing that's not surprising: In 2007, Google ranked number one on *Fortune*'s list of the best places to work.

Revisiting Our Management Innovation Agenda

Though Google is still a young company, and in many ways untested, its management model provides a few useful tips for anyone hoping to tackle the adaptability challenges I outlined in chapter 3:

Management Innovation Challenge	*Google's Distinctive Management Practices*
How do you guard against the dangers of hubris and denial?	Open up the strategy process— make sure it isn't dominated by the old guard; keep the hierarchy flat—don't insulate top management from the views of front-line employees who are in the best position to see the future coming; encourage dissent.
How do you create a steady flow of new strategic options?	Make it easy for folks to experiment with new ideas—give them time (the "20 percent" rule) and minimize the number of approval levels; build a "just try it" culture—emphasize "test and learn" instead of "plan and execute"; create outsized rewards for individuals who come up with game-changing ideas; don't truncate the business definition.
How do you accelerate the reallocation of resources from legacy projects into new initiatives?	Encourage people to work on "out of scope" projects—formalized with the 70/20/10 rule; give people the freedom to do market experiments so they can build a solid case for their ideas.

Whole Foods Market. W.L. Gore. Google. It would be hard to find three companies less alike: a retailer, a manufacturer of industrial products, and an icon of the Internet. My purpose in profiling these modern management pioneers was not to hold them up as paragons of "excellence" or "greatness"—I'll leave that judgment to others, and to time. Rather, my goal was to demonstrate that it really *is* possible to defy management orthodoxy and still run a successful business; that you *can* flout conventional management wisdom and still ship products on time, satisfy exacting customers, and deliver mouthwatering results.

Turns out, we *haven't* reached the end of management. We really *can* reinvent the way big companies are structured and run. There *isn't* any law that prevents large organizations from being engaging, innovative, and adaptable—and mostly bureaucracy free. Even better, it really *is* possible to set the human spirit free at work. So no more excuses. It's time for you to buckle down and start inventing the future of management.

IMAGINING
THE
FUTURE
OF
MANAGEMENT

PART THREE

Seven

Escaping the Shackles

"B UT WAIT," YOU MAY BE SAYING, "I'M NOT STARTING with a clean sheet of paper—and I'm not the CEO. My company's been around for a while and has an installed base of white-bread management practices. I don't have the option of building a newfangled management system from the ground up. And there aren't a lot of management heretics around here, either. How do I get the ball rolling, when my company's deeply conventional and has been for decades?"

What you need is a methodology for breakthrough management thinking. While innovation can never be entirely scripted, it is possible to increase the odds of a "eureka" moment by assembling the right ingredients. In the case of management innovation, these ingredients include:

- A disciplined process for unearthing and challenging the long-standing management orthodoxies that constrain creative thinking

- New management principles with the power to illuminate new approaches

- Insights drawn from the practices of "positive deviants"—organizations with management practices that are eccentric yet effective

Unblinkered thinking, fresh principles, and wisdom from the fringe—these are the foundations of a systematic approach to reinventing management. In this chapter and the two that follow, I'll discuss each of these creativity boosters in turn, and demonstrate how they can be used to stoke the fires of management innovation in *your* company.

Going to War with Precedent

To get started, you're going to have to cross swords with innovation's deadliest foe: the often unarticulated and mostly unexamined beliefs that tether you and your colleagues to the management status quo. All of us are held hostage by our axiomatic beliefs. We are jailbirds incarcerated within the fortress of dogma and precedent. And yet, for the most part, we are oblivious to our own captivity.

The Outsider's Advantage

Physicians, for example, long believed that ulcers were caused by spicy foods, stress, and booze. So strong was this belief that, when two Australian physicians, Barry Marshall and Robin Warren, proposed an alternate explanation—that ulcers were caused by an ignoble bacterium—the medical community reacted with snooty disbelief. After all, everyone *knew* that nothing could live in the stomach's sterile, acidic environment. It didn't help that Marshall and Warren were based at Royal Perth Hospital rather than at a prestigious research facility, nor that Marshall was a 30-something internist rather than a seasoned gastroenterologist.[1] Growing up, Marshall had always had a big dose of can-do spirit. (He once improvised a centrifuge by tying blood-filled test tubes to a ceiling fan.) As a young doctor, he was frustrated that he couldn't provide lasting relief to his ulcer patients. A clue to a potential cure came when Warren, a pathologist at Royal Perth, happened to show Marshall a biopsy taken from the lining of a patient's stomach. Using a high-powered microscope, Warren had noticed a number of small, corkscrew-shaped bacteria. Could they be the culprit? The physicians set out to accumulate more evidence and soon they had their smoking gun. The strange bacteria were present in virtually all of Marshall's ulcer patients, and absent in samples taken from patients with other maladies. Over the next several months, the pair tried to cultivate the offending microbes in the lab, but to no avail. Then, over a long Easter weekend, Marshall happened to leave one of his cultures unattended for six days, rather than the usual two. Upon returning to work, Marshall discovered that his Petri dish was alive with germs. When he couldn't induce ulcers in animals by feeding them the cultured bacteria, the intrepid researcher ingested a three-day-old dose himself. Sure enough, seventy-two hours later he awoke with all the grossly unpleasant symptoms of severe gastritis.

With his hypothesis seemingly confirmed, Marshall set about developing a treatment program using antibiotics and bismuth (the active ingredient in Pepto-Bismol). Within weeks this regimen had eradicated the ulcers in a majority of his patients. Thrilled, Marshall rushed off to a conference of microbiologists in Brussels and enthusiastically presented his findings. He was shocked, though, when the attendees threw up a wall of objections. More than a few pronounced him a "madman." Marshall was similarly rebuffed when he submitted his findings for publication in the *Lancet* and the *New England Journal of Medicine*—both of which refused to sanction his offbeat theory. It would be years before Marshall and Warren's groundbreaking work would change ulcer treatment protocols around the world. Finally, in 2005, more than 20 years after their first experiment, the two indefatigable researchers got the recognition they deserved and were awarded the Nobel Prize for medicine.

Why, one might ask, did this unlikely duo succeed where so many veteran researchers had failed? Marshall thinks he knows the answer: "The people who have a stake in the old technology are never the ones to embrace the new technology. It's always someone a bit on the periphery, who hasn't got anything to gain by the status quo, who is interested in changing it."[2]

Of course it's hard to think like an outsider when you've spent years swimming in the mainstream. If you had never heard of W.L. Gore, for example, would you have believed that a company could give every employee the right to say no to any request and still maintain operational discipline? Like fish that can't conceive of a world not immersed in water, most of us can't envision management practices that don't correspond to the norms of our own experience. Even our language is hostage to our paradigmatic beliefs. Consider, for example, how thoroughly the notion of hierarchy has infiltrated the lexicon of management. "Chain of command." "Pyramid." "Boss." "Subordinate." "Direct reports." "Organizational level." "Top-down." "Bottom-up." "Cascade." All these terms connote a formal scale of power and authority. Indeed, managers have as many ways of talking about hierarchy as Eskimos have of talking about snow. Now try to conjure up a vocabulary that describes the features of a "lattice" or networked organization. How many terms can you come up with? That's the problem: It's tough to imagine something we lack the language to describe.

Questioning Our Inheritance

Remember the old saw about the tendency of generals to refight the last war rather than the one at hand? Like experts in other fields, military leaders have a hard time dethroning out-of-date beliefs. One example: for nearly a century after the invention of the musket, European generals continued to arrange their infantry in formations better suited to pikes and bows than to flintlocks.[3] Two generations of commanders had to pass from the scene before new and more appropriate force formations finally supplanted traditional battlefield groupings. This anecdote illustrates two important characteristics of any dominant paradigm: first, it is usually bequeathed from one generation to the next; and second, the beneficiaries often take possession without questioning its provenance or its relevance to new contexts.

Think about it: How did you come by your basic beliefs about the best way to organize, motivate, lead, plan, and allocate resources? No doubt you were socialized and indoctrinated—in B-school lectures and management development programs, in coaching sessions with mentors and in conversations with colleagues. The fact is, you inherited most of your management beliefs from others. They came to you, secondhand, from celebrity CEOs, management gurus, and gray-haired professors—most of whom are either long-dead, long-retired, or long in the tooth. Now, with so much change afoot, it's time to reexamine your heirloom beliefs.

Temporary Truths

A glance back through history reminds us that time often proves conventional wisdom wrong. As it happens, the sun *doesn't* revolve around the earth. Infectious diseases are *not* caused by bad humors. And the world *wasn't* created in six days. The future has a way of making monkeys out of die-hards who cling too long to old certainties. Keep this in mind, and you'll find it easier to be skeptical about *your* management beliefs.

Consider, for a moment, just how wrong-headed early-20th-century managers were in their beliefs about motivation and pay. At the time, most executives assumed that once their employees had earned enough to buy food, shelter, and clothing, they would cease striving for more. In this view, if you increased wages beyond what was needed to meet life's basic necessities, employees would simply work less or become wastrels. One can understand, then, why Henry Ford's competitors reacted in horror when, in January 1914, the auto magnate doubled the pay of his production workers—from $2.50 to $5.00 per day. The results confounded Ford's critics. While employee turnover at Ford had been 31.9 percent *per month* in 1913, by 1915 it had tumbled to a mere 1.4 percent per month. Henry Ford's key insight: well-paid workers would be able to afford the goods of America's burgeoning industrial economy and would work energetically to fulfill their growing consumer appetites.

While it's easy to smile at the misguided beliefs of those who came before us, can we be sure that our management beliefs won't appear equally archaic a decade or two hence? For example, most 21st-century managers seem to regard the notion of an economically dependent and willingly biddable "employee" as an immovable cornerstone of corporate life. Yet the idea of spending your entire life working for someone else would have seemed strange, even repugnant to most Americans living before the Civil War. In the 19th century, America was a "republic of the self-employed," as Roy Jacques so aptly puts it.[4] Nine in ten white, male citizens worked for themselves. "Manufactures" as the census labeled them, typically employed no more than three or four individuals.[5] Most of the folks who labored in tanning sheds, bakeries, and smithies dreamed of one day setting up on their own, and many would eventually do so. Having escaped Europe's economic feudalism, America's 19th-century artisans and laborers would have been dismayed to learn that millions of their progeny would one day become permanent "wage slaves."

Fact is, the concept of the employee is a recent invention, not some timeless social convention. Indeed, one doesn't have to be a Marxist to be awed by the scale and success of early-20th-century efforts to transform strong-willed human beings into docile employees. The demands of the modern industrial workplace required a dramatic resculpting of human habits and values. To sell one's time rather than what one produced, to pace one's work to the clock, to eat and sleep at precisely defined intervals, to spend long days endlessly repeating the same, small task—none of these were, or are, natural human instincts. It would be dangerous, therefore, to assume that the concept of "the employee"—or any other tenet in the creed of modern management—is anchored on the bedrock of eternal truth.

Uncovering Shared Beliefs

Skepticism and humility are important attributes for a management innovator—yet they're not enough. To create space for management innovation you will need to systematically deconstruct the management orthodoxies that blind you and your colleagues to new possibilities. Here's how to get started. Pick a big management issue like change, innovation, or employee engagement, and then assemble 10 or 20 of your colleagues. Ask each of them to write down 10 things they believe about the nominated problem. Have them inscribe each belief on a Post-it note. Then plaster the stickies on a wall and group similar beliefs together. If a belief seems ungroupable, put it off to the side for the moment. It's the commonly held assumptions that require the greatest scrutiny. Since these beliefs seem noncontentious, they seldom get examined.

Let's say the problem you picked was adaptability. You asked each of your colleagues to write down 10 deeply held beliefs about the nature of change in large organizations. After clustering the submissions, the three most commonly held beliefs turn out to be the following:

1. It takes a crisis to provoke deep change.

2. You need a strong leader to drive change.

3. Change starts at the top.

How do you challenge these beliefs? The dilemma, of course, is that they seem empirically true: It usually *does* take a crisis to change a big company. Most successful change programs *are* driven from the top, usually by a new CEO. Everyone knows these things are true—they are facts, not assumptions. So your colleagues are going to be nonplussed when you ask them to question these maxims. They'll feel as if you're asking them to speculate on whether gravity is really true or just a convention. And in a way, that's exactly what you're urging them to do. Here's what you need to tell them:

To escape the straitjacket of conventional thinking, you have to be able to distinguish between beliefs that describe the world as it *is*, and beliefs that describe the world as it is *and must forever remain*. In 1900, it would have been accurate to say that human beings couldn't fly, but it would have been wrong to say they would never fly. What kept humankind earthbound for so long wasn't the law of gravity, but a lack of inventiveness. And so it is with management.

Not many of our management practices are grounded in natural law. While managers must contend with all the behavioral instincts that have been hardwired into human beings, this is not as much of a constraint as you might think. Reflect again on the way in which modern industry *manufactured* dutiful employees out of farmers, peddlers, and housemaids. It's not human nature that limits the pace and scope of management, it's our unexamined beliefs. Having explained this to your colleagues, you're ready to move on.

Ask your associates which of their assumptions about change *deserve* to be challenged—which beliefs reflect a reality they wish could be otherwise. After mulling this question over, your team decides they'd like to test the notion that it takes a crisis to change a big company. Clearly, customers, employees, and shareholders would be better off if deep change was more often proactive and less often reactive. Now ask your teammates whether they can think of any counterexamples to the general rule that deep change is crisis-driven. Are there companies that have changed direction without having to go through some sort of near-death experience? If, after a few minutes, no one has offered a counterexample, you should move on to the next question.

Getting at the "Why"

"All right then," you ask, "*why* does it take a crisis to provoke deep change? What, specifically, are the impediments to timely adaptation?" One of your colleagues ventures that denial is often the culprit. Heads nod in agreement. Another voice chimes in: "Denial *is* a law of human nature. We're all ostriches sometimes." Again there's a murmur of assent. Five or six folks lean back in their chairs—well, that's it: people are unnerved by disruptive change. Simple as that. Only it's not. Not by a long shot. This is where the work of deconstructing orthodoxies really begins—once you've elicited that first knee-jerk, can't-be-helped explanation for the way the world is.

Your next question catches folks off-guard: "Is denial an infectious disease, like an outbreak of *E. coli* from a bad batch of spinach? Does the virus of self-delusion infect *everyone* in a company? Or are there usually some folks who manage to escape the bug, who understand all too well the potential dangers of sticking with the status quo?" Now people are thinking. Someone pipes up: "Yeah, there's usually someone—usually a lot of people—who see the handwriting on the wall, but nobody pays attention to them." Soon folks are sharing personal stories about prophets who went unheeded, and disasters that could have been averted but weren't.

As the discussion heats up, your colleagues grab the initiative and start asking their own questions: "Why do prophets usually end up as martyrs?" "Why do the folks with 20/20 vision have to sit around waiting for top management to do something?" "Why are the visionaries writing position papers and blogs when they should be out inventing new business models?"

Suffice to say, if you encourage your teammates to keep asking "why," they'll eventually land on the *real* reason it takes a crisis to provoke big change: too much authority has been vested in too few people. When power is concentrated at the top, a few senior executives can hold the organization's capacity to change hostage to their own willingness or ability to change. The veterans at the top built the current business model, or got promoted for perfecting it. Their careers, skills, and mental models are inextricably bound up with the status quo, and they can scarcely imagine an alternative. Not surprisingly, they will often ignore or discount information that casts doubt on the current strategy.

Now you've arrived at a fundamental truth about social systems: the more you consolidate power in the hands of a few senior leaders, the less resilient the system will be. (If you're old enough, you'll remember the Soviet Union.) Hitting on this insight energizes the discussion. "So there's no law that says companies have to go through a crisis every five or ten years," ventures one of your teammates. Another colleague chimes in: "Yeah, but if you want to avoid a painful turnaround, you can't give top management a monopoly on setting strategy." This prompts another interjection: "In today's world it's tough to keep a strategy evergreen. Maybe the top team would actually welcome the chance to share the burden." "So what are we going to do?" someone asks. "How can we change this?" "How can we make our strategy process more bottom-up and less top-down?" Thus the journey of management innovation begins.

As the conversation unfolds, try to capture key points and post them to an internal Web site or circulate them by e-mail. As you broaden the conversation electronically, your peers will start to ask, "Why is our company run this way?" "Why can't we do better than this?" "What are the alternatives?" As the contrarian spirit spreads, the potential for management innovation will grow.

Asking the Right Questions

Rooting out dogma is all about asking the right questions—repeatedly. I've found the following lines of attack to be helpful in getting beneath the surface of long-held management beliefs:

1. Is this a belief worth challenging? Is it debilitating? Does it get in the way of an important organizational attribute (like strategic adaptability) that we'd like to strengthen?

2. Is this belief universally valid? Are there counterexamples? If so, what do we learn from those cases?

3. How does this belief serve the interests of its adherents? Are there people who draw reassurance or comfort from this belief?

4. Have our choices and assumptions conspired to make this belief self-fulfilling? Is this belief true simply because we have *made* it true—and, if so, can we imagine alternatives?

These questions are your pickax. If you're persistent, they'll help you break through even the most impenetrable of management orthodoxies.

Let's test these questions on another bit of dogma. When talking to senior executives about the need to encourage innovation, I often get the sense they'd like their employees to loosen up a bit, to think more radically and be more experimental, but they're worried this might distract them from a laserlike focus on efficiency and execution. Most companies have spent years honing their business processes, weeding out waste, and improving operational discipline. There is an understandable fear that some of these hard won gains will be lost if employees are given the latitude to flex policy guidelines, experiment with new methods, and incubate new projects. I've heard this concern expressed in a variety of ways: "Yeah, we want people to innovate, but we have to stay focused." "Innovation's well and good, but at the end of the day, we have to deliver." "If everybody's off innovating, who's going to mind the store?" These sentiments reveal a persistent management orthodoxy: *If you allow people the freedom to innovate, discipline will take a beating.* Mathematically expressed, this view holds that freedom plus discipline equals a constant—having more of one means having less of the other.

Let's go back to our first orthodoxy-busting question: *Is this belief worth contesting?* Absolutely! What company *wouldn't* like to have more innovation *and* more discipline? Might as well ask someone if they'd like to be rich *and* famous. On to question two, then: *Are there any counterexamples that challenge the assumption of an unavoidable trade-off?* Are there companies that have figured out how to double dip? In most organizations you can find a lot of disciplined execution in one place (on the factory floor, say), and a lot of free-spirited innovation somewhere else (in a design lab, for example). But is there any evidence that these virtues can coexist in the same place, at the same time?

Think back to Whole Foods, Gore, and Google. How would you rate these companies in terms of the freedom they cede to their employees? Higher than your company? Probably. Higher than most companies? Without a doubt. Indeed, at first glance, one wonders how these loose-limbed organizations manage to meet budgets and delivery deadlines.

First-line employees who set prices. People who take a day a week to work on whatever they like. Associates who can fire their leaders. A 50-to-1 span of control. All this sounds like a recipe for anarchy.

Separating the "What" from the "How"

To understand how these companies manage to radically empower their employees *and* deliver consistent results, it's necessary to distinguish between the *what* and the *how* of discipline. Everyone can agree that discipline is a good thing—it's an essential *what*. The problem is with the *how*.

In most organizations, control is exercised via standard operating procedures, tight supervision, detailed role definitions, a minimum of self-directed time, and frequent reviews by higher-ups. These mechanisms certainly bring people to heel, but they also put a short leash on initiative, creativity, and passion. Luckily, there are other ways of keeping things in check—other *hows*, if you will.

For example, while the in-store teams at Whole Foods have a significant degree of discretion over staffing, pricing, and product selection, they are also held accountable for the profitability of their various departments. Teams are assessed against monthly profitability targets, and when they meet those goals, team members receive a bonus in their next paycheck. Since the rewards are team-based, associates have little tolerance for colleagues who don't pull their weight. The fact that every team's performance is visible across the entire company is another incentive to work hard and stay focused. Turns out you don't need a lot of top-down discipline when four conditions are met:

1. First-line employees are responsible for results.

2. Team members have access to real-time performance data.

3. They have decision authority over the key variables that influence performance outcomes.

4. There's a tight coupling between results, compensation, and recognition.

Gore would also seem to suffer from a dangerous excess of freedom. Associates choose which teams to work on. They can say no to requests. And they allocate their dabble time as they see fit. But they also know they'll be reviewed by at least 20 of their peers at the end of each year—and that these assessments will determine their compensation. Then there's the discipline of "Real, Win, Worth." While Gore encourages grassroots innovation, associates have to build a solid business case before they can get serious funding. Add to this the fact that pensions are closely tied to Gore's share price, and one starts to understand why Gore is as disciplined as it is inventive.

And then there's Google—with its top-to-bottom anti-authoritarian vibe. Listen again to Shona Brown, Google's VP of operations: "We believe that if an individual feels something is more important than anything we might ask them to do, they should be able to follow their passion."[6] Can you hear *your* VP of operations saying something like that? Again, though, there are countervailing forces. Google's equivalent of Real, Win, Worth is "Learn fast, fail fast." Employees don't need a lot of sign-offs to try something new, but they won't get much in the way of resources until they've accumulated some positive user feedback. Then there's all that horizontal communication. Since every project has its own internal Web site, engineering teams get a lot of peer feedback. This transparency helps to weed out stupid ideas and beef up good ones—reducing the need for formal project reviews. On top of this, there's Google's reputational scoreboard. Titles don't mean much at Google. If you want to be a big kahuna, you have to develop a product that attracts millions of users—this helps to keep developers focused on real world problems. Finally, there are the Founders Awards. To get a big bonus, you have to build something that makes money for Google. All these mechanisms help to keep noses to grindstones.

In each of these cases, what at first glance looks like a slacker's paradise turns out to be anything but. Apparently, discipline and freedom *can* coexist, but not if companies rely on stick-instead-of-carrot methods for keeping employees in line.

As you can see, drawing a clear distinction between the *what* and *how* of a critical organizational imperative—like discipline—can be a useful tactic in uprooting management dogma. Individuals often defend the *how* of a hoary old management process simply because they haven't thought deeply about other ways of accomplishing the goals that process serves. Help them distinguish between the *what* and the *how*, give them some time to think, and new approaches are likely to emerge.

Exposing Self-Interest

Sometimes, though, a single counterexample—or even three—won't be enough to demolish a strongly held belief. When confronted with an unsettling anecdote, some of your colleagues are likely to protest that while "it might work there, it will never work here." When you're up against a belief that seems set in concrete, it may be helpful to ask, *whose interests does this belief serve?* For example, how does a reflexive belief in the danger of "excessive" employee freedom benefit those who hold that belief? Well, if the believers are managers, the answer is obvious: more freedom means less supervision, and less supervision means less authority—and, perhaps, fewer managers.

It's hardly surprising that most managers believe *you can't manage without managers.* Indeed, this may be the mother of all management orthodoxies. Yet despite the blatant self-interest that is buried in this belief, I can easily forgive anyone who struggles to imagine a world without supervisors and overseers. I struggle, too. I'm a management professor, after all. Who would I teach if not aspiring managers? Listen to Roy Jacques on this point: "[In a world without managers] academic organizational knowledge would be without a constituency, since it exists to train that specialized group called 'managers,' speaks most frequently from that group's perspective, and is structured institutionally to speak *to* managers *about* employees. Within present management discourse, managers represent 'the' organization; employees are merely a contingent resource need."[7]

Jacques then cheekily asks, "*To whom* [would] one address knowledge about self-managing employees, managers?" Touché. If employees were really self-managing, we wouldn't need managers—well, at least not so *many* of them.

Drawing attention to the ways in which deeply entrenched beliefs serve the interests of equally entrenched organizational factions may not win you new friends. On the other hand, there is value in exposing the political incentives that tend to perpetuate performance-limiting beliefs. It's OK if people want to defend the status quo, but they should be forced to do so on grounds other than self-interest.

Distinguishing Choices and Consequences

The fact that a belief serves the interests of a particular constituency doesn't make it wrong. While it's important to excavate political motivations, you'll need to dig deeper to determine whether or not a particular shred of dogma is a law of physics or merely an artifact of the way we've chosen to structure and run our organizations. So let's move on to our last set of questions: How have our choices contributed to the belief that freedom and discipline are mutually exclusive? Is this belief true simply because we have *made* it true? And if so, can we imagine alternatives that would free us from a tit-for-tat trade-off?

Here's a thought. Maybe we need "managers" because we have "employees." (Be patient, this is not as tautological as it sounds.) Think about the way computers are dependent on software. PCs aren't smart enough to write their own operating instructions, and they sit idle until a user sets them to work. Perhaps the same is true for employees.

Earlier, I talked about the invention of "the employee." What happened in this process, at the dawn of the 20th century? How did work life change as individuals left their farms and workshops to be absorbed into large-scale organizations? In manufacturing employees, did we manufacture a need for managers as well? I think so. If we understand how this came about, we will gain clues into how we might learn to manage without managers—or, at least, with a lot fewer of them.

In pre-industrial times, farmers and artisans enjoyed an intimate relationship with their customers. The feedback they received each day from their patrons was timely and unfiltered. Yet as industrial organizations grew in size and scale, millions of employees found themselves disconnected from the final customer. Robbed of direct feedback, they were compelled to rely on others who were closer to the customer to calibrate the effectiveness of their efforts and to tell them how they could better please their clients.

As companies divided themselves into departments and functions, employees also became disconnected from the final product. As tasks became narrower and more specialized, employees lost their emotional bond with the end product. The result? A diminished sense of responsibility for product quality and efficacy. No longer were workers proud craftsmen, now they were cogs in an industrial machine over which they had little control.

Size and scale also separated employees from their coworkers. Working in semi-isolated departments, they no longer had a systemwide view of the production process. If that system was suboptimal, they had no way of knowing it and no way of correcting it.

Industrialization also enlarged the gulf between workers and owners. While a 19th-century apprentice would have had the ear of the proprietor, most 20th-century employees reported to low-level supervisors. In a large enterprise, a junior employee could work for decades and never have the chance to speak one-on-one with someone empowered to make important policy decisions.

In addition, growing operational complexity fractured the information that was available to employees. In a small proprietorship, the financial scoreboard was simple and real time; there was little mystery about how the firm was doing. In a big industrial company, employees had a scoreboard, but it was contrived. It told workers how they were doing in their jobs, but little about how the company was doing overall.

With no more than a knothole view of the company's financial model, and only a sliver of responsibility for results, it was difficult for an employee to feel a genuine burden for the company's performance.

Finally, and worst of all, industrialization disconnected employees from their own creativity. In the industrial world, work methods and procedures were defined by experts and, once defined, were not easily altered. No matter how creative an employee might be, the scope for exercising that gift was severely truncated.

To put it simply, the pursuit of scale and efficiency advantages disconnected workers from the essential inputs that had, in earlier times, allowed them to be (largely) self-managing—and in so doing, it made the growth of an expansive managerial class inevitable.

To a large extent, employees need managers for the same reason 13-year-olds need parents: they are incapable of self-regulation. Adolescents, with their hormone-addled brains and limited life experience, lack the discernment to make consistently wise choices. That's why smart parents set boundaries on adolescent freedoms. Employees, on the other hand, aren't short of wisdom and experience, but they do lack information and context—since they are so often disconnected from customers, associates, end products, owners, and the big financial picture. Deprived of the ability to exercise control from within, employees must accept control from above. The result: disaffection. It turns out that employees enjoy being treated like 13-year-olds even less than 13-year-olds.

To bring timeworn beliefs to the surface, you'll occasionally need to play the role of an archaeologist. You'll need to use your pick and shovel to unearth the long-ago choices that have made our contemporary management beliefs and practices inevitable—for while the consequences of those choices may have been preordained, the choices themselves probably weren't. In the 20th century, thousands of executives *chose* to organize their companies along bureaucratic lines—a decision that in every case produced a multitiered management structure and the innovation-strangling effects of bureaucracy. Bill Gore, on the other hand, *chose* to build his company as a lattice—and the consequences of that decision are clearly visible today in Gore's weird but effective management model.

Disengaged employees. Hamstrung innovation. Inflexible organizations. Although we are living in a new century, we are still plagued by the side effects of a management model that was invented roughly a hundred years ago. Yet history doesn't have to be destiny—not if you are willing to go back and reassess the time-forgotten choices that so many others still take for granted. With the benefit of hindsight, you can ask: How have circumstances changed? Are new approaches possible? Must we be bound by the shackles of the past? These are essential questions for every management innovator.

The Value of Persistence

The deeper you dig into the hard mantle of management orthodoxy, the bigger the opportunity for radical innovation. This is true for two reasons. First, when you go deep, you have the chance to surface beliefs that haven't been examined in decades, or generations—beliefs that no one else is questioning, or dares to question. This can give you a big leg up as a management innovator. A few years back, who would have dared believe that it would one day be possible to develop complex software with a community of volunteers and virtually no managers? Seems that the hackers who invented the open source process were simply too dumb to know that you can't manage without managers.

Second, going deep helps you to build a nuanced understanding of what it will take to reinvent conventional management practices. It's not enough, for example, to wonder why your company can't manage without managers. To invent a management system that is less reliant on formally appointed managers, you must understand precisely *why* managers have been long regarded as indispensable. This deep understanding will help you focus your innovation efforts on foundational management challenges—like reconnecting employees with customers, with each other, and with the information they need to be self-managing.

Put simply, the deeper and more thoroughly you understand why you and your colleagues believe what you believe, the better and more robust your innovations will be. So keep digging.

Contrarian to the Core

Twenty-three-year-old Ricardo Semler didn't have a clean sheet of paper when, in 1982, he took over from his father as the CEO of a small Brazilian manufacturing company. Nevertheless, as Semco's new *presidente*, Semler's first move was to fire two-thirds of the company's senior management. Since then, he has been conducting one of the world's most radical experiments in employee self-management. At one point, for example, a Semco division of 800 employees had a single manager. Today Semco has "approximately" 10 businesses (Semler claims not to know the exact number), and more than 3,000 employees, up from 90 in 1982. The company's businesses are clustered around engineering services and high-end industrial products. If anything, Semco's management model is more radical than Gore's or Google's. It is defined, Semler claims, by the sum of all the conventional management practices the company forswears. A few examples:

- In a gesture that was more than symbolic, the company recently dismantled its headquarters building. HQ is now a small facility that looks like an airport executive lounge—people come and go, but no one is permanently stationed there.

- All workers, including assembly-line workers, choose their own hours—not only when to work, but how much to work.

- The company has no internal audit staff. No one double-checks expense reports. Instead, Semco works hard to cultivate a deep sense of honor and trust among its employees, and since employees share in the profits of unit, they have a big stake in rooting out fraudulent behavior.

- A substantial percentage of employees set their own salaries. In doing so, they are given data on comparative pay at other companies as well as access to Semco's own salary data. They know that if they ask to be paid "over the odds," their colleagues will expect a similarly outsized contribution, and profits will suffer.

- There are no policies governing employee travel—no restrictions on where people stay or which airlines they patronize.

A few Semler sound bites will give you a sense of his radical vision:

Semco has no official structure. It has no organizational chart. There's no business plan or company strategy, no two-year or five-year plan, no goal or mission statement, no long-term budget.[8]

The first principle to accept is that if an employee has no interest in a product or project, then the venture will never succeed. [Too often] workers are compelled to do jobs they could care less about, and that almost guarantees the company or product will never excel.[9]

Because of the fundamental tenet that we don't want anyone involved in anything that they really don't want to do, all of our meetings are on a voluntary basis, meaning that the meetings are known, and then whoever is interested can and will show up, and should also leave the moment they become uninterested.[10]

For a company to excel, employees must be reassured that self-interest, not the company's, is their foremost priority. At Semco, this is considered a form of corporate alignment. Without it, a company has to institute programs to pressure, exhort, and compel people to do their jobs.[11]

Why can't workers be involved in choosing their own leaders? Why shouldn't they manage themselves? Why can't they speak up—challenge, question, share information openly?[12]

You get the picture. Semco gives employees unprecedented control over their work lives, and then relies on personal integrity, peer pressure, financial self interest, and free access to information to help its staff members exercise their freedoms wisely. No one is treated like an adolescent. And not surprisingly, the managerial ranks have remained anorexic ever since Ricardo Semler sent his dad's lieutenants packing. Fact is, there's just not much for managers to *do* at Semco. If Semco sounds like a great place to work, it is. Not counting retirements, Semco's employee turnover is a scant 1 percent.

Semco is a Vegas-size, neon advertisement for management innovation. And it is also a reminder of just how many of our cobweb-covered orthodoxies we continue to honor as if they were God's commandments.

Semler claims that Semco is used as a case study in 76 business schools. If this is true, why don't more companies *feel* like Semco—or Google, or Gore? Why are examples like these so rare? Because, as I argued at the outset of this chapter, most managers have never taken the time and the trouble to deconstruct their management orthodoxies.

Additionally, it's easy to be intimidated by a management system that is both distinctive and intricate. Where does one start in building a management system like Gore's or Semco's? It's easy to forget that these funky management systems took decades to build. Management innovation isn't a six-month project; it's a never-ending search for better ways to emancipate and compound human capability. And it starts with the simplest of all questions, "Why?"

The sooner your company starts sloughing off its legacy management beliefs, the sooner it's going to become truly fit for the future. As we've seen, a few companies are already traveling light, having left a lot of their out-dated management baggage back there in the 20th century. In the end, there's really not much of a choice: you can either wait for tomorrow's management heretics to beat the orthodoxies out of your company, or you can start coaxing them out right now.

Eight

Embracing New Principles

YOU CAN'T REINVENT MANAGEMENT FOR THE 21ST CENTURY without some new management principles—big ideas with the power to inspire dramatic changes in tradition-bound processes and practices. Jim Lavoie, the CEO of Rite-Solutions, a young software company based in Middletown, Rhode Island, bumped into one such principle while driving his car.

The Power of a New Principle

The story begins in 1999 when Lavoie cashed in his stock options at a leading defense contractor and left to launch a start-up. Joining him in the new venture was Joe Marino, a longtime colleague who, like Lavoie, had risen to the rank of EVP within their previous employer. In those roles, both men had been frustrated by their inability to protect inventors from an overeager horde of rule-happy "preventers." Life would be different, they vowed, in their new company, which they christened Rite-Solutions. New ideas would always be welcome and everyone would have the chance to innovate.

Over the next five years, Rite-Solutions would grow to 150 employees and pass the $20 million mark in annual revenues. Yet with this success came a renewed concern on the part of Lavoie and Marino: how could they make sure that Rite-Solutions remained an energetic, innovative community, even as it grew?

The breakthrough came in October 2004, as Lavoie was sitting in his car listening to a roundup of the day's financial news. Wow, thought Lavoie, the stock market might be a great blueprint for building an innovative company. The market is inclusive—anyone can invest; it's fun—most investors avidly follow the progress of their portfolios; and the stock market is empowering—there's no über-investor telling individuals where to place their bets. Fired up by these insights, Lavoie quickly recruited a few lateral-thinking colleagues and challenged them to find a way of building a market-based innovation process within Rite-Solutions. When the new system finally went live, it encompassed three markets: the "Spazdaq," a market for risky ideas focusing on entirely new businesses and technologies; the "Bow Jones," a market for ideas "adjacent" to the company's current products and competencies; and a market for "Savings Bonds," ideas for short-term operational improvements.

To Lavoie's delight, the notion of a stock market caught on quickly, due in part, no doubt, to the scheme's tongue-in-cheek lingo. Over the next 13 months, 30 internal champions launched 44 "IPOs," each of which was a nascent idea in search of investors. In its first year, the new innovation platform added 10 percent to Rite-Solutions' top line and accounted for 50 percent of its new business growth. Here's how the markets work: To launch an IPO, a would-be entrepreneur prepares an "ExpectUs"—an offer document that outlines the value-creating potential of the new idea. Each new stock debuts at $10, and entrepreneurs don't have to seek top management's approval before launching a new security.

Every IPO has a "Budge-It" that is prepared by the entrepreneur. This document lists the short-term steps that must be taken to move the idea forward. The goal is to make it easy for volunteers to get involved, so each Budge-It task is structured in a way that allows it to be completed in a half day or less. Every employee gets $10,000 in fantasy money to invest across the three markets. Investors manage their own "Mutual Fun" portfolios and can buy and sell any stock at any time.

Each stock listing is accompanied by a threaded discussion that provides additional information to investors. Anyone can voice an opinion, positive or negative, or ask a question. By perusing these discussion boards, investors are able to judge which ideas are generating a positive buzz and which are languishing. Mutual Fun money flows to ideas that are attracting volunteer effort and moving steadily towards commercialization. Every week, a "market maker"—currently a retired CTO from a large IT company—revalues each stock based on the number of Budge-It items completed, inflows and outflows of Mutual Fun money, and the opinions expressed on the stock's discussion board. When an IPO gains momentum and breaks into the company's "Top 20" most valuable stocks, Rite-Solutions' "adventure capitalists"—Lavoie and Marino—accelerate the pace of Budge-It activity by awarding the initiative a real pot of money. When an idea finally springs to life and helps the company make or save money, those who have invested their time receive a share of the benefits, through bonuses or real stock options.

Thus far, the Bow Jones's stock with the largest market cap is "Rite-Away" (trading symbol: AWAY). This is an automated help-desk service that matches the most appropriate IT engineer with each incoming call. A female engineer listed the stock, which quickly attracted talent-and-time investments from every corner of Rite-Solutions. If a stock fails to generate enough interest, the market maker eventually de-lists it. But even the dogs of the Bow enjoy a little upside—anyone who takes the initiative to launch a new security gets credit for doing so in the company's annual employee evaluation process.

Lavoie calls Mutual Fun an "opinion game" whose aim is to provoke intelligent people to think—every day—about how to grow the company. The stock market gives every employee a voice in setting the company's strategy. "It lets us harvest the collective brilliance of *everyone*," says Lavoie, "which makes some of those tough strategic decisions a lot more obvious."

Rite-Solution's innovation bazaar may look weird when viewed through the prism of conventional management practice, but it demonstrates how a novel principle—market-based innovation—can help turbo-charge performance.

Unfortunately, management breakthroughs like this one are all too rare. The management practices that predominate in most companies are still based on a clutch of timeworn principles that trace their lineage back to the dawn of the industrial revolution. Yet what is true in other fields of human endeavor is also true for management: you can't solve new or chronic problems with fossilized principles. To build free societies based on self-rule, the 18th-century advocates of democracy had to renounce the time-honored principles of hereditary sovereignty. To untangle the story of life, Darwin had to abandon traditional views and conjure up a new theory based on the principle of natural selection. Similarly, physicists eager to understand the anomalies of the subatomic world had to look beyond Newton's clockwork laws to discover the principles of quantum mechanics. I believe we are at a similar juncture in the history of management. Put bluntly, there is no way to build tomorrow's essential organizational capabilities atop the scaffolding of 20th-century management precepts. To jump onto a new management S-curve, we're going to need some new management principles.

Unraveling the Management Genome

Have you ever asked yourself, what are the deepest principles upon which your management beliefs are based? Probably not. Few executives, in my experience, have given much thought to the foundational principles that underlie their views on how to organize and manage. In that sense, they are as unaware of their managerial

DNA as they are of their biological DNA. So before we set off in search of new management principles, we need to take a moment to understand the principles that comprise our current management genome, and how those tenets may limit organizational performance.

The practices and processes of modern management have been built around a small nucleus of core principles: standardization, specialization, hierarchy, alignment, planning and control, and the use of extrinsic rewards to shape human behavior. (See table 8-1.)

These principles were elucidated early in the 20th century by a small band of pioneering management thinkers—individuals like Henri Fayol, Lyndall Urwick, Luther Gullick, and Max Weber. While each of

TABLE 8-1

The principles of modern management

Principle	Application	Goal
Standardization	Minimize variances from standards around inputs, outputs, and work methods.	Cultivate economies of scale, manufacturing efficiency, reliability, and quality.
Specialization (of tasks and functions)	Group like activities together in modular organizational units.	Reduce complexity and accelerate learning.
Goal alignment	Establish clear objectives through a cascade of subsidiary goals and supporting metrics.	Ensure that individual efforts are congruent with top-down goals.
Hierarchy	Create a pyramid of authority based on a limited span of control.	Maintain control over a broad scope of operations.
Planning and control	Forecast demand, budget resources, and schedule tasks, then track and correct deviations from plan.	Establish regularity and predictability in operations; conformance to plans.
Extrinsic rewards	Provide financial rewards to individuals and teams for achieving specified outcomes.	Motivate effort and ensure compliance with policies and standards.

these theorists had a slightly different take on the philosophical foundations of modern management, they all agreed on the principles just enumerated. This concordance is hardly surprising, since they were all focusing on the same problem: how to maximize operational efficiency and reliability in large-scale organizations. Nearly 100 years on, this is still the only problem that modern management is fully competent to address.

Make no mistake; the diligent application of those industrial age principles has been a boon to economic prosperity. Yet if the goal is to create organizations that are highly adaptable and fully human, these principles are insufficient and often toxic. Specialization, for all its benefits, tends to limit the sort of cross-boundary learning that generates breakthrough ideas. It can also lead to parochialism and venomous turf battles. If not checked, the quest for ever greater standardization can metastasize into an unhealthy affection for conformance, where the new and the wacky are seen as dangerous deviations from standard operating procedures. An overemphasis on alignment and goal congruity can discourage individuals from pursuing "out-of-scope" opportunities and curtail the search for new strategic options. Elaborate planning-and-control rituals can lull executives into believing the environment is more predictable than it is, and desensitize them to discontinuities for which there is little precedent. Finally, a simple-minded belief in the effectiveness of monetary rewards can blind managers to the power of purpose and passion as mechanisms for engendering individual effort.

There is another, more general limitation to our shopworn management principles. While ostensibly they serve the goal of operational effectiveness, they minister to a need that is perhaps even dearer to top management's heart: predictability. One can fairly describe the development of modern management as an unending quest to regularize the irregular, starting with errant and disorderly employees. Regularity (achieved through standards, controls, plans, and procedures) makes management's job easier. It helps executives recognize and correct deviations when they occur. It allows business leaders to make predictions and then stick to them. It reduces the chance that middle managers will be caught out by their superiors. In other words, it helps the bureaucratic class maintain its self-comforting illusion of control. In the bible of modern management, "no surprises" is the first commandment.

Increasingly, though, we live in an irregular world, where irregular people use irregular means to produce irregular products that yield irregular profits. For example, while one can imagine a highly disciplined product development process yielding the "son-of-iPod," a line extension within Apple's family of iconic music players, it's unlikely that a rigid, mechanistic process would have ever hatched the iPod itself. In the 21st century, regularity doesn't produce superior performance.

During his reign as chairman of Pixar, the world's most successful animated film studio and now part of Disney, Steve Jobs regularly hired irregular people—one of whom was Brad Bird, an ex-Disney animator famous for getting *The Simpsons* off the ground. When he was approached to join Pixar, Bird was told that, "The only thing we're afraid of, is getting complacent. We need to bring in outside people so we keep throwing ourselves off balance." Encouraged by Pixar's appetite for the irregular, Bird signed on. Soon afterwards, he explained the logic of his appointment to a journalist: "I was brought here to cause a certain amount of disruption. I've been *fired* for being disruptive several times, but this is the first time I've been *hired* for it."[1]

Pixar is an exception. Most companies have deviance-abhorring, conformance-exalting management DNA; most are filled with executives intent on wringing the irregularities *out* of their organizations. Of course, deviations from the norm can destroy value, as when, for example, they impair product quality. Nevertheless, an organization that worships regularity with a single-minded devotion is likely to have trouble distinguishing between value-*destroying* irregularities and value-*creating* irregularities. The risk is that management systems designed to promote alignment and consistency end up culling out variations of *all* sorts—the good and the bad. With exactitude and invariability fast losing their power to generate above-average returns, companies are going to have to learn to love the irregular. In practice, this means rebuilding our management systems around *new* and unorthodox principles—just as Jim Lavoie did at Rite-Solutions.

Reinventing the Management Genome

So where do you start in reinventing the management genome? Where do you look to find the new management principles that will help your company meet the new challenges of the 21st century? Simple: you start by analyzing the DNA of things that *already* exhibit the cutting-edge qualities you want to build into your organization—things, in other words, that are adaptable, innovative, and highly engaging. For the purposes of this chapter, we'll focus on the challenge of adaptability, since there is no imperative more central to competitive success in a world of ever-accelerating change. To be adaptable, a company must, of course, be innovative and engaging as well. Thus by unwrapping the principles of adaptability, we will also gain insights into the prerequisites for building organizations that are intensely creative and deeply empowering.

What things, then, set the benchmark for adaptability? My nominations would be: life, markets, democracies, religious faith, and the world's most vibrant cities. All of these are far more resilient than big companies. So let's dig into these paragons of adaptability to see what we can learn.

Life: Creating Variety

Life is the most resilient thing on our planet. Despite meteor strikes, volcanic eruptions, extreme climate shifts, and wandering tectonic plates, life has not only persisted, it has flourished. In the process, it has become ever more complex and capable—this despite the fact that in the standard evolutionary model there is no CEO of life, no outside agency

directing the course of evolution. Life cannot predict, it can't anticipate, and it can't prepare for the future, but it can adapt, and it's adapting still. Under the pressure of poaching, for example, an increasing
percentage of male Asian elephants are being born without tusks.[2]

Life's capacity for adaptation is based on highly complex biochemical processes, yet the design rules for evolutionary "progress" are relatively simple: *variety* and *selection*. Life is constantly producing genetic
variety through mutation and sexual reproduction. "Gene flow"—the
genetic jumbling that occurs when two distinct populations intermingle—is another spoon stirring the genetic pot. Variety is how life insures
itself against the unexpected, and over the past 4,000 millennia our
planet has changed in some pretty unexpected ways. Yet all that change
has never outpaced life's capacity to adapt—not so far, anyway. Across
the eons, life has managed to strike a surprisingly effective balance between perpetuating mechanisms, such as the near-perfect transcription
of DNA in cellular division, and variety-inducing mechanisms such as
mutation and reproduction.

Geological data suggests that evolution has not been a steady and gradual process. During periods of environmental stress, evolution speeds
up, often moving faster than what random mutation and subsequent selection would seem to allow. One possible explanation: evolution occasionally equips organisms with apparently superfluous, reproductively
neutral features that turn out, quite by accident, to be highly useful
when conditions change. This is known as *pre-adaptation*. Feathers, for
example, may have been used as insulation long before they were used
in flight. Without pre-adaptation, it is difficult to imagine how some life
forms made the rapid leaps in functional capability that seem to be indicated in the geological record.

A species becomes extinct when it fails to adapt fast enough to
changes in their habitat. This risk is exacerbated when the population
is small and inbred. For example, about 90 percent of the world's commercial apple trees trace their lineage back to a single pair of parent
trees. With so little genetic diversity to draw upon, evolution has a hard
time producing the kinds of adaptations that would allow apple trees to

cope with environmental stresses. As a result, apple trees are highly susceptible to a wide range of threats, including apple scab, fire blight, and powdery mildew. The point: a genetically homogenous population reduces the "feedstock" for evolutionary progress. As a result, a negative shift in the environment can endanger an entire species.[3]

So what lessons does life hold for the prospective management innovator? What are the implications of *variety* and *selection* for 21st-century organizations? No doubt you're already drawing lessons, but let me highlight a few that seem particularly critical.

Experimentation beats planning. It is natural that human beings want to be "in control." Each of us hopes the future will unfold according to our plans. Yet in a world where the present is an increasingly unreliable guide to the future, competitive success depends less on *planning* for what will come next and more on continuously experimenting with what *could* come next. The only thing you can bank on is that the future is going to be surprising. Whether those surprises turn out to be good or bad for your company will depend largely on the extent to which it proactively invests in exploring alternatives to the status quo—by experimenting with disruptive technologies, exploring new ways of going to market, and reaching out to new sorts of customers. To be resilient, a company needs a lot of lightly scripted pre-adaptation. This is the logic behind Gore's dabble time and Google's 20 percent rule—policies that give associates the chance to pre-adapt rather than react. Too much of what gets done in most companies is in response to some already pressing issue; there's no slack, no space for improvisation, and no way to defend projects that aren't immediately useful. That's why so many companies end up on the wrong side of the change curve. Your job as a management innovator is to make sure that the management systems in your company encourage strategic pre-adaptation.

All mutations are mistakes. Most companies strive for operational perfection. Yet if nature were perfect, if every instance of DNA transcription were error-free, the process of evolution would come to a grinding halt. The lesson for management innovators is clear: not only must companies expand the scope of their strategic experimentation, they must also be slower to brand things "unworkable," "ridiculous," or "out-of-bounds." As every student of innovation knows, radical ideas always provoke incredulity at the outset. So you must ask, in what ways do my company's management processes reinforce a narrow view of what is sensible? How do they dissuade folks from coming forward with ideas that are out of the ordinary? There's a difference, of course, between ideas that are "stupid-stupid" (selling coffee online) and ideas that are "smart-stupid" (selling a caramel macchiato for four bucks a pop at Starbucks). Trouble is, you can't find this dividing line if you're using a decade's worth of industry dogma as your screening criteria. An evaluation process that weeds out every idea that fails to meet a narrowly defined test of feasibility will jeopardize your company's adaptability. As Steve Jurvetson, the noted venture capitalist, notes, "It's OK to be wrong most of the time if you're really right some of the time."[4]

You can build a company that is virtually error and mistake free. You can build a company that is highly adaptable. But you can't do both. In this sense, perfection is the enemy of progress.

Darwinian selection doesn't need SVPs. When it comes to picking which ideas to fund and which to kill, the selection process in most companies is anything but "natural." In Darwinian selection there is a single criterion that governs which genes get selected into the genome: reproductive success. Genes at risk of being cut have no one to lobby. There's no one who will entertain fears about cannibalization. Yet in most companies, there are all sorts of political biases that determine which ideas get selected into budgets and which ones get selected out.

This suggests another worthy goal for management innovation: depoliticizing decision making. In practice, this means that new ideas must be given the chance to compete openly for support, rather than being subject to the veto of a single executive or unit head. Conversely, there needs to be a process that allows ordinary employees to voice their opinions on top management's "pet projects." This is the logic behind the weight given to peer feedback at Gore and Google. Put simply, if you want to increase the survival chances of your company, you need to make sure that "natural" selection, not SVP selection, determines which ideas go forward, and which don't.

The broader the gene pool, the better. Managers tend to marry their cousins. Not literally, of course, but they often surround themselves with people whose life experiences mirror their own. Think about it. How many people hold senior executive positions in your company who are *not* engineers, *not* accountants, *not* MBAs, and *not* industry veterans?

The diversity of any system determines its capacity to adapt. Greater diversity—of thought, skills, attitudes, and capabilities—equals a greater range of adaptive responses. The risk in a fast-changing world is that a company becomes *overadapted* to a particular ecological niche. In the pursuit of focus, a company can impair its ability to adapt by hiring in a single mold, narrowing the scope of its innovation efforts, relying exclusively on a single business model, or failing to experiment with new operating models. As change accelerates, investing in diversity is not a luxury; it's a survival strategy.

There's a lot more to diversity than the shade of one's skin and the shape of one's genitals. What really matters is the sum total of one's life experiences. Despite all the rhetoric to the contrary, companies often put more effort into training the diversity *out* of people, through programs that indoctrinate employees in the "one best way," than they do into bringing fresh ideas *into* the company. A notable exception: IBM. In July 2006, the company launched an online "Innovation Jam" and invited more than 100,000 individuals—customers, outside consultants, and employee family members—to join in. Once they signed on, participants were given the chance to brainstorm ideas around the future of transportation, healthcare, the environment, finance, and commerce. For its part, IBM stuffed the site full of video clips, virtual tours, and background information on some of its most intriguing technologies. While not quite an "open source" approach to strategy creation, the Innovation Jam gave IBM access to a diversity of viewpoints that it simply could not have matched internally. In that sense, the Jam was a refreshing alternative to the incestuous management processes that companies typically use to generate strategy.

As the future unfolds, the competitive environment for business will increasingly "select in" companies that have learned how to rapidly evolve their core strategies, and "select out" firms that are less adaptable. Your goal is to help your company get inside the evolutionary cycle of its competitors. If life is any guide, this will mean reinventing management processes in ways that broaden the scope of experimentation, depoliticize strategic decision making, and enlarge the gene pool. These are critical design specs for a 21st-century management model.

Markets: Flexibly Allocating Resources

Evolution is a *sorting* mechanism that propagates "good" mutations while suppressing "bad" ones. In contrast, a well-functioning market is a *routing* mechanism that diverts resources from low-value uses to high-value uses. Economists have long agreed that lightly regulated markets are the most effective means for achieving *allocational efficiency*. In a regime of open markets, chronically underperforming companies lose customers and investors, and thereby, capital and employees. Markets then reallocate those resources to firms that can use them more productively. When markets work, no company can forever misuse society's resources. This is why the adaptability of national economies depends so critically on the existence of well-functioning markets.

By definition, markets are decentralized—they encompass thousands, or even millions, of economic actors. Yet markets are remarkably good at collating data from many disparate sources and summarizing that information in the form of prices. In this sense, markets divine the "wisdom of the crowd," to borrow James Surowiecki's simple phrasing.[5] What do folks think a certain stock is worth? What do they think a pair of designer jeans should sell for? Buyers and sellers trust the "fairness" of a price when it reflects a wide range of opinions and sentiments. Yet in large companies, managers place too much trust in the wisdom of the few—particularly when it comes to "pricing" the potential value of new strategic initiatives.

Markets are capable of solving highly complex allocational problems. At any point in time, New York City, a metropolis of more than 8 million inhabitants, has a scant three-day supply of food. In a sense, the city is always close to famine. New York's mayor could appoint a food czar, with a mandate to ensure that an adequate supply of victuals is always on hand, but such an idea is clearly absurd. New Yorkers don't starve thanks to the efficiency of a wide variety of markets—for vegetables, meats, beverages, and more—that respond almost instantly to the demands of restaurateurs, street vendors, and ordinary shoppers. Indeed, the Nobel Prize–winning economist Amartya Sen maintains that no democratic country with a market economy has ever experienced a serious famine.

Silicon Valley also excels in getting the right resources to the right people at the right times. Over a recent five-year span, the Valley's venture capitalists raised and invested more than $42 billion in 4,624 deals.[6] Yet there's no CEO of Silicon Valley Inc., and no investment committee making resource allocation decisions. No central authority decides how much to invest in nanotechnology, biotech, or the mobile web.

In essence, venture capitalists are independent brokers who compete to create value at the intersection of three markets: the market for new business ideas, the market for capital, and the market for talent. In an average year, a midsized VC firm will receive and review more than 5,000 business plans. For a large firm, the figure can be four or five times that. Venture capital firms vie with one another to attract capital and find the best start-ups to fund. Would-be entrepreneurs compete to get funding. Nascent business plans are typically sent to a dozen or more VCs, and it's a rare start-up that doesn't suffer a spate of rejections before finding a sponsor. Newly minted companies compete to hire the best engineers, sales reps, and senior execs, all of whom hope to sign up with the next Cisco, eBay, or Google. Markets work only to the extent that participants have access to relevant information. Silicon Valley's compact geographical dimensions and its dense matrix of interlocking social networks is a boon in this regard. With only a degree or two of social separation between them, it's relatively easy for the Valley's VCs, entrepreneurs, and engineers to take stock of one another across the negotiating table. All of this helps to make Silicon Valley one of the most economically vibrant places on earth.

By creating a forum where needs and solutions can find each other, markets expand the array of choices for buyers and suppliers alike—whether it's would-be entrepreneurs looking for funding, or lonely adults looking for a romantic encounter. A few years back, the *New York Times* ran an article about the growth in online markets for casual sex.[7] Craigslist, AdultFriendFinder, and other such sites have vastly expanded the market for short-term, intimate "relationships." Host to hundreds of thousands of personal ads, these online markets are much more efficient than their primary competitor—the local bar scene. Unlike a bar, the online markets are open all hours, offer a large selection of potentially willing partners, and reduce the risk of misconstrued intentions. When technology makes it easier for buyers and suppliers to find each other, markets expand—sometimes exponentially.

So what can management innovators learn from markets? First and foremost, this: resources (capital and talent) have to be free to seek the best returns. Resilience requires resource flexibility and history suggests this is best achieved with some sort of market mechanism. More specifically . . .

Markets are apolitical. Over the past 50 years, the New York Stock Exchange has outperformed most of the companies *on* the New York Stock Exchange. Why? Because markets are better at allocating resources than hierarchies. Hierarchies are very good at *applying* resources—laying out plans, sequencing activities, and meeting dead-lines—but they're lousy at *allocating* resources—or, more specifically, at *reallocating* resources from old strategies to new strategies.

It wasn't until 2004, for example, that Kodak finally faced up to the near-terminal decline of its film-based photography business and launched a $3 billion restructuring program. Not surprisingly, it took a new CEO to push the plan through. The fact that the move came so late suggests that Kodak's veteran managers simply couldn't bring themselves to disinvest from the company's legacy business.

Unlike big companies—most of which are organized more like the Soviet Union than the New York Stock Exchange or Silicon Valley—markets don't suffer from the resilience-sapping allocational rigidities outlined in chapter 3. Markets are apolitical and unsentimental. No broker or fund manager can compel folks to keep pouring money into an underperforming asset. Senior executives, in contrast, often have a personal stake in perpetuating the status quo. And therein lies the problem. It's tough for a company to stay in the vanguard when major funding decisions are controlled by the old guard.

Build a market and they will come. As of August 2006, eBay had more than 200 million registered users. In 2005, the company hosted more than 1.9 billion listings and facilitated the sale of over $44 billion of merchandise. The ease of doing business on eBay has created millions of first-time traders. Now think of the 5,000 business plans sent to the average VC each year. If Silicon Valley didn't exist, if there weren't hundreds of VCs eagerly culling through their e-mail for the next Yahoo! or YouTube, would all those business plans have been churned out? Would college kids be dreaming about becoming the next Tom Anderson, the English major who cofounded MySpace? Probably not. Markets can't generate new business models or new products, but they can create a powerful incentive for individuals to think up new things.

Now transfer this logic to the "market" for new ideas in your own company. Consider, for a moment, the options facing a politically disenfranchised frontline employee who hopes to win funding for a small-scale experiment. In most companies, that employee has only one option: to push the idea up the chain of command to the point where it can get considered as part of the formal planning process. Success in this case requires four things: a manager who doesn't peremptorily reject the idea as eccentric or out of scope; an idea that at first blush is "big" enough to warrant senior management's attention; executives who are willing to divert funds from an existing program in favor of the half-baked idea; and, finally, an innovator who has the necessary acumen, personal charisma, and political cunning to make all this happen. That makes for long odds. Given these imperfections in the internal market for innovation, it's no wonder that breakthrough ideas are undersupplied in large companies.

Most companies have no internal equivalent to Silicon Valley's innovation marketplace. VPs aren't receiving thousands of new business plans a year; there aren't hundreds of investors competing to fund the next big idea; and the best engineers don't have the freedom to abandon an essential but boring project for one that has more upside potential. While some companies, like Procter & Gamble, are getting better at sourcing innovation from outside their borders, few have built open innovation markets in-house.

Operational efficiency ≠ strategic efficiency. While companies have many ways of measuring operational efficiency, most are clueless when it comes to evaluating their strategic efficiency. After all, how can corporate leaders be certain that the current set of initiatives represents the highest-value use of talent and capital if there's no process for generating and examining a large population of alternatives? How can executives be sure that the right resources are lined up behind the right opportunities if capital and talent aren't free to move to more promising projects? The simple answer is, they can't.

When there's a dearth of new strategic options, or when talent and cash are "locked up" in legacy programs, divisional executives get to "buy" their resources at a discount, since they don't have to compete for resources against a wide array of unconventional alternatives.[8] Requiring that every project earn its cost of capital doesn't correct this anomaly. It is perfectly possible for a project to have a positive EVA, and still be a suboptimal use of talent and capital. The only way to raise a company's strategic efficiency is to create a resource allocation process based on market principles.

The allocational flexibility of markets points us to some additional design rules for building nimble companies. First, the process of evaluating and "pricing" new projects needs to be decentralized. No small group of nostalgic executives should be allowed to deep six a new and unconventional idea. Second, innovators should have access to multiple sources of experimental capital—analogous to all those VCs and angel investors looking to fund new business ideas. In any large company, there should be hundreds, or even thousands, of individuals who have the ability to make small, experimental bets on new ideas. And third, the more efficient the market for ideas, talent, and capital—that is, the easier it is for internal innovators and investors to find each other, and the fewer the constraints on the internal realignment of resources—the more adaptable a company will be.

Democracy: Enabling Activism

Over the past two centuries, no one-party state or autocratic regime has been able to match the resilience of the world's great democracies. Today, two-thirds of the world's states are either democracies or on a path toward democracy—double the percentage at the close of World War II.[9] Contrary to the assumptions of many development experts, democracy is as much a boon to third-world countries as it is to first-world nations. In their well-researched book, *The Democracy Advantage*,[10] Morton Halperin, Joseph Siegle, and Michael Weinstein argue that democracies outperform autocracies in even the poorest regions of the globe. Among developing countries, democracies are much less likely to experience severe economic contractions and humanitarian emergencies than authoritarian regimes.[11] Notes Michael Weinstein, "Democracies don't fall off the edge of the cliff and hit bottom the way autocracies do."[12]

Nevertheless, one can forgive a powerful CEO for doubting democracy's adaptability advantage. Democratic processes are notoriously slow and cumbersome. Only in a dictatorship, it could be argued, do leaders have the power to make the kind of split-second decisions that are required in a world of split-second change. Autocrats don't have to waste time building a consensus, and since they control the levers of power (the military, the press, and the civil service), they can make things happen *now*.

The problem, though, is that in an autocracy, the quality of decision making is highly dependent on the wisdom of a single individual, or a small cadre of senior leaders. That wouldn't be a problem if every company was led by the CEO equivalent of Lee Kuan Yew, the long-serving former Singaporean prime minister who used his near-dictatorial powers to transform a colonial outpost into a benchmark for Asian economic development. But in business, as in politics, leaders like Lee Kuan Yew are rare. If it were otherwise, totalitarian regimes wouldn't consistently underperform democracies.

In an autocratic system, there are few mechanisms for bottom-up renewal. As a result, change tends to come in belated, convulsive spasms, via revolutions and insurrections. In democracies, change usually starts at the grass roots, and compounds upwards as interest groups and political activists amass support for their policies. With change constantly bubbling up from below, democracies are able to avoid the periodic rebellions that typify political life in totalitarian regimes. The same, unfortunately, can't be said for most large companies, where it usually takes a financial crisis and a shareholder revolt to provoke a change in leadership and a strategy reboot.

Indeed, it often appears as if large companies have borrowed their change model from poorly governed third-world dictatorships, where the only way to change policy is to depose the despots. Yet a board-led coup is a highly inefficient way of changing corporate direction, since it usually occurs only *after* a company has lost a significant measure of momentum and money. Without democratic reforms, though, there is no alternative to this brutish and expensive way of re-vectoring strategy. That's why you, as a management innovator, need to understand the secrets of democracy's regenerative powers.

Accountability to the governed. Francis Fukuyama describes democracy as "a set of accountability mechanisms." According to Fukuyama, "all political systems have a degree of accountability, but some have more than others—and the ones that have more accountability are more resilient."[13] In a democracy, the political elite are prisoners of the populace. Every politician, no matter how stubborn or self-serving, knows that he or she must ultimately answer to the electorate.

In a democracy, power flows up and accountability flows down. Politicians are chosen by, and are accountable to, their constituents. Because of this, they must take account of a wide variety of viewpoints. In the corporate world, this pattern is reversed: employees are accountable upward, while authority trickles downward from the board. Top management is accountable only to the shareholders. Problem is, boards don't create value. Rather, it is the wisdom and imagination of employees, and the extent to which their sagacity is honored, that determines how much value gets created.

Shortly before he was booted out of his job as the chairman and CEO of Home Depot, America's largest DIY chain, Robert Nardelli told a television interviewer, "I really feel no one is more aligned with shareholders than me."[14] Well, of course Nardelli was aligned with shareholders—he had huge stock option grants that would pay off only if Home Depot's share price went up. (Though he, like many other CEOs, also did surprisingly well when the share price drifted sideways.) My guess is that Home Depot's shareholders would have been better served if their chairman could have bragged about being aligned with employees and customers. It seems to me that a CEO's *first* accountability should be to those who have the greatest power to create or destroy shareholder value—rather than to those who have a residual claim on the firm's profits.

How might a corporate leader evince such a sense of accountability? By spending a lot more time in dialogue with first-level associates— with the objective of learning rather than exhorting. By giving employees, rather than senior staff groups, the responsibility for designing the management processes that affect their work. By creating formal consultation mechanisms that involve a diagonal slice of the organization in every key decision. By setting up the kind of uncensored, Web-based discussion forums that tie folks together at Google. And, if they're really brave, by trimming the salary gap between the moguls and the minions. My point: executives who feel truly accountable to their employees will consult more broadly and listen more intently than those who don't. The payoff? A company where top management's self-serving and out-of-date beliefs are less likely to be impediments to change.

The right of dissent. In a democracy, political leaders have to face their critics. From town hall meetings to presidential news conferences, elected officials have to respond publicly to their most strident detractors. Day by day, they have to face up to the sort of criticism and damning information that is often ignored or suppressed in an authoritarian regime. Yet invariably this open and vigorous dissent improves the quality of decisions and ensures that bad policies get revisited and revised more quickly than would otherwise be the case.

Vociferous, honest dissent is not a hallmark of hierarchical organizations. As a consultant, I've often had the chance to watch a young team pitch a controversial idea to their CEO. In prep sessions, the team is invariably passionate and resolute. But once in the presence of the top dog, these bold heretics often morph into forelock-tugging supplicants. A raised eyebrow, a skeptical question and they're backpedaling and looking for the door. Adaptability requires alternatives. Alternatives require dissenters. So as a management innovator you have to ask yourself, do the management processes in my company encourage dissent, and if not, what can I do to change that?

Distributed leadership. Some wag once remarked that America was invented by geniuses to be run by idiots. Of course, the same is true for any constitutional democracy. Though glib, this statement reveals a central truth: America's resilience doesn't depend on the qualities of the man or woman who occupies the Oval Office—and thank God for that. While a few of America's presidents have been brilliant leaders and inspired statesmen, most have been something less. Critically, if democracies are more resilient than large companies, it's not because they are better led.

In a democracy, the pace of change depends only tangentially on the vision and moral courage of those in power. Social campaigners, industry groups, think tanks, and ordinary citizens all have the chance to shape the legislative agenda and influence political priorities. The legitimacy that democracy accords to activists is based on a belief that every citizen has the right to be a policy innovator, if he or she is so motivated. It also reflects a deep trust in the capacity of the electorate to choose wisely from among the many policy options that are, at any point in time, vying for their support. Rarely, though, do companies extend this sort of trust to their employees. Instead, they cling to the belief that institutional success depends disproportionately on the leadership qualities of the CEO and the senior executive team.

Every year, boards and executive recruiters spend countless hours in the search for the perfect CEO—someone who is visionary yet well grounded, courageous yet prudent, confident yet modest, firm yet flexible, and tough yet compassionate. Trouble is, there aren't many people who possess a full measure of these admirable and paradoxical qualities. The inventors of democracy recognized this fact and compensated for it by creating political processes that leverage the everyday genius of "ordinary" citizens. The real challenge, then, isn't to hire or grow great leaders, but to build companies that can thrive with less-than-perfect leaders.

Of course, democracies have problems. They are often immobilized by competing interests, and frequently spawn bloated, unresponsive bureaucracies. Yet in their capacity to adapt and evolve, we can discover additional design rules for 21st-century companies: leaders must be truly accountable to the front lines; employees must feel free to exercise the right of dissent; policy making must be as decentralized as possible; and activism must be encouraged and honored. Embed these principles in your company's management systems, and it will be a lot more adaptable than it is right now.

Faith: Finding Courage in Meaning

For more than 300 years, commentators have been predicting the end of religious faith. From Auguste Comte to Richard Dawkins, they have argued that faith must inevitably crumble as scientific certitude grows. Yet faith in a divine presence continues to be one of humanity's great common denominators. While some societies are more overtly religious than others, the majority of human beings share a belief in the transcendental.

The belief that science will one day displace faith is based on a mistaken assumption that religious belief is principally a set of mystical and misguided conjectures about how the natural world works. As the sunlight of scientific discovery breaks through the black night of ignorance, so the thinking goes, these primitive superstitions will evaporate like the dew beneath the summer sun. Yet religious faith is not chiefly concerned with the what, how, and when of natural phenomena. Rather, it is concerned with the *why* of existence. And while a few scientists may argue that the question of "why" is unanswerable and therefore not worth pursuing, they haven't yet convinced the rest of humanity to suspend its search for significance.

At the heart of spiritual faith is a bargain: in return for a commitment to realign one's life around a set of often inconvenient moral imperatives, the adherent is offered a theology which emphasizes the consequentiality of human choice within the limitless expanse of time and space. The message: you are more than protoplasm, more than artfully yet unintentionally arranged stardust. There is a purpose to your existence. Rodney Stark and Roger Finke, two sociologists who've studied the human foundations of faith, put it simply: ". . . religious explanations specify the fundamental meaning of life: how we got here and where we are going (if anywhere)."[15] In other words, they provide answers to the eternal question of "why?"

Of course it matters greatly what you put your faith *in*. Fascism and communism, the two great political faiths of 20th-century Europe, turned out to be disasters for humanity. Neither is history likely to exonerate the radical Muslims who have put their faith in a cult of death and revenge. Human beings will forever seek orientation and significance, in causes both noble and ignoble. Luckily, history provides countless examples of individuals whose quiet, life-affirming faith elicited virtue, spurred charity, and restored broken lives. Scholars have repeatedly found that religious faith enhances self-esteem, improves physical health, and enlarges the capacity of individuals to cope with the traumas of life.[16]

Faith has something to teach us about resilience—not because faith itself has survived, but because faith, to the extent it provides individuals with a sense of meaning, helps make *people* more resilient. Through the centuries, millions of lives have been transformed by the sense of significance that every deep-rooted faith system offers its adherents. Prophets, patriarchs, and saints have found in their sacred purpose the courage to endure deprivation and tragedy, and the impetus for extraordinary accomplishment. It is remarkable, though not, perhaps, surprising, that the best-selling hardback book in publishing history is Rick Warren's *The Purpose-Driven Life*. Turbulent times demand personal resilience, and resilience requires a sense of destiny—a goal that draws us forward, a pole star that keeps us oriented when all around us is changing. Without a narrative that creates drama and meaning, we are listless and rudderless. That's why *meaning* is a critical design rule for creating adaptable organizations. More specifically . . .

The mission matters. During Bill George's tenure as chairman and CEO of Medtronic, the world's largest maker of heart pacemakers and implantable defibrillators, the company achieved a compound annual shareholder return of 32 percent. In accounting for this extraordinary performance, George points to the transformational power of the company's mission: "to restore people to full life and health."[17] Says George, "The first thing that strikes any visitor to Medtronic is the mission. It is everywhere—in every building, hanging on the walls, and on cards in the wallets, purses and desks of employees. Next to it are patient photos—people from all walks of life, all ages, and all corners of the globe—all with Medtronic products implanted in them. They look happy and healthy."[18]

What higher purpose does *your* company serve? I hope you didn't answer, "shareholder wealth." In most companies, gains in the share price mostly benefit those at the top. Says Bill George, "The real failure in focusing on short-term [shareholder] value is the inability to motivate large numbers of employees to exceptional performance."

Actually, it is possible to motivate (at least some) people with money alone. But it's dangerous, as Enron's shareholders learned, when greed trumps higher-minded goals. Without a beneficent purpose, the temptation to overstep ethical boundaries in the pursuit of personal gain can be irresistible. Without a sense of destiny, the CEO and others may be tempted to act like mercenaries who are more interested in pumping up the share price than in building critical capabilities for the future. To serve shareholders well, a company must forever be on the way to *becoming* something more than it is right now. It must possess a mission compelling enough to overcome the gravitational pull of the past and spur individual renewal.

People change for what they care about. In the final analysis, there are no adaptable organizations, only adaptable people. While a company's management processes can either impede or encourage adaptation, it's the willingness of individuals to change that ultimately matters. Most books on change start from the premise that people reflexively resist change, and have to be manipulated, browbeaten, and cajoled into abandoning the serenity of the status quo. I have a different view. I believe most human beings welcome change. For all our reactionary tendencies, we are always looking for new experiences and new challenges.

Admittedly, there are folks who spend their days mindlessly polishing the deep grooves of habit. Yet even these souls are capable of change; they just haven't found anything worth changing *for*. In a world of here today, gone tomorrow ephemera, it's not easy finding something that merits the effort of self-renewal. Yet it's possible. And it doesn't require one to invent a new religion. Those who work at Medtronic find meaning in restoring human health. Googlers revel in their capacity to democratize knowledge. The associates at Whole Foods celebrate the value of healthy, nourishing cuisine.

Faith empowers transformation when there's an attractive bargain—genuine meaning and significance in return for devotion. What does that bargain look like for the people who drag themselves into your company every Monday morning? Is it inspiring or insipid?

You probably won't be given the chance to rewrite your company's mission statement any time soon. But that doesn't mean you can't get your colleagues to start thinking about your company's higher purpose. You should view your company's management processes—the budget reviews and planning meetings, the training events and brainstorming sessions—as opportunities to raise some purpose-oriented questions. Don't be afraid to ask your colleagues: What difference do we want to make in the world? What goals would be worth taking personal risks for? What accomplishments would justify the ten hour days and interrupted weekends that seem to be par for the course in our company? What do I want to tell my kids I do every day, besides working hard and making shareholders rich? It is regrettable that such questions seldom get asked in most companies. As a management innovator, you must change this.

Cities: Increasing the Odds of Serendipity

Cities are resilient. Athens, Instanbul, London, Tokyo, New York, Shanghai, San Francisco—these great cities seem almost immortal. They are standing waves in the rushing torrent of human history. A great city is a cultural kaleidoscope, where the potential for surprise lurks around every corner. A stroll through an unfamiliar neighborhood, a gallery opening, a new play, the latest indie band, hot clubs, concerts, lectures—a city is an amusement park for the mind. At times, when wandering through Greenwich Village or London's West End, I have wondered why street life is so much more interesting and energizing than corporate life. Surely, though, if we can get at what makes a great city vibrant and irresistible, we ought to be able to make life inside our companies a bit less like Main Street and a bit more like SoHo or Notting Hill.

Historically, every notable city had a locational advantage—it flanked a harbor, or bisected a trade route. Yet a strategic location is no longer enough to make a city great. Today, the most resilient cities are those that attract the "creative class"—the writers, technologists, artists, filmmakers, publishers, video-game developers, and fashion designers whose imagination and ingenuity fuel the creative economy.

The geography of creativity has been studied closely by the sociologist Richard Florida, who believes there is a strong correlation between a city's financial and cultural well-being, and its ability to attract creative capital.[19] Since curious and iconoclastic minds are the catalysts for economic growth, cities that attract more than their fair share of the creative class are bound to do better than those that don't. The implication for city planners: worry less about building a great "business climate," and more about building a great "people climate."

As a "new urbanist," Florida is part of a growing network of architects, scholars, and planners who have been working to unravel the secrets of urban vitality. The movement's patron saint is Jane Jacobs, whose 1961 classic, *The Death and Life of Great American Cities*, launched a full frontal attack on the imperial plans of the era's preeminent urban architects. Jacobs regarded cities as essential to the creation of "new pools of economic use," which formed, she believed, when diverse sets of people were given the chance to interact and discover opportunities to trade information, goods, and ideas. In Jacobs' view, the conventional components of urban "renewal"—broad boulevards, grand plazas, vertical tenements, segregated business districts, and soaring freeways—seemed designed to undermine, rather than facilitate, the sort of intimate, street-level interaction that creates economic and cultural value.[20] Like Jacobs, who died in 2006, the new urbanists are suspicious of elaborate, top-down plans. Instead, they put their faith in a clutch of simple rules—principles that history has shown to be the real foundations of urban vitality.

Diversity begets creativity. In a city, it's the diversity of cultures, perspectives, skills, industries, building styles, and neighborhoods that stoke the fires of innovation. When like meets like, there is no creative spark; but when like collides with unlike, there is often a small *frisson* of inspiration. If cities produce more innovation than the suburbs, it's because they are more diverse—they possess more raw material for the machinery of human imagination.

In his research, Florida ranked U.S. cities on two scales: the size of the high-tech sector within the local economy, and the degree of cultural diversity. When he compared the rankings, he found that all the top ten high-tech centers also appeared on the list of America's 18 most culturally diverse cities. His conclusion: diversity attracts the sort of creative capital that spawns high-tech innovation.[21]

Not surprisingly, mavericks and rebels are drawn most strongly to the cities that tolerate their eccentricities. This helps to explain why a few cities, like New York and London, have long been nuclear reactors for human creativity—their diversity, along with a constant flow of new arrivals, fuels an ongoing chain reaction of discovery and invention.

Samsung gets the importance of diversity. In a bid to become a design powerhouse, this once quintessentially Korean company set up design centers in London, Los Angeles, San Francisco, Tokyo, and Shanghai. In addition, it regularly sends its designers on learning sabbaticals to cities such as Frankfurt, Florence, Athens, and Beijing. As Samsung has immersed itself in diversity, its reputation for breakthrough design has soared. In 2004, the company won more Industrial Design Excellence Awards than any American or European firm—the first Asian company to achieve this feat.[22]

Diversity can no longer be just a buzzword. It must become an active search for the idiosyncratic and the peculiar, the weird and kooky, the colorful and the bizarre. In concluding her signature volume, Jacobs posed a rhetorical question: "Does anyone suppose that, in real life, answers to any of the great questions that worry us today are going to come out of homogenous settlements?"[23] She might just as well have asked, "Does anyone suppose that pathbreaking innovations will come out of intellectually homogenous companies?" Management innovators must look at every management process and ask, how can we use this to infect our colleagues with new attitudes and unconventional perspectives?

You can organize for serendipity. The way a city is laid out can either encourage or inhibit the serendipitous encounters that spur innovation. Jacobs suggested three strategies for increasing the odds of value-creating happenstance that seem particularly relevant to 21st century organizations.[24] Let's consider each one briefly and see if we can imagine a corporate counterpart. First:

> The district, and indeed as many of its internal parts as possible, must serve more than one primary function; preferably more than two. These must insure the presence of people who go outdoors

on different schedules and are in the place for different purposes, but who are able to use many facilities in common.

Jacobs' goal here is to maximize the opportunities for different sorts of folk to interact—by creating places where people with contrasting needs and objectives will bump into each other. Visit Google, and you'll see a lot of public spaces that seem to serve multiple purposes. On one visit, I noticed a grand piano, a billiards table, several large whiteboards, and a sandwich station all within a few meters of one another—an odd sight if you're used to seeing offices that contain rows of sterile, carefully ordered cubicles. Yet the eclecticism of the furnishings suggested a conscious attempt to create opportunities for unscripted interaction.

Jacobs' second design rule for serendipity:

Most blocks must be short; that is, streets and opportunities to turn corners must be frequent.

Shorter blocks and more intersections create more potential routes from point A to point B, and increase the odds that residents from adjacent streets will run into one another on the sidewalk.

The analogy here for managers is less about street design than project design. There's not much chance for serendipity if reporting relationships and job definitions force people to work with the same small cluster of colleagues for months at a time. An extensive use of short-duration teams, with individuals frequently rotating among teams, is one way of keeping the "blocks short."

And rule number three:

The district must mingle buildings that vary in age and condition, including a good proportion of old ones so that they vary in the economic yield they must produce. This mingling must be fairly close-grained.

Different kinds of buildings—office towers, shops, renovated warehouses, town homes, hotels, and restaurants—support different types of activity, and attract different sorts of users. Thus, if buildings of a single type predominate in an area, opportunities for dissimilar sorts of individuals to interact will be limited.

A few years back, a business school I know decided to physically segregate its faculty by discipline. Each department—marketing, economics, finance, strategy, and HR—was given its own floor within a sprawling facility. Ironically, at the same time, the school was trying to promote more cross-discipline collaboration. Companies often make the same mistake. By physically isolating functional and staff groups, they aggravate rather than ameliorate the serendipity-limiting effects of specialization.

But Jacobs' point goes deeper than this. Buildings can be ranked by their rents. Start-ups and noncommercial activities often can't afford to carry a big rent burden, so they typically get pushed out to the city's periphery. The result? A city whose core is sterile and uninteresting. It's worth quoting Jacobs further on this point:

> As for really new ideas of any kind—no matter how ultimately profitable or otherwise successful some of them might prove to be—there is no leeway for such chancy trial, error and experimentation in the high-overhead economy of new construction. Old ideas can sometimes use new buildings. New ideas must use old buildings.
>
> Flourishing diversity anywhere in a city means the mingling of high-yield, middling-yield, low-yield and no-yield enterprises.[25]

The same is true in companies. New ideas can't afford the same overhead costs, can't meet the same risk hurdles, and can't deliver the same short-term payback as incremental extensions of old ideas. Management systems and overhead allocation rules that don't recognize this will choke off innovation. Just as importantly, folks who are working on bleeding edge ideas need to be rubbing shoulders every day with people who are responsible for churning out more of the same, and vice versa. As is true for cities, everyone gains when the new and the quirky are neighbors with the tried and the true.

No pigeonholes. In part, great cities are able to reinvent themselves because they make it easy for *individuals* to reinvent themselves. Filled as they are with escapees from the stultifying conventions of small-town life, cities are oblivious to peculiarity. The world's creative centers are filled with self-made men and women—folks like Russell Simmons, Masayoshi Son, Donald Trump, Oprah Winfrey, Lakshmi Mittal, Steve Jobs, and Larry Ellison. In progressive cities, aptitude counts for more than provenance, and today's dropouts, misfits, and goofballs may well be tomorrow's media mavens, property kingpins, and cultural icons. Cities are filled with people on the make, scrambling up and skidding down the slippery slope of fame and fortune. New arrivals quickly learn that the city's anonymity allows them to try on different value systems and pursue their eccentric passions. In cities, elastic social conventions and permeable hierarchies create space for personal growth and reinvention.

Here's how Robert Park, a pioneering sociologist, put it more than 80 years ago: "In a small community, it is the normal man, the man without eccentricity or genius, who seems most likely to succeed. The small community often tolerates eccentricity. The city, on the contrary rewards it."[26] Put simply, a great city offers urban adventurers the chance to explore the limits of their own capabilities in a way a village simply can't.

Think about the conventions of behavior, interaction, expression, and dress that predominate in your company's culture. Do they reward eccentricity or stifle it? Are people respected for the value they add, or for the titles and credentials they hold? Does the hiring process put a premium on people who've had unique life experiences, or zero in on those who fit a mold? Does passion score highly in making job appointments, or does experience always get the nod? As a management innovator, you have to make sure that your company's management systems aren't frustrating the kind of social mobility and personal growth that is central to creating an adaptable organization.

Let's step back and briefly review our 21st-century management principles. I've emphasized what I believe are the five key design rules for building companies that are truly fit for the future. This is the *new* DNA that must be injected into your company's management processes and practices.

Life ⟶ *Variety*

Experimentation beats planning.

All mutations are mistakes.

Darwinian selection doesn't need SVPs.

The broader the gene pool, the better.

Markets ⟶ *Flexibility*

Markets are more dynamic than hierarchies.

Build a market and the innovators will come.

Operational efficiency ≠ strategic efficiency.

Democracy ⟶ *Activism*

Leaders are accountable to the governed.

Everyone has a right to dissent.

Leadership is distributed.

Faith ⟶ *Meaning*

The mission matters.

People change for what they care about.

Cities ⟶ *Serendipity*

Diversity begets creativity.

You can organize for serendipity.

Pigeonholes are for pigeons, not people.

These tenets are both timeless and timely. They stand in marked contrast to the legacy principles that comprise the current management genome. Creating and maintaining a healthy tension between the control-oriented principles of the 20th century and the adaptability-enhancing principles of the 21st, isn't going to be easy. Indeed, the more one learns about what it is that makes things adaptable, the more one is tempted to question the very foundations of modern management theory. After all, when compared to large companies, the most adaptable things on the planet are either *under*-managed or, *Mon Dieu*, *un*-managed.

Yet there's every reason to believe that the contrasting creeds of modern management and *post*-modern management really *can* coexist in your company. After all, Google's management system may look semi-anarchic, but the company's massive computing centers still deliver nanosecond search results 24 hours a day, 7 days a week, with nary a glitch. Likewise, Gore's embrace of democratic principles doesn't get in the way of its ability to serve demanding customers like Nike and P&G. And Whole Foods' community ethos doesn't prevent it from delivering mouthwatering profits quarter after quarter. Augmenting the management genome won't be easy, but it's certainly possible.

Putting the Principles to Work

How do you put our 21st-century principles to work? Perhaps you can already imagine a way forward—but if not, here's a suggestion or two. Get 30 or 40 of your colleagues together and divide them into four or five teams. Have each team pick a critical management process to focus on. (Planning, budgeting, recruiting, and training are particularly good candidates for this exercise.) Now ask each group to outline the primary characteristics and features of their chosen process. Specifically, they should ask:

- Who "owns" this process? Who has the power to change it?

- What purpose does this process serve? What contribution is it supposed to make to business performance?

- Who gets to participate in this process? What voices get heard?

- What are the inputs to this process? What data gets considered?

- Whose opinions get weighted the most heavily? Who has final decision-making authority?

- What decision tools are used? What kind of analysis gets done?

- What are the criteria for decision making? How are decisions justified?

- What events or milestones drive this process? Is it calendar-driven or real-time?

- Who are the "customers" of this process? Whose work does it most directly impact?

The goal is to develop a relatively detailed "as is" description of each team-nominated process.

Once they've mapped their particular process, ask the team members to imagine how that process might be redesigned to reflect the new management principles that have been discussed in this chapter. If they struggle to come up with bold process innovations, you can spur their thinking by tossing out a few questions:

- *Life/Variety:* How would you introduce a greater diversity of data, viewpoints, and opinions into this process? How would you design the process so that it facilitates, rather than frustrates, the continual development of new strategic options and encourages relentless experimentation?

- *Markets/Flexibility:* How would you redesign this process so that it exploits the wisdom of the market, rather than just the wisdom of the experts? How might this process be used to help speed up the reallocation of resources from legacy programs to new initiatives? How could we make it easier for innovators to get the resources they need to advance their ideas?

- *Democracy/Activism:* How would you change this process so that it encourages, rather than discourages, dissenting voices? How would you make this process more responsive to the needs and concerns of those working on the front lines? How do we give folks on the ground a bigger voice in shaping policy and strategy?

- *Faith/Meaning:* How would you use this process to help focus attention on the higher order goals our company claims to serve (or should be serving)? How could this process help employees to identify and connect with the goals they care about *personally*?

- *Cities/Serendipity:* How could this process be redesigned in a way that would help our company to become an even more exciting and vibrant place to work and a magnet for creative talent? How could this process be used to facilitate the collision of new ideas?

Give the teams several hours to mull over these questions. Ask them to come up with a menu of detailed changes they would like to make to their chosen management process. Then post these suggestions on an internal Web site and challenge others in your company to add to the list.

I've led exercises of this sort with a wide variety of management teams around the world. I'm invariably surprised by how willing people are to challenge the thinking behind long-venerated management rituals. Equally heartening is the fact that many of the suggested fixes are often quite revolutionary.

Nevertheless, you'll need to be patient as the dialogue unfolds. Remember, it took decades for companies like GE, DuPont, and Ford to fully operationalize the essential management principles of the industrial age. Similarly, the task of reinventing management for the 21st century is going to take time. But what you can and must do is to get your colleagues thinking and talking about the opportunity to reinvent your company's management DNA.

Nine

Learning from the Fringe

B Y NOW, I HOPE YOU'VE JETTISONED SOME OF YOUR hand-me-down beliefs and have started to reshuffle your management DNA. If you have, your agenda for management innovation should be coming into focus. Nevertheless, you may feel that your ideas aren't yet bold enough, or focused enough, to give your company a big head start in tackling tomorrow's make-or-break business challenges. So where else might you look for inspiration? Where can you find examples and analogies that will help your company build a bona fide management advantage? Here's a suggestion: look someplace weird, someplace unexpected, far beyond the boundaries of "best practice." Why? Because uncommon insights usually come from uncommon places.

185

New Vantage Points,
New Perspectives

Take the case of Mary Parker Follett—arguably the 20th century's most prescient management thinker. Born in Quincy, Massachusetts, in 1868, Follett's life was bracketed by the American Civil War and the Great Depression. A contemporary of Frederick Winslow Taylor, her views on management were decidedly post-industrial. Consider a few of the points she made in *Creative Experience*, a book first published in 1924:

- Leadership is not defined by the exercise of power, but by the capacity to increase the sense of power among those who are led. The most essential work of the leader is to create more leaders.

- Adversarial, win-lose decision making is debilitating for all concerned. Contentious problems are best solved not by imposing a single point of view at the expense of all others, but by striving for a higher-order solution that integrates the diverse perspectives of all relevant constituents.

- A large organization is a collection of local communities. Individual and institutional growth are maximized when these communities are self-governing to the maximum degree possible.[1]

Servant leadership. The power of diversity. Self-organizing teams. Follett's shrewd insights into the nature of leadership didn't come from a survey of turn-of-the-century management practices; instead, they grew out of her experience organizing community centers in Boston's Roxbury neighborhood. Vested with little formal authority and faced with the challenge of melding the interests of several fractious constituencies, Follett developed a theory of management that was starkly at odds with the prevailing wisdom at the time. Although she never held a corporate job, Follett is today regarded as one of management's greatest oracles. Her experience holds an important lesson for contemporary management innovators: you are unlikely to see the future if you're standing in the mainstream.

Positive Deviants

To glimpse the future of management, you must search for "positive deviants," organizations and social systems that defy the norms of conventional practice. In management as in science, it's the anomalies that point us toward new truths. Yet it's often difficult to see the anomalies for what they are, since by definition they don't fit into our preexisting mental categories. Like conventionally trained physicians who often dismiss the wisdom of tribal healers, modern managers often doubt they have anything to learn from organizations that are unlike their own.

Anomalies defy logic. That's why they're usually ignored, or dismissed as irrelevant. If forced to make sense of W.L. Gore's weirdly effective organization, a myopic CEO would likely respond, "Yes, well, Gore is a privately held company"—as if that single fact allows Gore to defy all the usual laws of management. Google would probably get the brush-off as well. "Unlike my company," a convention-loving CEO might argue, "Google doesn't have billions of dollars tied up in inflexible factories"—as if it's immobile capital, rather than immobile mind-sets, that blocks strategic renewal.

Anomalies are discomforting. Their very existence is an affront to conventional wisdom. Yet as an innovator, you must resist the temptation to explain them away. Your goal, after all, is not to validate today's management practices, but to reinvent them. That's why we must now set off in search of exotic organizational life forms.

First stop, Jobra, Bangladesh, home to the Grameen Bank. Since its founding in 1976, the bank has been a pioneer in microfinance. Its mission, to extend credit to the severely impoverished, is based on a belief that the poor are poor not because they lack useful skills, but because they lack capital. Acting on this belief, the bank makes small loans to five-person syndicates with no requirement for collateral and virtually no documentation. Ninety-five percent of the borrowers are women, who use the bank's money to start small businesses such as basket weaving, embroidery, and poultry breeding. Microcredit gives these microscale entrepreneurs the chance to improve the well-being of their families and raise their own social standing. In essence, the bank is a co-op, since 94 percent of the bank's equity is owned by its borrowers. In 2006, the Grameen Bank had more than 2,185 branches and had 6.4 million borrowers. Since its inception, it has dispersed 5.6 billion dollars, and despite its unorthodox lending practices, its loan recovery rate is better than 98 percent.

So what do you make of this peculiar bank? Does it challenge you to think differently about the way your company does things? It should. After all, why should a desperately poor woman in a developing country have an easier time getting cash to fund a new idea than the average first-level associate in your company? If the Grameen Bank can make millions of unsecured loans to individuals with no banking history, and with little in the way of paperwork, shouldn't your company be able to find a way to fund the glimmer-in-the-eye projects of ordinary employees? As we'll see, the world is filled with aberrant organizations whose practices make management-as-usual seem quaint at best, and antediluvian at worst.

Finding the Fringe

In your hunt for management mutants, you'll need a search strategy. Start by identifying the head-scratching management problem you want to address, and then look for offbeat organizations that have come up with a novel solution, or offer a useful analogy. You will recall that in chapter 3, I introduced a trio of next-generation management problems. I then broke each one down into three contributing problems—

three specific pathologies that prevent companies from being adaptable, innovative, and highly engaging. For the purposes of this chapter, we'll focus on six of these subsidiary problems. After summarizing each one, we'll go hunting for useful lessons from the fringe.

Problem #1: In most companies, the farther down employees sit in the organization, or the more unconventional their views, the harder it is for them to get a hearing. This often contributes to denial at the top.

Challenge #1: How do you create an organization where everyone's voice gets heard and ideas compete solely on their merits? How do you build a *democracy of ideas?*

———

Problem #2: Most companies exploit no more than a fraction of their employees' imagination, due in part to a sort of "creative apartheid."

Challenge #2: How do you turn ordinary employees into extraordinary innovators? How do you *amplify human imagination?*

———

Problem #3: Allocational rigidities frequently impair a company's capacity to fund the future. This puts a brake on the work of strategic renewal.

Challenge #3: How do you accelerate the redeployment of capital and talent? How do you *dynamically reallocate resources?*

———

Problem #4: Positional biases and inattention to competing viewpoints often lead to poor decision making at the top.

Challenge #4: How do you ensure that decisions fully reflect the collective knowledge of the organization? How do you *aggregate collective wisdom?*

———

Problem #5: Executive knowledge and capability often depreciate faster than management power and influence, often with unfortunate consequences.

Challenge #5: How do you keep top management's out-of-date beliefs from impeding strategic renewal? How do you *minimize the drag of old mental models?*

———

Problem #6: Too much management and too little freedom sap the initiative of employees and leave little time or energy for innovation.

Challenge #6: How do you turn an army of conscripts into a community of volunteers? How do you *give everyone the chance to opt in?*

As you ponder each of these 21st-century management challenges, see if you can think of an example or an analogy that might embolden your thinking or hint at a potential solution. Here are a few ideas to get you started.

Challenge #1: Creating a Democracy of Ideas

Look around your company. What do you think correlates most highly with an individual's position in the corporate hierarchy? Salary? Years of experience? Authority? Perks? These are all things that vary proportionately with organizational rank. But what about wisdom, foresight, and imagination? These attributes are only weakly correlated with the gradient of executive power. Why, then, are the views of senior executives so often granted a higher coefficient of credibility than the convictions of mid- and lower-level employees? Overweighting the views of those who are furthest away from customers, and have most of their emotional equity invested in the past, is hardly a recipe for building a resilient enterprise.

Now try to imagine what a *democracy* of ideas would look like. Employees would feel free to share their thoughts and opinions, however politically charged they might be. No single gatekeeper would be allowed to quash an idea or limit its dissemination. New ideas would be given the chance to garner support before being voted up or down by senior executives. The internal debate about strategy, direction, and policy would be open, vigorous, and uncensored. Maybe this sounds hopelessly romantic, but such a *thoughtocracy* already exists—not in any big company, but on the Web.

The Internet has decisively destroyed the power of the elites to determine what gets published and who gets heard. The result? An explosion of online opinion, comment, advice, and insight. Over the past three years, the number of blogs tracked by Technorati, a blog-indexing site, has mushroomed from a few hundred thousand to more than 50 million. As I'm writing this, each day sees the creation of 175,000 new blogs and the addition of 1.6 million new posts to existing blogs. As it expands, the blogosphere is also getting more organized. One can search for blogs that focus on a particular topic or contain specific content. Technorati displays a real-time list of the top 100 subject matter categories and makes it easy to see which topics are generating the highest volume of new postings. More interestingly, the company also assigns each blog an "authority" score based on the number of times it has been referenced by other blogs. In the blogging world, "authority" doesn't come from above, nor can it be purchased with a big marketing budget. The only way to win credibility online is to write stuff a lot of people want to read.

Unfortunately, the explosion of "citizen media" hasn't been matched by equally dramatic changes in the market for ideas inside most large companies. While many organizations solicit ideas via some sort of electronic suggestion box, or run online discussion boards that facilitate knowledge sharing, few companies invite employees to publish hard-hitting internal blogs or host open-to-all online discussions on key decisions. Yet the real distinction between the Web's thoughtocracy and the slightly autocratic world of big-company politics doesn't hinge on the use of technology. Rather, it is centered on a disparity in values: while the Web was founded on the principle of openness, the most honored virtue among senior executives seems to be control. Most companies have elaborate programs for top-down communication, including newsletters, CEO blogs, webcasts, and broadcast e-mails; yet few, if any, companies have opened the floodgates to grassroots opinion on critical issues.

For example, can you imagine any of the following actually happening in your company?

The CEO uses an internal discussion board to solicit advice on who should become your company's new chief marketing officer.

The head of product development opens up an online forum to discuss why launch dates are so often missed, or why a new product failed to meet its targets.

The board of directors hosts an online discussion on executive pay, or the strengths and failings of the top team.

Business unit plans are published on an internal Web site, and employees from across the company are asked to critique them.

New ideas are dangerous, particularly to those with a stake in the established order. That's why Soviet authorities limited the use of photocopiers, and why many governments censor the Web. It's also why the notion of an open market for opinion makes executives nervous. As a manager, what does it mean to be in control if you can't script the conversation? What does it mean to be in charge if your views have to compete with everyone else's views? What does it mean to be the boss if anyone can publicly disparage your ideas, your decisions, or even your IQ?

Most executives are happy to solicit the views of trusted colleagues in private. Some are willing to host town hall meetings. Many will field e-mail questions from employees. Yet in all these settings, the conversation is still circumscribed. In a one-on-one meeting with a subordinate, it is easy to squelch dissent. A physical town hall meeting is limited to the people present and bounded in time. A CEO who has the power to select which e-mails to answer publicly and which to ignore will be tempted to avoid tendentious or embarrassing issues. In other words, executives are comfortable when communicating *to* the front lines or fielding queries *from* the front lines. What worries them, though, is the prospect of frontline employees grabbing the microphone (so to speak) and communicating, en masse, with *other* employees. One-to-many communication is OK, and many-to-one is tolerable—but many-to-many? That's how insurrections start.

Of course, this is precisely what makes discussion boards and blogs so powerful—they allow individual points of view to coalesce and compound. In an online forum, a single brave dissenter creates a license for others to protest and object, thus lowering the threshold of courage for all those who might otherwise have been afraid to speak up. As others join the fray, a snowball of dissent starts rolling downhill. This, of course, is what senior management fears. Suddenly, instead of facing skeptics one at a time, or in controlled circumstances, executives have to confront a mob of disgruntled employees. For many business leaders, that's a seriously discomforting notion—but then again, no one ever said a democracy of ideas would be tranquil.

If you want to dramatically increase the quality of dialogue and decisions in your company, you have to think boldly. What if your company *encouraged* people to write critical in-house blogs (and allowed them to do so anonymously if they wished)? What if it encouraged employees to read and respond to those blogs? What if it tracked the number of responses each posting generated (its "authority index"), and then required senior executives to respond to those that generated the most comment? What if it appointed an employee jury to award a monthly prize for the best posting, as a way of rewarding the most thoughtful, amusing, or courageous contributors? Sure, there are downsides: Attacks will get personal. Dirty laundry will be aired. Internal criticism will occasionally leak outside. Yet one must weigh these costs against the price that is paid when dissent is pushed underground, when opportunities to improve the quality of big decisions are missed, and when employees who feel unable to speak out on key issues simply stop caring.

Oftentimes, employees who don't feel empowered to speak up internally will do so externally. When, in early 2006, Microsoft announced yet another delay to Vista, its long-overdue update to the Windows operating system, the clearest-headed (and most impassioned) critique of the company's woes didn't appear in any of the world's leading business magazines. Rather it showed up on Mini-Microsoft, a blog that is edited by someone who claims to be a Microsoft employee. In March 2006, "Who da'Punk" (that's the blogger) posted a short essay entitled, "Vista 2007. Fire the Leadership Now." In a matter of days, the post had attracted more than 500 comments, many from Microsoft employees. While a few were angry attacks on individual executives, many more were thoughtful, detailed commentaries on the company's product-development process and management systems. If not a manual for getting Microsoft firing on all cylinders, the comments were a comprehensive diagnostic readout. Ramble around Mini-Microsoft, and you'll see a lot of comments like the following: "If it means anything, I think you're serving a valuable purpose for fellow employees. Without your forum, there's no sanity check for individual observations." Or, "Your blog has provided an avenue for exchanges that were hitherto impossible." Or, "This blog is awesome simply because it IS anonymous, and people can post without fear of retaliation." To be clear, I don't think Microsoft is any less hospitable to dissenters than other big companies. But like its peers, it has a long way to go to create a truly open marketplace for ideas.

Challenge #2: Amplifying Human Imagination

As human beings, we cannot help ourselves—we *have* to create. It's a primeval urge, only slightly less irresistible than the urge to procreate.

Whether laying out a garden, improvising a recipe, redecorating a room, plinking at the piano, or scribbling a verse of poetry, we are happiest when doing that which no other species can do—mindfully, joyfully creating. It is through creativity that each of us asserts our humanity and individuality. Given this, those of us who are alive in the early decades of this new millennium have much to celebrate, for it has never been easier for human beings to indulge their creative yearnings.

Throughout history, only a tiny fraction of humanity has possessed the economic means to pursue their creative passions. Paint and canvases, parchment and pens, stone and chisels, musical instruments, tutors and studios—prior to the 19th century, these were expensive luxuries. While a few gifted artists were fortunate enough to find patrons, most were not. Looking back across the centuries, one can only speculate on the quantity of creative capital that has gone to the grave unexploited. Blessedly, our age is different.

Digital technology is rapidly democratizing the tools of creativity and emancipating human imagination. Thanks to Photoshop, Type-Pad, GarageBand, Final Cut Express, Pro Tools, VideoStudio, Home Designer Pro, and thousands of other creativity-boosting applications, there is less and less that stands between creative vision and creative expression. New technology is not only unleashing human imagination, it is amplifying it as well. The infinite malleability of software allows human beings to do things today that were impossible even a decade ago, from mixing digital music loops, to producing "high dynamic range" images, to creating new characters and scenarios in video games, to mashing up new Web services—and much more besides. We are the first generation in history that can honestly say, "We are limited only by our imagination."

Consider. At the moment, nearly 2 million video clips are being uploaded to YouTube each month, and more than 100 million clips are being viewed every day by visitors to the site. In the past 60 days, more than 1.6 million individuals have wandered through the 65,000 acres of *Second Life*, a virtual world built almost entirely by its residents. Around the globe, tens of thousands of avid video gamers are using sophisticated editing tools to produce new characters and settings for popular games such as *Unreal Tournament* and *World of Warcraft.* Tens of thousands of photographers are getting valuable feedback on the photos they've uploaded to Flickr. Hundreds of indie bands are building word-of-mouth buzz on MySpace. Thousands of individuals are building new applications using Google's mapping software and satellite images.

Make no mistake, your company is filled with video bloggers, mixers, hackers, mashers, tuners, and pod casters. They can draw from a near limitless set of tools and resources in their quest to create. So here's my question: What has your company done to help all these ingenious people become fully empowered *business* innovators? Has it given every employee access to a comprehensive suite of business innovation tools? Do associates have access to a global database of customer insights, and competitor intelligence? Can they download detailed financial statistics in order to explore the profitability implications of changes in pricing, promotional spending, staffing, or other operating variables? Do they have online access to comprehensive maps of key business processes so they can analyze opportunities for reconfiguring workflows? Is it easy for employees to mock up new product designs using computer-aided design software? Is there an internal Web site that helps individuals to gather feedback on their creative ideas? Trust me, your employees are exercising their creativity *somewhere*, it just may not be at work.

As creativity tools proliferate, the distinction between "pro" and "amateur" is fast disappearing. When you upload a clip to YouTube, no one asks if you're a film school grad or a self-taught videographer. When you write a blog, no asks whether you have a journalism degree or just an incisive mind. In the creative commons, one's reputation is a function of aptitude—not credentials, connections, or years of experience. Yet in many companies, professional and hierarchical distinctions still disenfranchise thousands from getting involved in product development, business model innovation, promotional design, and a host of other "creative" tasks. Given the right tools, and the opportunity to contribute, just about everyone in your company is a potential member of the "creative class."

Challenge #3: Dynamically Reallocating Resources

What can be done to correct the tendency of companies to overinvest in the past at the expense of the future? Is there some way of setting resources free in a large organization? How would one create a market that connects "out-there" ideas with small doses of experimental capital? These are tough questions. But again, an example or two from the fringe can point us toward some potential answers.

Every CEO knows you have to "invest in the future." Most also realize that the pressure to deliver quarter-by-quarter earnings growth makes line executives wary of backing projects that have long-odds or a leisurely payback. As a work-around, companies have set up venture funds, incubators, and CEO slush funds to funnel investment into new and uncertain projects. A centrally administered innovation fund is a step in the right direction, but it's still a far cry from the kind of vibrant market for experimental capital that exists in Silicon Valley.

For would-be entrepreneurs, there are several advantages to having a multiplicity of potential funding sources. First, competition among investors helps to bring down the cost of funds. If a VC demands too large an equity share, a founder can seek financing elsewhere. Second, more investment options mean more funding conversations and, therefore, more opportunities for the entrepreneur to adjust and refine a still-nascent business model. Third, a diversity of funding sources increases the likelihood that an entrepreneur will find an investor with the expertise to provide wise counsel after the venture is launched.

While Silicon Valley provides one useful analogy, Zopa provides another. Funded by some of the same investors who launched eBay, this U.K.-based business brings lenders and borrowers together online. Think of it as a bank without the bankers. Let's suppose you have £5,000 to invest. You could sink your money into a deposit account at an old-style bank, but given the large spreads banks need to cover their equally large overheads, you probably won't be thrilled with the interest rate you'll be offered. Alternately, you could register with Zopa.com and ask them to help you lend out your 5,000 quid. At Zopa, lenders specify the interest rate they'd like to receive and the duration of the loan—12 months, 24 months, or longer. They also choose whether to lend to "A"- or "B"-class borrowers. When borrowers register, they undergo a computerized credit check. Zopa filters out the deadbeats and assigns everyone else to one of two risk categories depending on their credit score. Generally, lenders earn higher interest rates when they make loans to B-class borrowers. Every potential borrower also picks a desired interest rate and termination date. To facilitate price setting, borrowers and lenders can review the terms of recently consummated loans. As offers and bids are received, Zopa's clever software works to match supply and demand. Hence the acronymn: Zone of Possible Agreement. To minimize a lender's exposure to risk, each loan is spread across at least 50 borrowers. Zopa makes money by charging borrowers and lenders a half-percent fee of each loan's value, and by taking a commission when borrowers purchase repayment insurance.

In its first year of operation, Zopa's lenders earned an average of 6.75 percent on their invested funds, around two percentage points higher than what they would have received from Britain's "high street" banks. Likewise, the interest rate charged borrowers was several percentage points less than what traditional lending institutions would have demanded.

As a first-generation, social-lending marketplace, Zopa's success is by no means assured; nevertheless, the genie of peer-to-peer banking is out of the bottle. If it's not Zopa that scales up the idea work, some other upstart will.

By now, I hope you can see the connection between Zopa's peer-to-peer banking model and the problem of dynamically allocating talent and capital in large companies. Depending on the size of your organization, there are somewhere between a few dozen and few thousand individuals who control a discretionary budget of more than $100,000 per year. Within some constraints, these folks can choose whether to use these funds to hire additional staff, raise promotional spending, acquire capital equipment, or add to the year-end bonus pool. Imagine now that all these budget holders were given permission to invest up to 2 percent of those funds in any idea, anywhere across the company, that they found attractive. Investments could be made in cash, or in increments of staff time. Now you have the beginnings of a corporatewide network of angel investors.

Does this sound nutty? I hope not. Many companies devote 5 or 10 percent of their revenue to R&D. Why not set aside a small share of discretionary funding for ideas that don't pop up at the right time or in the right place to make it into the formal budgeting process? My guess is that a community of hundreds of midlevel managers spread out across a large company would, in the aggregate, make better investment decisions than a few folks in a new ventures unit. Of course, as in all markets, there would have to be some ground rules.

To be eligible for funding, an innovator would have to prepare a prospectus and have it vetted by a peer review panel. Assuming the idea met some basic tests of logic and feasibility, the innovator would then be free to solicit funding from the company's "band of angels." Ideas would be posted on an internal Web site, along with an "elevator pitch" video clip. In addition, there would be a beauty contest each month where internal entrepreneurs could pitch their ideas to an audience of potential financiers. Innovators would be allowed to use the funds they raised to buy themselves out of their current responsibilities and/or hire other folks from across the company on short-term assignments. A portion of the cost savings or revenue gains from successful projects would be credited back to the investor's budget, to be used in backing other new ideas. Thus investors who backed successful projects would get more to invest in subsequent periods. Investors would also have the option of joining together in syndicates to fund larger or more risky projects. Additionally, entrepreneurs would be allowed to come back for additional rounds of funding if a project met its initial objectives. In such a system, no shortsighted executive, no manager worried about cannibalization, and no risk-averse boss would be able to sink a good idea.

Challenge #4: Aggregating Collective Wisdom

Everyone knows that in most cases, a lot of people are smarter than a few people. That's why most of us would rather live in a democracy than a dictatorship, and prefer open markets to central planning. Yet if you think about how decisions are made in large companies, you could be forgiven for believing that executives have a predilection for authoritarian systems and command economies. If this seems an overly harsh verdict, go back and review the critical decisions your company has made over the past decade—the big acquisitions, new product programs, C-level appointments, and so on. In each case, ask yourself, what percentage of the organization's collective wisdom was brought to bear in making the decision? How many individuals got the chance to weigh in? The answer to both questions: Not enough.

Why are so many executives reluctant to exploit the power of collective wisdom? Maybe it's because they feel it would undermine the rational for their stratospheric salaries: they get paid the big bucks to make the big calls. Maybe it's because they've bought into the myth of the CEO as monarch—a cartoonish distortion often perpetuated by the business media. Maybe it's because they've been lucky enough to make some admirable calls in the past and ascribe their success to good judgment rather than good fortune. Or maybe they've simply never thought about how one applies the principles of democracy and free markets to strategic decision making. Whatever the cause, companies often pay an "ignorance tax" when magisterial decisions are uninformed by the collective intelligence of the masses.

In one large-scale study, senior executives judged nearly a quarter of their decisions to have been wrong.[2] (An independent audit would probably have put the figure higher.) Another study found that misplaced confidence frequently leads CEOs to significantly overpay for acquisitions.[3] The point is, it's virtually impossible for a small cadre of senior executives to accurately estimate the costs and benefits of any complex strategic decision. For example, imagine trying to calculate the potential returns on a billion-dollar investment in China. One would need to make assumptions about exchange rates, Chinese economic growth, government policy, the actions of competitors, consumer behavior, and a host of other variables. This is precisely the sort of valuation problem where the "many" usually outperform the "few." Again, let's take an example from outside the corporate sphere.

There's little that is chancier than a golf tournament. Although Tiger Woods has won 30 percent of golf's four annual "major" championships since turning pro, it's hard to predict when and where he'll win his next title. It's even harder to set the odds on players who are less gifted. Yet William Hill, a leading U.K. bookmaker, is quite happy to take bets on future golf tournaments. At the moment, the odds of Tiger winning the next Open Championship are 3.5:1 *off*. If you wager a pound on Tiger and he triumphs, you'll get £4.50 back—your £1 stake plus £3.50 of winnings. If you bet against Tiger and he loses, you'll win 38 pence on top of your £1 wager. The odds on Phil Mickelson are longer, at 11:1. If Luke Donald, the top-rated English player prevails, you'll earn a fat £35 for every pound you put down. These odds are probability estimates based on two kinds of data: the expert opinion of "odds compilers" who work for the bookmakers, and market data as reflected in the actual bets made by golf-mad punters. Having set an initial price on a particular outcome, bookmakers adjust their odds over time as additional bets are placed and public opinion reveals itself.

In other words, there is more wisdom embedded in the average sports bet than there is in the typical corporate investment decision. That seems crazy to me. You wouldn't buy a stock if its price had been set by five analysts, yet companies often make big financial bets based on the views of fewer than a dozen senior executives. The potential solution:

an internal "market for judgment" that harnesses the wisdom of a broad cross-section of employees in setting the odds on the success of future projects.

How might this work? Suppose your company created a market in which employees could buy and sell contracts based on their beliefs about the returns to a prospective project. Let's say you work for a retailer, and your company is thinking about opening a store in Shanghai—its first in China. A team has been on the ground for the past year working on a launch plan, and has now published its views and a detailed pro forma. The team believes that the new store, and the six more scheduled to open over the next 18 months, will achieve a 15 percent compounded return on investment over five years. As an employee, you have the option of buying a contract that will pay out $100 if the project achieves this target, but if the project falls short of this number, the contract will pay nothing. Obviously, the more confident you are in the initiative, the more you will be willing to pay for the contract. On the other hand, if you're bearish on your company's China plan, you have the option to go short and sell the contract. In both cases, though, you'll have to find someone to take the other side of the transaction. Let's say that prior to groundbreaking, the average trading price on the Shanghai contract is $35. This means that for every investor who thinks there's a 35 percent chance that the project will exceed the 15 percent threshold, there's someone else who believes there's a 65 percent probability it won't. To keep things simple, let's assume for the moment that there are only two people in the market, you and your colleague, Susan. You're convinced the China venture will succeed so you go long on the contract. Susan, who is less optimistic, goes short. If the project is a winner, you'll receive $100—your $35 plus Sue's $65. If the project fails, Susan gets back her bucks, plus your $35.

A market of this type could be opened at any point during the initial planning for a new project, provided relevant details are made available to all employees. Project members would be free to buy and sell contracts, but their trades would need to be publicly disclosed. Contracts would continue to trade over the five-year project term. If the first store was a blowout success, the price on the contracts would go up. In that case, you might find that your $35 contract was now worth $70. You could either lock in your gains by selling the contract, or hang tight until the five-year mark.

The purpose of such a market is not to rob top management of its decision-making authority, but to provide it with more information. Suppose your company is now six months away from breaking ground in China, and the Shanghai contracts are trading hands at $15. It's obvious that most employees think the China venture is going to fail. Of course, top management can still proceed, but they would be wise to reconsider the details of the plan, for should the project ultimately fail, the board will want to know why they chose to ignore the voice of the market. (If the project gets scuppered, the contracts pay out nothing.)

Today, you can find online prediction markets covering just about everything—from the opening box office take of a soon-to-be-released movie, to the district-by-district outcome of forthcoming congressional elections, to the chance that peace will break out between Israel and the Palestinians. Thanks to the power of collective intelligence, some of these markets have demonstrated uncanny predictive powers. For example, Intrade, a Dublin-based pioneer in predictive markets, correctly called 33 out of 34 of the U.S. senate races in the 2004 election. Only in Alaska, where trading was thin, did the wisdom of the market falter.

Every day, companies bet millions of dollars on risky initiatives: new products, new ad campaigns, new factories, big mergers, and so on. History suggests that many of these projects will fail to deliver their expected returns. Ironically, many companies have invested millions of dollars in IT systems that move data from the periphery to the center. The hope: more data will help top management make better decisions. But there's a big difference between data and knowledge. Rather than working to perpetuate the myth of the omniscient executive, IT managers should be searching for ways to collect and correlate the organization's distributed wisdom. A little more humility at the top, and a lot more bottom-up knowledge aggregation, could substantially reduce the ignorance tax *your* company has to pay. Who would have guessed that a bookie could provide inspiration for management innovation?

Challenge #5: Minimizing the Drag of Old Mental Models

Earlier, I argued that companies miss the future when top management's intellectual capital depreciates faster than its authority. Indeed, I believe that a misalignment between power and perspicuity is the most frequent and deadliest cause of strategic maladaptation. Analyze a company caught behind the curve, and you will invariably find an organization where senior management has retained its influence but lost its foresight.

For example, in the early years of this decade, at least some of Samsung's meteoric growth in the mobile phone business came from Nokia's reluctance to manufacture two-piece "flip-phones," the design favored by its Korean rival. In the 1990s, Nokia's sleek, one-piece "candy bar" phones were coveted lifestyle accessories, and earned the company numerous design awards. Yet Nokia's compact product architecture made it hard to enlarge the size of the display without significantly increasing the overall dimensions of the phone. At first, this wasn't a problem, but as people started to use their phones to send messages, take photographs, and surf the Web, the limits of a tiny, claustrophobic screen became ever more apparent. Samsung's solution: a two-piece design where the display overlapped the keyboard until the phone was unfolded. To Asian customers, the flip-phone was a handy but far-from-earthshaking innovation. Nokia's chief product engineer, on the other hand, viewed the flip-phone as design heresy. Having helped invent the mini-brick phone, Nokia's head of design doggedly defended its virtues and repeatedly shrugged off requests from Nokia's Asian marketers for a rejoinder to Samsung's customer-pleasing design. Eventually Nokia would come out with a two-piece design, but not before surrendering millions of dollars in lost revenue to Samsung. In this case, Nokia's capacity to adapt literally hinged on a hinge.

An ideal management system would be one in which power was automatically redistributed when environmental changes devalued executive knowledge and competence. Two things work against this. First, in a hierarchical organization, authority is bestowed from above and can only be revoked from above. Not surprisingly, corporate leaders are often reluctant to admit they've made a hiring mistake, and therefore can be slow to take corrective action. Second, the allocation of power tends to be binary—an executive is in full control up until the moment he or she is dismissed. Because it's expensive and disruptive to move someone out of a big job, the reallocation of managerial power tends to lag declines in executive effectiveness.

Most people find it hard to imagine an organization in which authority is a fluid commodity, flowing smoothly toward leaders who add value and away from those who don't. Yet this is how the Web already works. In the online world, power and influence are the product of de facto leadership, rather than de jure appointments. Hierarchies get built from the bottom up, not from the top down. In that sense they are "natural" rather than "proscribed."

Within the open source software community, for example, one finds something that looks very much like a pyramid. At the top sits Linus Torvalds, the Finnish programmer who wrote the core of what ultimately became the Linux operating system. The rest of Torvalds's iceberg is best described by Professor Steven Weber, a keen student of the open source phenomenon:

Torvalds depends heavily on a group of lieutenants who constitute what many programmers call "the inner circle." These are core developers who essentially own delegated responsibility for subsystems and components. Some of the lieutenants onward-delegate to area-owners (sometimes called "maintainers") who have smaller regions of responsibility. The organic result looks and functions like a decision hierarchy . . . Torvalds sits atop the pyramid as a benevolent dictator with final responsibility for managing disagreements that cannot be resolved at lower levels.

The decision hierarchy for Linux is still informal in an important sense. While programmers generally recognize the importance of the inner circle, no document or organization chart specifies who is actually in it at any give time.[4]

It is this hierarchy that ultimately decides which bits of computer code get incorporated into Linux and which don't. Developers who believe they've crafted a clever piece of software can submit their work to one of the Torvalds's "maintainers" for review. After soliciting a wide range of opinions on the proffered code, the deputy will render a judgment on whether or not to include the patch in the Linux "kernel." In cases when there's a serious disagreement over whether to adopt the patch, the decision gets escalated to one of Torvalds's long-serving lieutenants, and if necessary, to the famous Finn himself.

While the Linux community has a couple of layers of hierarchy at the top, it would be wrong to picture Torvalds as a CEO, since his power is entirely contingent on the support of his deputies and a legion of Linux programmers. Within the open source community, as in all true communities, it is the leader who depends on the "followers." Virtually all of the Linux code base, which includes millions of lines of software, has been written by volunteers. As the godfather of Linux, Torvalds is far more dependent on those contributors than they are on him. Critically, Torvalds has no control over the Linux programmers. No one tells them what to work on. Instead, they devote themselves to the bugs, patches, and features they find most interesting.

Moreover, every Linux volunteer has the right to "fork the code." A programmer whose work has been excluded from the Linux core can launch a new open source project and invite others to pitch in. In other words, no one has to accept the decision of the reviewers. In this sense, the Linux hierarchy is entirely upside-down. The moment Torvalds stops being responsive to his army of open source partisans, his power will start to ebb away.

In a traditional pyramid, executives are under no obligation to justify their decisions to the "plebes." Not so for Torvalds. On those rare occasions when he is forced to make a decision, Torvalds goes to great lengths to explain his reasoning to the broader Linux community. He has also been quick to admit mistakes when unfolding events have cast doubt on previous decisions. Torvalds understands that in a community of peers, people bow to competence, commitment, and foresight, rather than to power. The fact that Torvalds has retained his position at the center of the Linux galaxy for more than a decade, without any formal mandate, makes him a worthy role model for aspiring 21st-century leaders.

While the value of hierarchy as an organizing tool will wane in the years to come, it will never disappear. Some people, at certain times and on certain issues, will always wield more authority than others. Yet embedded in this pedestrian fact are some crucial questions: How is that authority gained? Under what circumstances can it be lost? And what limits the ways in which it can be exercised? Within the Linux sodality, power is *granted from below*, unbuttressed by formal positions and titles. Power is *easily lost*—it happens every time a community member opts out or chooses to fork the code. These are decisions that cannot be reversed by Torvalds or anyone else. Finally, the exercise of authority is constrained by the necessity for *consultation and transparency*. Servant leaders can't afford the luxury of making capricious decisions, and must extend "due process" to every well-intentioned individual and plausible idea. Like W. L. Gore's power-from-the-people leadership system, the open source development model helps keep power and value-added tightly coupled. Within Gore and Linux, anyone with an out-of-date mental model will soon be out of power as well—an enormous boon for adaptability. As a management innovator, you goal is to ensure that the same can be said for *your* company.

Challenge # 6: Giving Everyone the Chance to Opt In

If there was a single question that obsessed 20th-century managers it was this: How do we get more out of our people? At one level, this question is innocuous—who can object to the goal of raising human productivity? Yet it's also loaded with industrial age thinking: How do *we* (meaning "management") get *more* (meaning units of production per hour) out of *our* people (meaning the individuals who are obliged to follow our orders)? Ironically, the management model encapsulated in this question virtually guarantees that a company will *never* get the best out of its people. Vassals and conscripts may work hard, but they don't work willingly. This is a crucial distinction, for in a world where prosperity depends on creativity, an enthusiastic workforce will consistently outperform one that is merely industrious.

Can you remember any instance in which something that was *assigned* to you brought you more joy than something you *chose* to do? No? Well, neither can anyone else in your company. Human beings are most enthusiastic when they're doing the things they *want* to do.

The success of the open source software movement is the single most dramatic example of how an opt-in engagement model can mobilize human effort on a grand scale. How big is the open source phenomenon? Really big. In mid-2007, SourceForge.net, a Web site that caters to open source developers, listed nearly 150,000 open source projects with 1.6 million contributors. All that was needed to un-dam this cataract of creativity was a technology that allowed individuals to find and collaborate with other eager contributors. Suddenly, individuals from across the planet could sync up in boundary-spanning communities of passion.

It's little wonder that the success of open source has left a lot of senior executives slack-jawed. After all, it's tough for managers to understand a production process that doesn't rely on managers. In a 1998 memo, later leaked to the press, a young Microsoft engineer, Vinod Valloppillil, conveyed perfectly the sort of wide-eyed awe that is often experienced by command-and-control types when they are first exposed to the anomaly of open source: "The ability of the OSS [open source software] process to collect and harness the collective IQ of thousands of individuals across the Internet is simply amazing . . . to compete against OSS, [Microsoft] must target a process rather than a company."[5]

Understanding why otherwise busy software engineers are willing to contribute their time to OSS projects can help us understand some of the necessary components of a successful opt-in system. Surveys of open source developers reveal a diverse mix of personal motivations. Many coders are energized by the aesthetic appeal of writing an elegant piece of code that solves a complex problem in a simple way. Others get fired up by the prospect of taking on the commercial software establishment—they're eager to contribute to a project that makes great software available to everyone for free. A substantial proportion of coders are IT professionals who are working on problems that are important to their day jobs. As Weber puts it, they're scratching an itch. Finally, virtually every OSS programmer is motivated by the chance to build reputational capital. A developer whose patch or fix gets incorporated into an open source application usually gets a mention in the program's credits file. The first version of Linux, for example, credited 78 developers from 12 countries. Like professors vying to get published in prestigious journals, coders hanker for the peer recognition that comes from making a visible contribution. In other words, OSS contributors volunteer for a wide variety of reasons. The lesson: a successful opt-in system is one that allows contributors to take their "psychic income" in a variety of currencies.

A lack of central authority is another critical feature of the open source model. Since there's no project kingpin parceling out tasks, interesting problems are likely to get tackled by more than one developer. To a traditionally trained manager, this parallelism may seem wasteful—but what's worse, some duplicated effort or a suboptimal solution because too few options got generated?

The OSS model also makes it easy for people to contribute. First, the raw material for creativity—the code base—is open to anyone. Second, there is no prejudice about who is and who isn't qualified to contribute— if your code measures up, you're good enough. And third, the approval process is transparent and largely apolitical. There's little chance that someone's hard work will fall victim to an arbitrary decision.

At this point you may be wondering who has to work on the "boring stuff." A lot of software development involves fixing bugs—hardly glamorous work. Yet when you have a large enough pool of talent to draw from, you quickly find that what is a tedious chore for one person is an engrossing brain-teaser for someone else. Moreover, hackers often reserve their highest praise for colleagues who take on the scut work that others shirk.

Opt-in is more than a model for Web-based volunteerism. It is at the heart of Google's 20 percent policy and Gore's principle of self-chosen commitment. And there are other examples. At Linden Lab, the company behind *Second Life*, engineers choose what to work on from a large database of essential tasks. This allows teams to form organically, on the basis of mutual interests. Philip Rosedale, Linden Lab's founder and CEO, says his goal is to get everyone behaving like an entrepreneur. The secret is to let people set their own direction. "That's what entrepreneurs do," says Rosedale. "You have to take risks and you have to expect to be held accountable." His simple charge to Linden's engineers: "Tell everybody in an e-mail every week what you are doing, then make some progress of some kind and tell everybody in an e-mail how you did it." That, he claims, is Linden's "organizational scheme."[6]

The freedom to scratch your itch. Credit for your contribution. Peer review. That's the opt-in formula—and it isn't rocket science. So if your company isn't exploiting the power of volitional commitment, you need to get busy. But be prepared for some push back. The most likely demurral: it's inefficient to let people follow their bliss. Here's how I'd respond to that objection.

It's true, self-direction may reduce efficiency, if by "efficiency" you mean the speed and economy with which individuals carry out work that has been assigned to them by others. By definition, if employees are working on the things *they* care about, they may be giving less attention to the things their superiors care about. But this is a myopic definition of efficiency. It fails to account for the costs of malicious compliance when employees are ordered to do things they don't want to do. It ignores the bureaucratic overhead—the reporting, auditing, and supervision—that is necessary to keep people focused on things they find unrewarding. It doesn't include the potential value of all the discretionary effort that bored employees choose *not* to supply. It omits the responsiveness costs a company incurs when employees who know what to do spend weeks or months running a gauntlet of approvals. Neither does it take account of the opportunities that get missed because associates have so little self-directed time. So yes, there are efficiency advantages in doling out assignments from on high. But are they large enough to cover the costs of disenchanted and disengaged employees? I doubt it—not in the long run. If your company is going to thrive in this new century, it must build a management system that allows an ever-growing percentage of employees to devote an ever-increasing proportion of their time to projects of their own choosing. The payoff: an ever-growing sense of commitment and passion.

Bringing the Fringe Back Home

Here are a few questions that should help you and your colleagues extract maximum value out of your journey to the fringe:

1. Which of our problems (like spurring creativity or allocating resources more effectively) has this particular management deviant solved in an unconventional way?

2. What are the methods, incentives, and infrastructure that comprise this atypical "solution"? How, exactly, has this renegade organization managed to sidestep the pathologies that afflict our company?

3. Are there any deep principles that underpin their approach? What are the "big lessons" that we should take away from this case (like the power of opt-in or the advantages of aggregated wisdom)?

4. What are the checks and balances that keep these counterintuitive practices from becoming counterproductive? How does this maverick organization mitigate the downside of its anomalous practices?

5. How would we translate these quirky practices into our company? What exactly would we change in our core management processes? (It may be useful to ask: If we outsourced one of our core management processes to this oddball organization, how would it get retooled? What changes would we expect?)

6. What would be the primary impediments to adopting these renegade practices in our own company? What would be the most likely objections and how would we answer them?

By the way, your lessons will carry a lot more weight if they are the product of a shared experience. So when you set out to explore the fringe, make sure you invite along the executives who are responsible for your company's core management processes. A secondhand account of a deviant management practice is never as compelling as a first-person encounter.

A final piece of advice: don't be overawed by the parade of positive deviants I've presented in this chapter. Instead, go searching for your own. Once you start looking beyond the usual doyens of best practice, you'll discover a veritable circus of management oddballs. As you explore the fringe, see if you can find amazing feats of managing and organizing that don't involve managers and organizations. When you do, you'll know you have found the fringe—and there you will catch a glimpse of the future.

BUILDING THE FUTURE OF MANAGEMENT

PART FOUR

Ten

Becoming a
Management
Innovator

O VER THE PAST DECADE, JUST ABOUT EVERY COMPANY on the planet has been hard at work reinventing its *business* processes—inbound logistics, inventory management, customer fulfillment, technical support, and the like. Yet few companies have devoted a similar degree of energy and imagination to the challenge of reinventing their *management* processes. There are, though, a few notable exceptions.

- Over the past few years, General Electric has been hard at work reinventing its core management processes—financial reviews, management development, strategic planning, and executive assessment—around the challenge of raising the company's organic growth rate.[1] CEO Jeff Immelt is determined to make GE the world's largest growth company.

- In recent years, Procter & Gamble has turned its R&D process inside out in an attempt to open up its development pipeline to

215

ideas and technologies sourced from outside the firm.[2] P&G's chairman, A. G. Lafley, has said that he expects 50 percent of the company's future products to be based on concepts and technologies acquired from third parties.

- As we saw in chapter 2, Whirlpool, the global leader in domestic appliances, has spent the better part of a decade redesigning its management processes to make them catalysts for product and business model innovation.[3] The once-stodgy manufacturer is now widely viewed as a benchmark for companies intent on making innovation a core competence.

These three widely reported cases demonstrate that even 100-year-old industrial giants can reengineer their management DNA. Nevertheless, at this point you may be looking for a few pointers on how to turn revolutionary management thinking into revolutionary management doing. In this chapter, we'll delve into two recent examples of groundbreaking management innovation. I'll describe in detail the often exhilarating and sometimes exasperating work of turning new management ideas into new management practices. I'll also draw out a few key lessons that will help *you* to become a high-impact management innovator, and that will help your company leap onto the next management S-curve.

Building a Growth Engine at IBM

To be adaptable, a company must be capable of spawning new businesses. For a host of reasons, this is a daunting challenge for most incumbents. As a consequence, it's usually newcomers who grab tomorrow's opportunities. Often, the real problem for an established company is not a dearth of ideas, but management processes and practices that reflexively favor "more of the same" over "new and different." While the green shoots of a new business idea may occasionally push their way up through the compacted soil of management indifference and skepticism, few companies are truly satisfied with their success at launching new businesses. And in 1999, IBM's then-chairman, Lou Gerstner, was more dissatisfied than most.[4]

With over 320,000 employees and revenues of $91 billion, IBM is the world's largest information technology company. But during the late 1990s, its top-line growth slowed alarmingly as the behemoth struggled to keep pace with the industry it had once dominated. Having taken over the top job in 1993, Gerstner shepherded Big Blue through a remarkable comeback, but as the new millennium loomed, investors wondered whether IBM, after years of retrenchment and cost-cutting, had lost its knack for growth. While the reformed company was lean and efficient, it seemed to be missing out on a wide range of exciting opportunities—from the boom in life sciences computing, to the explosive growth of open source software, to the rapid proliferation of handheld and mobile computing devices. To many, it looked like IBM was leaving billions of dollars on the table.

During the first six years of Gerstner's tenure, IBM had won far more patents (12,773) than any other company in America, and yet it had consistently failed to convert this technological prowess into new businesses. While IBM's celebrated labs had produced such industry-defining technologies as the router and the relational database, nimbler outfits like Cisco and Oracle had seized on those breakthroughs and turned them into highly profitable businesses. By at least one measure, IBM seemed almost disinterested in growth: Instead of using its profits to seed new businesses, IBM spent billions during the 1990s buying back its own shares. This inflated the share price, but did nothing to pump up the top line. As the tech boom peaked in 1999 and 2000, IBM's badly sputtering growth engine nearly ground to a halt—producing a measly 1 percent growth in revenues.

On a Sunday afternoon in September 1999, the problem finally boiled over. Gerstner was working at home, reading a monthly report, when he came across a footnote explaining that an embryonic effort to build a business in life sciences computing had been scuppered to meet quarterly earnings goals. Having intervened personally to get the venture started, Gerstner was angry to discover it had been summarily terminated. He wondered whether such seemingly insignificant budgetary trade-offs might be at the heart of IBM's growth problem. The chairman and CEO dashed off a flinty memo to his staff. Why was it, he demanded, that IBM was systematically missing new growth opportunities? Determined to get IBM back on a growth path, the former McKinsey consultant asked a team of his top lieutenants to track the problem to its source and report back to him with recommendations for fixing it.

Over the next three months, a task force comprising 12 senior leaders worked to unearth the deep roots of IBM's lackluster growth. By interviewing scores of employees who had worked on ill-fated new business ventures, the detectives hoped to uncover the ways in which IBM's management processes were undermining the company's growth efforts. As one might expect of IBM, the probe was wide-ranging and thorough.

On December 1, 1999, the task force huddled with Gerstner and laid out its findings. "It was a painful process," acknowledges Mike Giersch, vice president of corporate strategy. "We had to admit that we had screwed things up."[5]

Gerstner's turnaround had staunched IBM's record losses and had inculcated a laserlike focus on achieving near-term profitability. But with their heads down, managers frequently failed to spot emerging growth opportunities. While Gerstner had worked hard to make IBM more customer-centric, most of these efforts were focused on satisfying existing customers, rather than on winning over new customers. Then there was the fear factor. Top management's unyielding demands for fact-based analysis and detailed financial forecasts dissuaded all but the most incautious managers from embracing the uncertainty and risk of investing in a new business.

The task force's analysis showed that when an executive finally did summon up the courage to launch a new business, IBM typically burdened the zero-dollar start-up with the same expectations for near-term earnings that it laid on its billion-dollar legacy businesses. Thus, to win funding, new business programs had to promise impossibly ambitious financial returns. When, almost inevitably, a nascent business missed its initial targets, its budget would be quickly whittled away. Finally, and perhaps most damningly, the task force found that new ventures often failed because they didn't attract first-rate talent. Given the high mortality rate of new business ventures, most aspiring managers preferred to build their careers within the relative safety of IBM's long-established businesses.

While the team's critique was harsh, it wasn't directed at any particular executive or business unit. Having missed so many opportunities, across so many sectors of the computer industry, the team could only conclude that IBM's growth malaise was a systemic problem, and not an individual failing. As Giersch remembers it, the conversation among the top team "was never about who should be hung." Moreover, since the diagnosis came from a group of seasoned IBM leaders, rather than from outside consultants, it felt authentic. Yet no one could escape the inevitable conclusion: to get better at inventing new businesses, IBM was going to have to dramatically reinvent its management processes and values.

While the diagnosis was clear enough, the outlines of a solution were anything but. Acutely aware of IBM's deliberate and conservative culture, Gerstner and his deputies wondered what could be done to help new business teams intercept fast-moving opportunities—without disrupting IBM's smooth-running profit machine. What kind of a management system would let new businesses leverage IBM's vast resources while simultaneously freeing them from the pressure for immediate returns?

Over the next five years, IBM's response to these thorny issues would take shape in the form of a new management process aimed at nurturing "emerging business opportunities." From its launch in 2000, the EBO process, as it was dubbed, rapidly evolved into a comprehensive system for identifying, staffing, funding, and tracking new business initiatives across IBM. In the program's first five years, IBM launched 25 new businesses. Three misfired and were wound up, but the remaining 22 were delivering $15 billion in annual revenues by the end of 2005. Through the EBO process, IBM built a multibillion-dollar business that offered sophisticated infotech tools to life sciences clients engaged in drug discovery and development. It forged a sprawling business in "pervasive computing," which utilizes IBM software and technology to embed wireless-computing capability in devices ranging from smartphones and PDAs to store checkout systems and home appliances. It grew a highly successful business built around the Linux operating system. Most critically, the EBO initiative helped rebalance the company's management systems. Today, managers across IBM value new business creation as highly as operational excellence.

All of this required a sustained campaign of management innovation, focused on the growth impediments Gerstner's team had identified back in its original study. Indeed, the EBO process is best understood in terms of the deep-seated management problems it addresses.

Problem: In established companies, no one "owns" new market space. In most companies, an executive who misses an earnings target gets pummeled in the next monthly or quarterly business review. Yet seldom does anyone take a career hit when a start-up runs away with a new billion-dollar opportunity.

IBM took a big step toward plugging this accountability gap when Gerstner promoted John Thompson, the chief of IBM's software group and a widely respected leader, to the position of vice chairman and designated him the company's new growth czar. A 32-year company veteran, Thompson's mission was monumental: help IBM identify disruptive technologies, industry trends, and embryonic markets, and transform them into billion-dollar businesses. With this appointment, IBM had, for the first time in its history, a top-ranked executive who owned the white spaces and was responsible to the chairman for filling them.

One of Thompson's first steps was to orchestrate a set of wide-ranging conversations aimed at identifying an initial portfolio of new business candidates. This first go-round yielded several EBOs, like open source software and "pervasive computing," that were low-hanging fruit—big opportunities where IBM was struggling to marshal its resources, but still had the chance to catch up. The next challenge: finding credible leaders to head up the newly minted EBOs. Not surprisingly, few executives seemed interested in the job. But after some gentle arm-twisting by Thompson, a few experienced managers signed on. Each new EBO leader was asked to provide a monthly progress report to Thompson and other top IBMers. In another first, IBM's major growth initiatives were now getting the same sort of executive attention the company lavished on its major business lines.

Upon Thompson's retirement in September 2002, Bruce Harreld, IBM's chief strategist, took over as the point man for new business development. Like Thompson before him, Harreld had a direct link to IBM's top brass, including Sam Palmissano, the new chairman. Under Harreld's leadership, the corporate strategy group worked steadily to develop a more rigorous and far-reaching approach to identifying emerging opportunities. Today, the team conducts regular conversations with IBM's R&D leaders and with the executive teams who run IBM's major divisions. It also helps IBM's sales organizations host conversations with leading-edge customers, with the goal of identifying industry discontinuities that can open up new market opportunities. Every year these forums generate hundreds of new business ideas that are then screened by the strategy group. To qualify for EBO status, an opportunity must have the potential to generate more than $1 billion in annual revenue, though there's no expectation that an EBO will produce profits in the first year or two of its existence.

Problem: New business incubators provide a "safe haven" in which to grow new businesses, but often isolate new ventures from the critical skills that reside within the operating units. It's not easy to grow a new business inside of an existing business. Managers who are working 12-hour days to satisfy current customers and deliver short-term results are likely to regard the pursuit of an untested market opportunity as a risky diversion of energies from the central task of "running the business." And even when a new venture manages to garner a modicum of support, there's always the risk that it will be hobbled with operating practices and assumptions that are better suited to running a large, predictable business than pioneering new markets. Because of this, companies often set up corporate incubators, which, at least in theory, provide fledgling businesses with a more nurturing environment. Yet in practice, these new business enclaves seldom prove to be a panacea for lackluster growth.

Fortunately, Thompson and Harreld recognized the dangers of sequestering the company's growth initiatives in a corporate crèche. They knew that new business incubators often ended up as orphanages, filled with ventures for which operating units felt little or no responsibility. If IBM's EBOs were going to beat out a swarm of upstart competitors, they would need to leverage the customer relationships, development expertise, and bleeding-edge technologies that resided within IBM's major divisions. This wouldn't happen if the EBOs were the wards of a few senior staffers.

After wrestling with this problem for several months, Harreld's team landed on a solution—a hybrid structure that divided the responsibility for an EBO's success between the corporate strategy office and a "host" division. In practice, this means assigning each EBO to the business unit that is able to contribute the most in terms of customer access and technical expertise. A senior executive from the relevant division serves as a surrogate parent to the EBO, allocating resources to the venture and ensuring that it stays on track through the ups and downs of the budget cycle. The EBO team itself is physically located within the guardian division, rather than at corporate HQ—making it easy for the EBO team to access local expertise.

While the EBOs may be sprinkled across IBM, they get a lot of oversight from Harreld and his team. Each EBO is reviewed monthly in a meeting chaired by Harreld and attended by the EBO leader and a top executive from the host division. At the outset, each new EBO receives a bucket of funding from corporate coffers—usually a few million dollars. But as the business matures, its parent division is expected to assume an ever increasing share of the funding burden. In this way, EBOs enjoy the best of both worlds: they are able to avoid the short-term profit pressures that put a squeeze on the rest of IBM, and because they are based within IBM's key operating divisions, they can leverage critical business unit resources.

Problem: It's difficult to get senior executives to devote themselves to un-proven, but potentially promising, opportunities. In most companies, executive power and prestige are highly correlated with the size of the business one runs. As a result, large businesses tend to attract first-rate executive talent while new businesses often get staffed with second stringers. So it was at IBM. Recognizing this, Thompson and Harreld worked hard to recruit some of IBM's fastest-rising stars to lead the EBOs. At the beginning, it wasn't an easy sell. Why would someone running a billion-dollar business want to take on an internal start-up with a meager staff? But slowly the message sank in—the chairman had made growth IBM's number one priority, and the company needed battle-tested leaders who were willing to take on the challenge of building new businesses.

Ultimately, IBM would draw most of its EBO leaders from the company's 300-member senior leadership team. Rod Adkins, for example, was managing IBM's $4 billion Unix computing division when he signed up to pilot the pervasive computing EBO. The upside for Adkins and other EBO leaders? Enormous visibility at the very top of the company; permission to pull in resources from across the IBM empire; freedom to defy conventional thinking; and the right to recruit their own team from IBM's best and brightest. As most of the EBO leaders quickly learned, this wasn't a bad return for taking on the risk of building something new.

Thompson and Harreld knew that little businesses wouldn't grow into big businesses without the fertilizer of top management attention—hence the top-level monthly review meetings. In a typical meeting, Harreld and his staff challenge the EBO team to come up with better ways of testing critical hypotheses, to be more creative in finding ways to share risk with third parties, and always—always—to move faster in getting early market feedback. An EBO review often runs for a half day or more. Multiply this by the dozen or more EBOs that may be in the corporate portfolio at any point in time, and it works out to a significant measure of parental care and attention. While the meetings are collegial, they can be exhausting for the EBO team. On this point, listen to Jan Jackman, general manager of the Retail on Demand EBO: "They are low-serial-number people, and none of them take it easy on you. But those reviews are invaluable. We are getting insights from IBM's top thinkers."

Problem: New business initiatives seldom survive a budget crunch unscathed. Thompson and Harreld realized that embedding the EBOs within IBM's operating divisions entailed a risk: when times got tough, as they always did, line managers might starve the EBOs of capital and talent in order to meet their own short-term financial targets. That was why divisional EVPs had to show up for the monthly review meetings—it reminded them of their responsibility to support the fledgling ventures. In a bid to further moderate the near-term focus of IBM's senior executives, top EBO support was made a component of their annual performance evaluation. This rejiggering of top-level priorities was a significant boost to the EBO program.

While Harreld's strategy team used the monthly review process as a stick to ensure continuity in EBO funding, the team also held out a carrot: the promise that an EBO's revenues would flow back to the sponsoring division.

Recognizing that earnings-obsessed executives might nevertheless find a way to subvert the EBO process, Harreld asked IBM's corporate bean counters to provide monthly reports on the investment going into each EBO, as well as its expenses and revenues. "Finance kept the line honest," says Gerry Mooney, who currently manages the EBO process and reports to Harreld. "It prevented people from moving the EBO money around."

Problem: There is no surer way to undermine a new business venture than to measure it by the profits generated, rather than by the learning accumulated. IBM's top-level growth team understood that when it comes to building a new business, you have to learn before you earn. Given this, they wanted to counter the debilitating assumption that if you're not holding a new venture accountable for profits, you're not holding it accountable for anything. Many of IBM's past growth efforts had stalled when an early push for profits limited a venture's potential upside by prematurely truncating the learning and experimentation that would have, in time, yielded a more powerful, and better targeted, business model.

As is true for most companies, IBM's mainstream project review process puts a big premium on analytical certitude, financial precision, and current period results. Fully aware that these biases would be toxic to their efforts to build new businesses from the ground up, Harreld's group crafted a new evaluation scheme better suited to the messy job of creating new markets.

In an EBO's early stages, the monthly review process emphasizes learning and experimentation. Progress is tracked by a set of short-term, learning-oriented metrics that include the number of customers contacted, the pace of product development, and the number of pilots underway. As the EBO ramps up, new milestones are established around the number of "design-ins" (which occur when a new product or service gets formally adopted by a customer) and first-time orders. The EBO process encourages bold moves and breakthrough thinking, but it also instills discipline and control. No one gets away with making a vague promise about "increasing mindshare." A typical goal might center around the number of business partners enrolled or customer pilots launched. The EBO process has made it clear to everyone across IBM that innovation doesn't imply a lack of accountability, but it requires accountability for different sorts of things than would be expected of a mature business.

While EBO leaders are not expected to provide precise profit forecasts, they are expected to be very explicit about their hypotheses, lest unstated and untested assumptions lead the venture into an expensive dead-end. The ethos of the EBO process, repeatedly driven home by Harreld and his colleagues, is to fail early and fail small. With this in mind, the monthly review meetings are an opportunity to reassess critical assumptions in light of customer feedback and shifts in the external environment. Oftentimes EBO teams are exhorted to move faster, but just as frequently they are encouraged to step back and revisit some foundational assumption that has started to look shaky.

In recent years, IBM has been challenged by major shifts in customer demand that have depressed growth rates in some of its legacy businesses. Adding to the pressure was the decision in 2004 to sell off the company's margin-challenged personal computer division. The EBO process and other, more recent, growth initiatives have helped IBM to offset the revenue-deflating effects of these changes in its business mix. Just as importantly, there are distinct signs that IBM's growth efforts have started to change the company's management DNA. The first bit of evidence is the fact that despite key personnel changes, the EBO program has continued to thrive. In addition, many of IBM's divisions are now running their own EBO-like processes. Then there are all those managers across IBM who've been exposed to the pro-growth principles of the EBO initiative. This includes not only the growing number of EBO leaders and alumni, but all those who've worked on EBO teams. As the growth message takes root in IBM, behaviors are beginning to change. Growth is now a regular topic of conversation in the hallways and at the company's planning meetings.

The saga of IBM's EBO process offers aspiring management innovators several important lessons.

Lesson #1: To tackle a systemic problem, you need to understand its deep roots.

You can't build a management process as sophisticated and successful as IBM's EBO system without first acquiring a detailed understanding of the problems you're trying to address. Think of all the effort that early task force put into identifying the systemic impediments to organic growth within IBM—they conducted a three-month-long investigation that examined more than two dozen cases of premature death among IBM's portfolio of enfeebled growth initiatives. Without this forensic inquest, Harreld's team might well have opted for some sort of quick fix, a spiffed-up skunk works, for example, rather than facing up to the challenge of inventing an entirely new and far-reaching management process. You will need to be equally painstaking in your own diagnosis.

Lesson #2: It's often easier to augment than supplant.

Harreld didn't try to uproot any of IBM's existing management processes. He realized that each served a valuable purpose and had powerful defenders. Rather, he built an entirely *new* management process, one that dovetailed with the old and helped offset the short-term bias of IBM's management culture. The goal was to improve IBM's ability to manage a perplexing paradox—how to stay focused on today's business while building tomorrow's. This is one of those trade-offs that most companies struggle to get right. Doing so requires the creation of a counterbalance to the incentives that currently drive management behaviors. The goal is not to blow up the old management process, but to supplement it with a new process that challenges managers to be more thoughtful and balanced in managing delicate trade-offs.

Lesson #3: Commit to revolutionary goals, but take evolutionary steps.

Bold new management processes—like IBM's EBO methodology—never emerge fully formed. Instead, they are assembled, piece by piece, through a process of trial and error. When you're trying to change the deep, near-instinctive, nature of a large organization, you're going to encounter a few setbacks along the way. Yet every reversal brings new knowledge—and with it, the chance to refine your approach. And so it was with the EBO initiative. As Adkins acknowledged, "The EBO process wasn't a natural or normal thing for IBM." Yet each time Harreld and his team encountered a new obstacle, they improvised a new solution.

Lesson #4: Metrics are essential.

As with other forms of innovation, the goal of management innovation is to improve business results. Given this, it is crucial you develop clear metrics that can be used to assess and validate the impact of your management innovation. At IBM, important metrics included the number of EBOs launched, the number of early design wins, the level of investment, the pace of product development, and, ultimately, revenue growth. If you can't describe the payoff to your bold new management idea in a way that resonates with your company's chief financial officer, or with investors, you won't get or deserve much support.

Lesson #5: Keep at it.

It takes time to change a company's management DNA. Even today, years after the program's inception, IBM is still refining its EBO process. It's not by accident that the world's small band of serial management innovators—companies like GE, Procter & Gamble, and IBM—have typically been led by CEOs who viewed themselves as long-serving stewards of the future, rather than by short-tenure mercenaries who couldn't see beyond the next quarter. While some management experiments can be conducted in a matter of days, and with a minuscule budget, reshaping deeply engrained management behaviors often takes months, if not years. When, in 1999, Whirlpool's chairman challenged his colleagues to create a company where innovation came from everyone, every day, he also promised that this would remain his number-one priority for the next five years. Like John Thompson and Bruce Harreld, he understood that when it comes to building new management capabilities, perseverance pays.

At this point, you may be thinking, OK, all this makes sense, but I'm not the vice chairman, nor the chief strategy officer. The CEO hasn't given me a mandate to solve some big and vexing management problem. I don't even have the power to convene a task force. Where do I start if I'm more serf than lord-of-the-manor? How much of a management innovator can I be with the limited power and resources I have at *my* command? The short answer is, more than you think.

Exploiting Collective Wisdom at Best Buy

While the genesis of IBM's EBO process holds important lessons for would-be management innovators, it would be a mistake to believe you need a license from the chairman to shake up the status quo. Consider the case of Jeff Severts, a vice president at Best Buy, America's leading consumer electronics retailer. Severts's inaugural management experiment cost a mere $50 and didn't require a single sign-off, yet it generated lessons that continue to reverberate through Best Buy's Minneapolis headquarters.

Having joined Best Buy in November 2001, Severts was appointed vice president of consumer and brand marketing in 2004—a job that put him in charge of the company's extensive advertising efforts. Severts relished his new role, but was discomforted to learn that his reputation was now inextricably linked to Best Buy's monthly sales performance. As long as the company outperformed its forecast, he was a hero—but when demand softened, he found himself buried under an avalanche of criticism. For Severts and his ad team, the internal reaction to a down month was as disconcerting as it was predictable: "The current advertising stinks. We're not making our budgets. It's marketing's fault."[6]

Severts understood that this knee-jerk reaction was rooted in Best Buy's forecasting and compensation system. Since store managers, along with their district and regional supervisors, were rewarded on the basis of their performance against demanding sales targets, any revenue shortfall directly threatened their compensation—and quickly landed the marketing team on the hot seat.

While Severts readily acknowledged that advertising played an important role in generating demand, he couldn't help but wonder whether big variations from the plan might be the result of poor forecasting rather than ineffective marketing. Based on this hunch, Severts started digging into how the company assembled its sales forecast, known internally as the "Version." Here's what he found.

Best Buy compiles its sales forecast on a rolling, 12-month basis. "Version 1" is issued in March, at the beginning of the company's fiscal year. An updated "Version 2" follows in April, "Version 3" is published in May, and so on throughout the year. Every month, each of Best Buy's eight merchant teams (the folks who order the computers, digital cameras, video games, DVDs, and other doodads that fill the company's cavernous stores) contributes a forecast for its product group. These projections are then aggregated into an overall corporate revenue target. As he compared forecasted and actual sales from previous years, Severts discovered that it was not uncommon for the merchant teams to miss the mark by as much as 10 percent—even when looking just 30 days out. While some of this "error" could be attributed to the inherent volatility of consumer demand, Severts wondered whether there were other factors that might be undermining the accuracy of the forecasts. While the merchants were encouraged to forecast robust growth, they also wanted to set targets that they could actually meet or, better yet, handsomely exceed, since this would maximize their chances for a fat bonus.

If the forecasts were subtly influenced by the interplay of measurement systems and self-interest, so too were the merchants' buying decisions. A merchant who ordered too much gear would get dinged for the costs of excessive inventory, while a merchant who ordered too little ran the risk of missing out on a big upside. In Severts's view, both the forecasts and the purchasing decisions were distorted by human emotion.

As he dug deeper, Severts discovered there were others within Best Buy who had similar doubts about the merchants' crystal ball. Saddled with the responsibility of providing guidance to investors, Best Buy's finance group generated its own forecasts, but those estimates were not widely referenced outside the finance function. Across the company it was widely assumed that the merchants knew their businesses best. As a result, their forecasts carried the most weight.

In working to disentangle the multitude of factors that impinged on Best Buy's forecasts, Severts found himself becoming ever more pessimistic about the chances of actually transforming the company's approach to projecting revenues. The forecasting process was entwined with a number of key management systems, including budgeting, performance measurement, compensation, and purchasing. Given this, any proposal for a major change would likely be met with stiff resistance, as people had so much vested in the existing process. As an "ad guy," Severts knew that he was poorly positioned to take on the merchant groups, which comprised some of Best Buy's most respected and powerful executives. Severts was also experienced enough to know that big changes to core management systems usually produced unintended consequences—not all of them good.

Severts had given up on finding a simple solution to the forecasting problem when, in late 2004, he happened to sit in on a talk given by James Surowiecki, the *New Yorker* business columnist whose book, *The Wisdom of Crowds*, was climbing the bestseller list. In his presentation to a cross-section of Best Buy leaders, Surowiecki argued that large groups of people "are often smarter than the smartest people in them." When it comes to predicting events that are driven by a multitude of variables, a diverse group of nominally informed individuals often has an advantage over a few "experts."

Severts was intrigued by Surowiecki's logic. It wasn't that Best Buy lacked data—after all, the company tracked everything from hour-by-hour, same-store sales to national consumer confidence. The problem, though, was that any single individual, or any small group of individuals, could only process a tiny fraction of that information. A crowd, however, could take in an almost limitless harvest of data.

In any company, Severts reasoned, there's always a large reservoir of information that can't be easily captured or shared. For example, a Best Buy associate might spot unsold mobile phones piling up in a Memphis warehouse, or a store manager might notice a sudden slowdown in the demand for digital cameras. But those bits of intelligence wouldn't necessarily show up in the statistics that informed top management's decisions. A crowd not only has access to the usual sorts of data, the kind that gets captured in corporate reporting systems, but it can also leverage information that never shows up in a formal report. Nor is a crowd likely to fall prey to the kinds of systematic biases that Severts believed skewed Best Buy's forecasts. That's because most people in a "wise crowd" don't have a big personal stake in the outcome.

As Severts mulled over the "wisdom of crowds" thesis, an idea began to take shape: perhaps there was a way for Best Buy to aggregate the views of many employees in making its forecasts. It wasn't long before Severts was pitching his embryonic scheme to Best Buy's EVP for strategy, Kal Patel, an executive with a reputation for supporting unconventional ideas. Patel urged Severts to develop his plan further, and promised to provide air cover if any were needed. This positive reaction emboldened Severts. Maybe he wasn't thinking big enough. While accurate forecasts were important, he reckoned that Best Buy faced other strategic issues where the wisdom of the masses might have an even bigger payoff.

At the time, Best Buy was embarking on an ambitious plan to tailor each of its stores to the needs of particular customer segments. In support of this new strategy, know internally as "customer centricity," the company had invested millions of dollars in refitting its stores and retraining its staff. Senior executives had also promised Wall Street that this new approach to market segmentation would enhance margins, improve customer loyalty, and fuel organic growth. Yet despite all the hype, Severts sensed that some of his colleagues were unconvinced by the new strategy—they weren't sure that the uplift in margins and revenue would be sufficient to offset the increased investment. Most skeptics, though, seemed unwilling to take a public stand, given the big bet the company was making on customer centricity.

Openly questioning a settled strategy is hardly ever a wise career move, but Severts thought it might be possible to overcome the risks by creating a mechanism that would enable people to voice their opinions anonymously. After all, Severts reasoned, while it's easy to shoot one messenger, it's hard to shoot an entire flock of messengers. Yet when he floated the proposal to some of his colleagues, the prospect of enabling associates to criticize the customer centricity strategy, even anonymously, was so politically poisonous that he failed to find any volunteers to help launch the initiative. It was then that Best Buy's chief marketing officer, Mike Linton, gave Severts a sage bit of advice: if you want to test a new idea, test it first on yourself.

Soon, Severts was casting about for an opportunity to test his hypothesis within his own group. As head of marketing, he was responsible for managing Best Buy's $1 billion gift-card business. In this role, he oversaw a small team that prepared monthly forecasts of gift-card sales. On average, the team's estimates were off by 5 percent, making them more accurate than the merchant forecasts. And unlike the merchants' predictions, the gift-card estimates didn't get rolled up into Best Buy's formal forecast; instead, they went directly to Severts. These factors seemed to make the gift-card forecasting process an ideal candidate for a management experiment. Before proceeding, though, Severts had to convince his gift-card team to back the test. This turned out to be a tough sell. The team was highly doubtful that a bunch of people who knew nothing about the gift-card business could out-forecast the experts.

Eventually, Severts persuaded his colleagues to participate, and on January 21, 2005, he sent out an e-mail to several hundred Best Buy employees, inviting them to submit their guesstimates for Best Buy's gift-card sales for the following month. To help them calibrate their estimates, he provided them with a single trend line: gift-card sales over the previous 12 months. To spur participation, he offered a modest incentive: the individual making the most accurate guess would win a $50 gift card. By January 31, the deadline for making predictions, Severts had received 192 submissions. On March 4, when February's gift-card sales were audited and finalized, he found that, true to form, the team's estimate was off by 5 percent; the crowd's average estimate, on the other hand, was off by less than one-half of 1 percent. In other words, the crowd's forecast was 10 times more accurate than that of the experts. As Severts put it in an e-mail reporting the results: "The crowd wins!"

The gift-card team was rather less ecstatic over the results. Not surprisingly, they regarded the crowd's victory as an affront to their own business acumen, and felt that they had been publicly humiliated. Faced with a snowballing morale problem, Severts realized that his zeal for the experiment had clouded his ability to anticipate the obvious fallout. He dealt with the problem by telling the group what he believed to be true: that while they, as individuals, were better informed than anyone in the throng, the crowd, given its numbers, had a wider range of data and insights upon which to draw. He then promised to conduct additional experiments that would pit large groups against other experts within Best Buy, "so this one result won't hang on our necks alone."

As Severts looked around for a suitable experiment, his mind circled back to Best Buy's forecasting process. While the notion of a customer centricity experiment had been a bit too politically charged, and the gift-card experiment could be written off as an anomaly, Severts felt that a positive outcome in a broader forecasting-focused experiment would be hard for folks to ignore.

Thus in August 2005, Severts sent out a second mass e-mail, inviting colleagues from across Best Buy to estimate the company's sales for the 2005 holiday season, which ran from "Black Friday" (the day after Thanksgiving) to the end of December. Again, he gave people a minimal amount of background data: net revenue for the previous fiscal year's holiday period, and year-over-year revenue growth for the first three months of the current fiscal year. He also doubled the incentive: this time there would be a $100 gift-card award for the person who came closest to the actual number.

In addition, Severts made a noteworthy tweak to the experimental design. There was no reason, he believed, for the crowd's forecast to remain static. People should have the ability to alter their estimates when things changed in the external environment. To this end, Severts set up an Excel spreadsheet on a corporate-access server. The document listed each of the participants (anonymously, via a user ID) and their respective predictions. Severts encouraged each forecaster to submit an initial estimate and then follow up once a week with a revised estimate. Now it would be possible to see how the crowd's expectations changed over the course of the 14-week experiment, a period that encompassed Hurricane Katrina, a big run-up in oil prices, and an end-of-year surge in consumer confidence.

This time around, Severts was under no illusion: the stakes were high. The crowd wasn't competing against a small group within Severts's business unit; it was up against Best Buy's vaunted merchant teams. Put simply, it was the rabble versus the oracles.

In late August, more than 350 people had submitted first-round estimates of holiday sales. On January 6, after a final audit, Severts sent out an e-mail announcing the results: the merchants' August forecast had proved to be 93 percent accurate. The crowd's forecast, on the other hand, which had also been made four months prior to the holiday season, had turned out to be 99.9 percent accurate!

Strangely, though, the accuracy of the crowd's average forecast had deteriorated slightly during the course of the experiment. The crowd's final estimate, just before the sampling was locked down on November 24, proved to be 98 percent accurate. Still, the crowd beat the merchants' late-November forecast, which had been 94 percent accurate. Severts speculated that the crowd had become slightly less accurate over time because the number of people making estimates had dwindled over the three-month span of the experiment. Despite sending out a weekly tickler to the participants asking them to update their estimates, only 60 dedicated prognosticators submitted a forecast in week 6—a number that would hold steady for the final eight weeks of the experiment. As the crowd turned into a clique, some of the diversity required to create an accurate estimate had undoubtedly evaporated. Moreover, roughly 40 percent of the final forecast group comprised people from the merchant and finance units—so the crowd's estimate was partly influenced by the views of Best Buy's official seers. That said, the results were still exceptional.

Overweighting the opinions of "experts" is an orthodoxy that runs deep in most companies, including Best Buy. Even after sharing the results of his first two experiments, Severts recalls that a number of people in Best Buy regarded the crowd's performance as "black magic." But many more understood the blunt implications of the high-profile experiment: here was a new way of making decisions, a methodology that mostly avoided the personal biases and incomplete knowledge that compromised the judgment of a single individual or team.

Best Buy's top management team greeted the results of the two experiments with enough interest that Severts was able to substantially ramp up his management innovation efforts. By the spring of 2006, he had assembled a team of volunteers and had a $50,000 budget to set up an internal system that would support a dynamic stock-trading game around future events and the outcome of key strategic decisions. Many senior executives seemed genuinely excited about the chance to tap into the wisdom of Best Buy's 100,000-plus associates through a carefully structured opinion market.

Unlike Bruce Harreld, Severts started out as a freelancer—he had no one's authority to leverage but his own. Instead of launching a major change program, he designed a couple of low-cost, low-risk management experiments. This example of middle-out management innovation provides would-be management heretics with a few more essential lessons:

Lesson #6: Minimize your political risks.

Mike Linton's advice—stay away from the customer centricity strategy—probably saved Severts from starting a firestorm that would have torched his idea and his career. Likewise, it would have been foolhardy for Severts to start off by impugning the foresight of Best Buy's powerful merchants, particularly since their forecasts heavily influenced their pay. Compensation is the third rail of management innovation. If you're not a C-level executive, or don't call the chairman "dad," you need to think twice before proposing changes to management processes that impact pay. Wisely, Severts started with a small-scale experiment within his own function. The advantages of this low-profile approach were twofold: First, it limited the risk of political fallout; and second, it allowed Severts to refine his design before experimenting with other, more politically sensitive, management processes.

Lesson #7: Start with volunteers.

No one was compelled to participate in Best Buy's forecasting experiments. Rather, Severts used e-mail lists to recruit people who were sympathetic to his idea and eager to be part of the initiative. This was a smart move. Putting together a formal task force, like the one that kicked off IBM's EBO initiative, typically requires a high-level sign-off. To secure this sort of approval, the innovator is often required to justify the experiment in advance—not an easy task when the new management idea challenges cherished privileges and prerogatives. By making it easy for folks to participate, Severts made it hard for anyone to block his experiment. Following this logic, you should design your initial management experiment in a way that minimizes the number of permissions you need to get, while maximizing the chances of learning something new and useful.

Lesson #8: Make it a game. Keep it informal.

This is another strategy for deflecting the objections of the old guard. It's hard to know in advance whether a new management idea will turn out to be a big success or a bust. So it's in your interest to downplay, rather than overplay, the significance of your innovation. Severts set up his first experiment as a lighthearted competition, with a small "door prize" for the winner. This kept the stakes low—not only for Severts, but for his coconspirators as well. Additionally, you want people to view the results objectively—even when they are personally discomforting. By keeping your experiment informal and unofficial—more like a game than a "pilot project"—you minimize the risk that opposition hardens before the results are in, and before the data has the chance to speak for itself.

Lesson #9: Run the new process in parallel with the old.

Severts lacked the power to overhaul the existing forecasting system— and a good thing, too. It's risky to dump an entrenched process in favor of something that's still unformed and untested. Like Bruce Harreld at IBM, Severts didn't start by trying to rip out a time-honored management process. You would do well to follow his lead. Before you tear up the old tracks, lay down some new tracks and run the trains in parallel for a while. Work to accumulate enough learning and support so that the need for change becomes obvious to all, and thereby inevitable.

Lesson #10: Iterate.

Like every smart researcher, Severts looked for a way to validate his initial hypotheses cheaply and quickly before raising the ante. His first experiment cost a scant $50 and absorbed only a couple hours of his time. When this initial test proved promising, Severts doubled up. The second experiment cost him $100 and burned up 40 hours of management time. The third experiment, which involves the development of a robust online opinion market, will soak up $50,000 and take a year or more to play out. While at the outset, Severts might have wished for a big budget and a clear mandate, he now believes that a high-profile launch "would have absolutely been the wrong way to do it."

Let's recap our rules for management innovators:

To solve a systemic problem, you need to understand its systemic roots.

At least initially, it's easier, and safer, to supplement an existing management process than supplant it. (Run the new in parallel with the old.)

Commit to revolutionary goals, but take evolutionary steps.

Be clear about the performance metrics your innovation is designed to improve.

Start by experimenting in your "own back yard," where the political risks are the lowest.

Whenever possible, rely on volunteers.

Diffuse potential objections by keeping your experiments fun and informal.

Iterate: Experiment, learn, experiment, learn.

Don't give up: Innovators are persistent!

Heed these lessons and instead of merely fuming at your company's retrograde management processes, you'll be able to start reinventing them.

Eleven

Forging
Management 2.0

NY MANAGEMENT EXPERIMENT THAT YIELDS A counterintuitive result is valuable. Like a crowbar, it can help you to pry up the floorboards of management ortho-doxy. Yet however indispensable, a single bold advance, like bottom-up forecasting, is unlikely to go far enough given the daunting challenges that lie ahead. What is needed is a top-to-bottom remodeling of modern management's creaking edifice of principles, processes, and practices. When measured against this goal, even the kind of focused effort that produced IBM's EBO process falls short. In the end, isolated initiatives and one-time projects are no substitute for a sustained, companywide campaign of breakthrough management innovation.

Today, I know of no company that has mounted such a crusade. It would seem that many managers have resigned themselves to the sub-optimal trade-offs and organizational incompetencies that are as the inevitable side effects of our early-20th-century management model. Like those afflicted with a lifelong ailment, they can scarcely imagine an existence free from infirmity. Yet as we've seen, it's not only possi-ble to imagine radical departures from the management status quo, it's possible to turn those ideas into profit-producing practices.

Now, with a battalion of new business challenges massing on the horizon, it's time for companies to start taking management innovation as seriously as they take other sorts of innovation. If, as I have argued, we are reaching the limits of management as we know it, then tomorrow's winners will be the companies that forge the future of management. In this effort, the work of every inspired volunteer will be needed, but sooner or later, management innovation has to go mainstream.

From Inspiration to Capability

Unfortunately, there's no well-thumbed manual that will help your company become a serial management innovator. Yet with a little thought, it's possible to sketch out a broad blueprint for making management innovation less of an aberration and more of a systematic capability. Herewith, a few essential building blocks:

The Courage to Lead

You can't build a management advantage unless you have the guts to tackle problems that others are too timid or too shortsighted to take on. When, in 2006, GE's chairman, Jeff Immelt, challenged his colleagues to double the company's organic growth rate to roughly 8 percent per year, he had to tell them that no company of GE's size had ever managed such a feat. There was no "how-to" guide they could reference for advice. Undeterred, Immelt challenged GE's leaders to write their own textbook.

To build a capacity for relentless management innovation, you must be willing to ask, "What new management challenge, if mastered, would give us a unique performance advantage?" Throughout its storied history, GE has often asked itself this question. As a consequence, it has regularly set itself new puzzles to solve: How can we bring management discipline to science? How can we grow outstanding leaders? How can the center add value to a disparate set of businesses? How can we build a boundaryless organization? How can we grow a behemoth? And every time GE has come up with an answer, it has pulled ahead of its competition. Yet no divine authority has appointed GE as the world's management bellwether. And there's no law that says your company has to be a follower. You don't have to be big or revered to be a management pioneer—but you can't be fainthearted. You must be willing to venture off the map.

An Inescapable Conversation

In previous chapters I described the formula for management innovation: commit to a bold goal; deconstruct your orthodoxies; embrace powerful new principles; and learn from the positive deviants. These are the sparks that will set imaginations alight. Your job is to gently fan those embers. The goal: a carefully controlled burn that will ultimately rid your company of deadwood management practices by creating space in which the tender shoots of innovation can take root and grow. How do you get the flame burning brightly? Not by designing some top-down, all-encompassing transformational initiative. You don't need a hydrogen bomb. What you need is a steady breeze that will help the flames of management innovation to spread. You need to get people throughout your company talking about the opportunity to reinvent the technology of management. You need to get them thinking about how they can turn management itself into a competitive advantage. Management innovation must become an inescapable topic—a part of every serious discussion about your company's future.

You might start by asking the participants in this year's planning or budgeting process to nominate a big management challenge that, if successfully addressed, would give your company a performance advantage.

You could invite a cross-section of business leaders to a daylong session focused on surfacing your company's management orthodoxies. (You can use the discussion template laid out in chapter 7.) Work hard to surface the deeply held beliefs that stand in the way of unprecedented performance breakthroughs. Once you've identified five or six toxic orthodoxies, go online and solicit ideas from across the company on what could be done to lay those hoary old beliefs to rest.

Get your colleagues involved in a discussion of new management principles. Identify the institutions or systems that embody the capabilities you're hoping to build in your company. Create a speaker series and invite in experts who can help your peers learn from these exemplars. Whenever you're asked to lead a meeting, take 15 or 20 minutes and get a discussion going around "next-generation" management principles. Ask your colleagues: If we wanted to create a company that was as good at experimentation as life itself, what would we do differently? If we wanted to build a company that was as restlessly innovative as Silicon Valley, how would our management processes need to change? If we wanted to make our work environment as engaging for our employees as Times Square or Covent Garden is for out-of-towners, where would we start? Take every opportunity you can to get your associates thinking more deeply about their managerial DNA and how it may need to change.

There are many ways to get the management innovation conversation started. In one company, a few enterprising activists built a "hospital" in the corporate training center. In each of ten or so beds, they placed an effigy of a once-healthy competitor who was currently struggling for survival. From the end of each gurney hung a "medical" chart outlining the patient's declining financial health and the strategic missteps that had landed it in the ICU. In a nearby "morgue" lay the artfully arranged remains of several industry stalwarts that had succumbed to the forces of change and closed their doors forever. The purpose of this elaborate staging? First, to warn colleagues about the dangerous pathogens of success—like arrogance and denial—that so often cripple even the stoutest of companies; and second, to spur the sort of management innovation that could protect their own company from these dangers. Over the course of several months, more than 3,000 employees toured the ward, as did the company's board of directors. This ingenious bit of theater helped drive home an essential, if often ignored, truth: there is little in the management systems of most companies that prompts proactive strategic renewal. Ultimately, the much-talked-about exhibit spurred a large-scale volunteer effort aimed at reworking the company's core management processes.

Remember: most of your colleagues *want* to work for a company that is forever ahead of the curve, that celebrates creativity in every guise, and elicits human creativity and passion. Problem is, they don't know how to build such a company, captives as they are of a moss-covered management model. If you can help them understand that history is not destiny, and if you can create occasions for them to question their hand-me-down beliefs, then you'll soon have an army of allies ready to help you build a company that's fit for the 21st century.

A Focus on Causes, Not Symptoms

To cure a crippling disease, drug researchers have to uncover the genetic flaws or disease mechanisms that cause the malady. The same is true for organizational "diseases"—the incapacities that stem from our inherited management beliefs. Here, too, a painstaking analysis of first causes is essential to inventing a cure. An illustration, if you will.

Recently, a CEO asked me for advice on how to make his company more resilient. Over the previous few years, he had seen a number of competitors go to the wall when they couldn't break free of a rapidly decaying business model. With the help of a close colleague, I convened a number of cross-company discussion groups and asked each multilevel team to analyze several internal examples of "strategic inertia." Why, I wanted to know, had their company been slow off the mark in exploiting a number of new business opportunities? Why had it failed to respond on a timely basis to several critical market shifts? Why, in several cases, had it continued to invest in an initiative long after it had become obvious that the project was fatally flawed?

Working with each team over the course of several days, we teased out a list of likely culprits, and then hosted a Web-based forum that helped us to expand upon this initial list. Ultimately, the participants in these discussions identified more than 100 "enemies of adaptability," which were then distilled down to a handful of systemic barriers. One impediment was a lack of "genetic diversity" among the senior executive group, most of whom had spent their entire career in one industry. Another barrier was a restrictive tangle of standard operating procedures that made it impossible for first-line associates to proactively respond to changing circumstances. Each impediment encompassed more than a dozen subsidiary causes.

While enhanced adaptability is the sort of problem one *works at* rather than *solves*, this sort of careful, consensus-oriented causal analysis is critical in focusing and sustaining a company's management innovation efforts. Today, there are hundreds of individuals in this company who are deeply aware of the *specific* management challenges that must be surmounted to build a perpetually resilient company. They have a diagnostic readout, like a panel of blood tests, that helps them focus their management innovation efforts.

To ensure that your company's management innovation is sufficiently broad-based, you may want to construct a simple matrix. The first dimension should contain a list of the impediments that handicap your organization's capacity to grow, adapt, or achieve some other performance objective. The second axis should encompass each of your company's key management processes. For each cell you must ask: How does this management process exacerbate this particular disability? Whenever you find a causal link, unpack your innovation tools: What are the orthodoxies that underlie this management process? Could it be reinvented around new, more constructive principles? Can we learn anything from the fringe that might suggest a new approach? This sort of detailed mapping will help to ensure that you're tackling systemic problems systemically, rather than piecemeal.

Accountability

In many companies, the major staff groups, such as HR, finance, and planning, employ hundreds, if not thousands, of people. Yet how many of those folks feel personally responsible for helping their company build a bona fide "management advantage"? In my experience, most are focused on compliance and efficiency issues. Yet if you want to create a capability for fast-paced management innovation, you must hold internal process owners responsible for breakthrough innovation. To this end, the most important question a CEO can ask a functional head is this: What share of your budget and headcount is focused on initiatives that could help our company build a decisive management advantage? The not-so-subtle implication—if you can't figure out a way to turn all this expensive and time-consuming work into a source of competitive advantage, you're going to be outsourced. In the same way that line executives are held accountable for the health of their product pipelines, corporate staffers need to be held accountable for the health of their management innovation pipelines.

One suggestion: have senior staffers meet quarterly to review one another's innovation performance. Questions to consider should include:

- Are we generating a robust flow of new management ideas and experiments? (Remember, innovation is a numbers game—it often takes a lot of experimentation to come up with an idea that will really make a difference.)

- Are we experimenting broadly enough? Are there any innovation "black spots"? Are there management processes, or sub-processes, where there are few if any ongoing experiments? If so, why is this?

- Are our experiments bold enough? Do they represent a significant departure from the management practices of our competitors? Would they surprise the competition?

- Which experiments should we scale up now, which should we abandon, and which need to go through another round or two of development?

- In aggregate, will this portfolio of experiments enhance our company's financial performance? Will it move the needle? If not, how do we amp up our innovation efforts?

The executives who administer your company's key management processes should have at least some of their compensation based on their innovation performance. The message needs to be unmistakable: "We expect you to be just as innovative as the folks who work in R&D and new product development—because your contribution to our competitive advantage is potentially even more important than theirs."

Permission to Hack

Perhaps the most important thing you can do to help your company reinvent its management processes is to give "ordinary" employees and lower-level managers the opportunity to "hack" those processes. No, this doesn't imply letting the janitorial staff tear up the employee handbook. What it does imply is creating a forum in which anyone across the company is free to suggest alternatives to the management status quo. This could be as simple as opening up a threaded conversation around a provocative question, such as: "What management practice or behavior does most to drive really great people out of our company?" Or, "Which of our management practices does the most to destroy employee initiative?" If you're more ambitious, you could post a detailed map of key management processes online—what's the timeline, who gets involved, what data get used, what decision criteria get applied, what are the success metrics for this process, and so on. Then you could ask folks to annotate the process with specific suggestions aimed at making it more conducive to the management advantage you're seeking to build: stop doing this, start doing that, get other folks involved here, change the timing, re-vector the purpose—whatever. Suggestions that attract a lot of support would require a formal response from the process owner. Alternatively, the users who offer the most interesting ideas could be given the chance to get directly involved in reinventing the process. Set up a task force of opinionated "users" and let them design a radically restructured process. Use this as a straw man in debating potential changes. After all, why shouldn't employees have the right to help design the management processes that govern their work lives? Again, what's important here is the overall principle: management innovation is too important to be left to the experts.

Working from the Future Backward

What does the future of management look like to you? This is the question I posed at the beginning of chapter 1. It wasn't rhetorical. In this new century, as in the one before, the most consistently successful companies will be the management pioneers—the companies that write the new rules of management for a new age. To take the lead, your company needs a vision of management's future.

I bet your CEO has a point of view about your company's strategic direction—or enough of one to placate the board and the analysts. But does he or she have a point of view about your company's *management direction*? Is there a consensus in your company around the ways in which the technology of management will need to be reinvented in the years to come? A broad vision is important for several reasons. It helps to legitimize grassroots innovation. It gives that innovation a focal point. And it serves notice to those who would reflexively defend the status quo.

Given that, there are two questions that every business leader in your company should be able to answer. First, what, in broad strokes, will be the new and distinguishing characteristics of our management system five years hence? And second, how will the way in which we manage give us a competitive advantage? Don't expect the answers to these questions to emerge from a two-day executive offsite, or from some corporate-level study group. Instead, the vision should take shape organically as the conversation about the future of management unfolds within your company. You can help this process along, though. Post the foregoing questions on your company's intranet. Use them to kick off staff meetings. Come back to them at the end of every management innovation powwow. And then mine all those conversations for convergent ideas, recurring themes, and shared dreams. Crystallize these into a set of shared beliefs and use that to spur further conversation. Keep doing this, and a consensus view will start to emerge.

Management 2.0

What may help you in this process is a stalking horse, a point of view about the future of management that your colleagues can debate and react to. So far, I've resisted the urge to share my own vision for the future of management. Mostly this is out of modesty. The future of management has yet to be invented, and when it arrives, I expect to be surprised—as astonished, perhaps, as those 19th-century farmers and craftsmen who watched Carnegie, Ford, and Sloan build their imperial and relentlessly methodical empires.

Nevertheless, I believe you can glimpse the future of management in the social revolution that is now gathering pace on the Web. It wasn't by accident that most of the "fringe" examples discussed in chapter 9 were Internet-enabled. After all, the Internet is the most adaptable, innovative, and engaging thing that human beings have ever created. In many ways, the Web *is* the new technology of management. Let me explain.

While the familiar tools and methods of modern management were invented to solve the problems of control and efficiency in large-scale organizations, we can envision management as serving a more general objective: multiplying human accomplishment. In a sense, the goal of management is to first amplify and then aggregate human effort—to get more out of individuals than one might expect by providing them with the appropriate tools, incentives, and working conditions, and to then compound those efforts in ways that allow human beings to achieve together what they can not achieve individually. We can portray these goals on two vectors (see figure 11-1). Companies gain a performance advantage when they invent better ways of amplifying and

FIGURE 11-1

Dimensions of managerial effectiveness

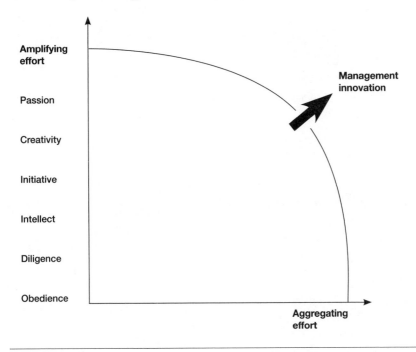

aggregating effort—when they push out the frontier of individual and collective achievement. This is the goal of management innovation.

What does this have to do with the Web? Simple: the Internet amplifies creativity and aggregates effort through pervasive, real-time connectivity (aided, of course, by all the new social technologies that allow people to chat, opine, share, and collaborate online). In chapter 9 I discussed some of the ways in which the Web emancipates human imagination. But the Web is also a tool for aggregating creativity—into things like Linux and *Second Life*, things that have a real economic value, where the whole is more than the sum of the parts.

In the 1990s, Web 1.0 was little more than a giant compendium of static Web pages. In the 21st century, Web 2.0 is being built around new "architectures of participation," such as social networking sites, wikis, and folksonomies. Where old social structures were configured like trees or wheels, with most connections running vertically or to a central hub, the social anatomy of the Net is an "all-channel," "end-to-end" network where everyone is (potentially) connected to everyone else. Here, horizontal processes for control and coordination largely substitute for vertical processes.

For thousands of years, markets and hierarchies were the only alternatives when it came to aggregating human effort. Now there's a third option: real-time, distributed networks. It is telling that the Internet was not created by, nor is it managed by, a hierarchy. Neither will you find many hierarchies among the thousands of novel organizational life forms that have proliferated online. Listen, for example, to how Eric Raymond characterizes the open source community: "[It] is an evolving creative anarchy, in which there are thousands of leaders and tens of thousands of followers linked by a web of peer review and subject to rapid-fire reality tests."[1]

I've been inside a lot of large companies—and this description wouldn't fit any of them. Indeed, even now, many managers find it difficult to understand how such an "organization" can produce one of the world's most complicated products—a computer operating system. Like a first-time visitor to Italy, they can scarcely believe that something so chaotic actually works. But that's the point. The power of the Internet lies in its capacity to facilitate coordination without the stultifying effects of hierarchy and bureaucracy.

The Web has evolved faster than anything human beings have ever created—largely, because it is *not* a hierarchy. The Web is all periphery and no center. In that sense, it is a direct affront to the organizational model that has predominated since the beginnings of human history. No wonder managers feel a little queasy when they venture into the far reaches of cyberspace, like space travelers who've arrived on a planet where up is down and left is right. It is a bit disorienting to realize that, as David Weinberger puts it, "Our biggest joint undertaking as a species [the Internet] is working out splendidly, but only because we forgot to apply the theory that has guided us ever since the pyramids were built."[2]

The Web is a near-ideal medium in which to culture new strains of social organization. From Craigslist to MySpace to FaceBook to *Second Life* to eHarmony, from instant messaging to podcasting, blogging, video chat, and virtual worlds, the Internet is radically changing the ways in which people find romance, manage friendships, share insights, learn, build communities, and more. For the moment, though, most of this joyous and frenzied experimentation is taking place outside the plush-carpeted hallways of the corporate old guard.

I find this ironic. While no company would put up with a 1940s-era phone system, or forgo the efficiency-enhancing benefits of modern IT, that's exactly what companies are doing when they fail to exploit the Web's potential to transform the way the work of management is accomplished. Most managers still see the Internet as a productivity tool, or as a way of delivering 24/7 customer service. Some understand its power to upend old business models. But few have faced up to the fact that sooner or later, the Web is going to turn our smoke-stack management model on its head.

Why, exactly, is the Internet so adaptable, innovative, and engaging? Because . . .

Everyone has a voice.

The tools of creativity are widely distributed.

It's easy and cheap to experiment.

Capability counts for more than credentials and titles.

Commitment is voluntary.

Power is granted from below.

Authority is fluid and contingent on value-added.

The only hierarchies are "natural" hierarchies.

Communities are self-defining. Individuals are richly empowered with information.

Just about everything is decentralized.

Ideas compete on an equal footing.

It's easy for buyers and sellers to find each other.

Resources are free to follow opportunities.

Decisions are peer-based.

This may not be a detailed design spec for a 21st-century management system, but I doubt it's far off. Argue with me if you like, but I'm willing to bet that *Management 2.0* is going to look a lot like *Web 2.0*.

Most of us grew up in a "post-industrial" society. We are now on the verge of a "post-managerial" society, perhaps even a "post-organizational" society. Before you object, let me assure you that this doesn't imply a future without managers. Just as the coming of the knowledge economy didn't wipe out heavy industry, so the dawning of a post-managerial economy won't produce a world free of executives and administrators. Yet it does herald a future in which the work of managing will be less and less performed by "managers." To be sure, activities will still need to be coordinated, individual efforts aligned, objectives decided upon, knowledge disseminated, and resources allocated, but increasingly, this work will be distributed out to the periphery.

While Management 2.0 won't completely supplant Management 1.0, the two versions aren't entirely compatible. There are going to be conflicts. Indeed, I think the most bruising contests in the new millennium won't be fought along the lines that separate one competitor or business ecosystem from another, but will be fought along the lines that separate those who wish to preserve the privileges and power of the bureaucratic class from those who hope to build less structured and less tightly managed organizations. Richard Florida sees the same battle shaping up. In *The Rise of the Creative Class*, he puts it bluntly: "The biggest issue at stake in this emerging age is the ongoing tension between creativity and organization."[3] This is, perhaps the most critical and intractable management trade-off of all, and therefore, the one most worthy of inspired innovation.

It will take more than advances in technology to issue in the post-managerial age. As I noted earlier, management and organizational innovation often lags far behind technological innovation. Right now, your company has 21st-century, Internet-enabled business processes, mid-20th-century management processes, all built atop 19th-century management principles. Without a transformation in our management DNA—in line with principles I outlined in chapter 8—the power of the Web to transform the work of management will go unexploited.

Fit for the Future

That's enough prognostication. My goal in writing this book was not to predict the future of management, but to help you invent it. At every turn, I've argued that the technology of management *must* be reinvented, and *will* be reinvented. The only question is: *Who's* going to do the reinventing? By now you should understand that the payoff goes far beyond beating your competitors, or guaranteeing yourself a footnote in the annals of management history. There is a deeper, nobler reason to take on the challenge of management innovation—and an historic opportunity. For the first time since the dawning of the industrial age, the only way to build a company that's fit for the future is to build one that's fit for human beings as well. *This* is your opportunity—to build a 21st century management model that truly elicits, honors, and cherishes human initiative, creativity, and passion—these tender, essential ingredients for business success in this new millennium. Do that, and you will have built an organization that is fully human and fully prepared for the extraordinary opportunities that lie ahead.

Notes

Chapter 1

1. Stuart Kauffman, *At Home In the Universe: The Search for Laws of Self-Organization and Complexity* (New York: Oxford University Press, 1995), 149–190.

2. L. G. Thomas and Richard D'Aveni, "The Rise of Hypercompetition from 1950 to 2002: Evidence of Increasing Structural Destabilization and Temporary Competitive Advantage," 2004, unpublished manuscript.

3. Thomas S. Kuhn, *The Structure of Scientific Revolutions*, 3rd ed. (Chicago: University of Chicago Press, 1996), 7.

4. Frederick W. Taylor, *Shop Management* (New York: Harper and Row, 1903), 3.

5. Frederick W. Taylor, *The Principles of Scientific Management* (New York: Harper and Row, 1911), 7.

6. Ibid.

7. Max Weber, *The Theory of Social and Economic Organization*, ed. and trans. A. M. Henderson and Talcott Parsons (New York: Free Press, 1947), 337.

8. Summarized in Daniel A. *Wren, The History of Management Thought*, 5th ed. (Hoboken, NJ: Wiley, 2005), 228.

9. Hearings before Special Committee of the House of Representatives to Investigate the Taylor and Other Systems of Shop Management under Authority of House Resolution 90 (Washington, DC: U.S. Government Printing Office, 1912), 1387.

Chapter 2

1. Henri Fayol, *Industrial and General Administration*, trans. J. A. Coubrough (Geneva: International Management Institute, 1930).

2. This figure does not include the brands that Procter & Gamble acquired in its 2005 acquisition of Gillette.

3. Dominic O'Connell, "Do Not Disturb: Mr. Watanabe Is Taking Over the World," *Car*, June 2006.

4. MacGregor Knox and Williamson Murray (eds.), *The Dynamics of Military Revolution, 1300–2050* (Cambridge: Cambridge University Press, 2001).

5. Ibid., 175–194.

6. Ibid., 54.

7. Ibid., 55.

8. Carl von Clausewitz, *On War*, eds. and trans. Michael Howard and Peter Paret (Princeton, NJ: Princeton University Press, 1976), 529.

9. Knox and Murray, *The Dynamics of Military Revolution*, 71–72.

10. Reconstructed from the author's handwritten notes.

11. For more on how Whirlpool built its innovation engine, see Jan W. Rivkin, Dorothy Leonard, and Gary Hamel, "Change at Whirlpool Corporation (A), (B), and (C)," Harvard Business School, Case nos. 9-705-462, 9-705-463, and 9-705-464, April 9, 2005.

12. Michael Arndt, "Creativity Overflowing," *BusinessWeek*, May 8, 2006.

13. On this point, see Nicholas Carr, *Does IT Matter?* (Boston: Harvard Business School Press, 2004).

Chapter 3

1. Peter Medawar, *Advice to a Young Scientist* (New York: Harper & Row, 1979), 13.

2. Frederick Winslow Taylor, *The Principles of Scientific Management* (New York: Harper and Row, 1911).

3. You may want to start with: Danny Miller, *The Icarus Paradox: How Exceptional Companies Bring About Their Own Downfall* (New York: HarperCollins, 1990); Clayton M. Christensen, *The Innovator's Dilemma: When New Technologies Cause Great Firms to Fail* (Boston: Harvard Business School Press, 1997); and Donald N. Sull, *Revival of the Fittest: Why Good Companies Go Bad and How Great Managers Remake Them* (Boston: Harvard Business School Press, 2003).

4. Some of the material in this section is drawn from: Gary Hamel and Liisa Välikangas, "The Quest for Resilience," *Harvard Business Review*, September 2003.

5. Larry Rother, "An Unlikely Trendsetter Made Earphones a Way of Life," *New York Times*, December 17, 2005.

6. Pekka Himanen, *The Hacker Ethic and the Spirit of the Information Age* (New York: Random House, 2001).

7. Towers Perrin, *Winning Strategies for a Global Workplace: Executive Report*, 2006.

8. Ibid., 11.

Chapter 4

1. Portions of this chapter are based on material that first appeared in the following publications: Julia Boorstin, "No Perservatives, No Unions, Lots of Dough," *Fortune*, September 15, 2003, http://money.cnn.com/magazines/fortune/fortune_archive /2003/09/15/toc.html; Charles Fishman, "Whole Foods Is All Teams," *Fast Company*, April/May 1996, http://www.fastcompany.com/magazine/02/team1.html; Charles Fishman, "The Anarchist's Cookbook," *Fast Company*, July 2004, http://www.fastcom pany.com/magazine/84/wholefoods.html; Daniel McGinn, "The Green Machine," *Newsweek*, March 21, 2005, http://www.msnbc.msn.com/id/7130106/site/newsweek/;

and Marianne Wilson, "Retail as Theater, Naturally," *Chain Store Age*, May 2005, http://www.chainstoreage.com/archives/preview.

2. Boorstin, "No Preservatives, No Unions, Lots of Dough."

3. Fishman, "Whole Foods Is All Teams."

4. Ibid.

5. Data quoted by John Mackey in his online blog. http://www.wholefoods.com /blogs/jm/archives/2006/11/conscious_capit.html.

6. Boorstin, "No Preservatives, No Unions, Lots of Dough."

7. John Mackey, "Rethinking the Social Responsibility of Business," http:// www.wholefoods.com/blogs/jm/archives/2005/09/.

8. Fishman, "The Anarchist's Cookbook."

9. S. C. Gwynne, "Thriving on Health Food," *Time*, February 23, 1998, p. 53, http://www.time.com/time/magazine/article/0,9171,987856,00.html.

10. Fishman, "The Anarchist's Cookbook."

Chapter 5

1. Portions of this chapter are based on material that first appeared in the following publications: Michael Kaplan, "You Have No Boss," *Fast Company*, October/ November 1997, http://www.fastcompany.com/magazine/11/noboss.html; Dawn Anfuso, "Core Values Shape WL Gore's Innovation Culture," *Workforce*, March 1999; Alan Deutschman, "The Fabric of Creativity," *Fast Company*, December 2004, http:// www.fastcompany.com/magazine/89/open_gore.html; Ann Harrington, "Who's Afraid of a New Product?," *Fortune*, November 10, 2003, http://money.cnn.com/magazines /fortune/fortune_archive/2003/11/10/352851/index.htm.

2. Douglas McGregor, *The Human Side of Enterprise* (New York: McGraw-Hill, 1960).

3. This and subsequent quotations from Bill Gore are drawn from his unpublished paper, "The Lattice Organization—A Philosophy of Enterprise."

4. Unless noted otherwise, this comment and all others attributed to Gore employees are drawn from interviews conducted by the author.

5. Kaplan, "You Have No Boss."

6. Herrington, "Who's Afraid of a New Product?"

7. Dawn Anfuso, "1999 Innovation Optima Award Profile: W.L. Gore and Associates," http://www.workforce.com/archive/feature/22/17/46/index.php?ht=dawn%20an fuso%20gore%20dawn%20anfuso%20gore.

Chapter 6

1. Portions of this chapter are based on material that first appeared in the following publications: John Battelle, *The Search: How Google and Its Rivals Rewrote the Rules of Business and Transformed Our Culture* (New York: Portfolio, 2005); Alan Deutschman, "Can Google Stay Google?," *Fast Company*, August 2005, http://www.fastcompany .com/magazine/97/open_google.html; Ben Elgin, "Managing Google's Idea Factory,"

BusinessWeek, October 3, 2005, http://www.businessweek.com/magazine/content/05_40/b3953093.htm; Ben Elgin, "So Much Fanfare, So Few Hits," *BusinessWeek*, July 10, 2006, http://www.businessweek.com/magazine/content/06_28/b3992051.htm; Keith H. Hammonds, "How Google Grows and Grows and Grows," *Fast Company*, April 2003, http://www.fastcompany.com/magazine/69/google.html; Steve Levy, "Living By Google Rules, *Newsweek*, April 11, 2005, http://www.msnbc.msn.com/id/7369181/site/newsweek; Eric Schmidt and Hal Varian, "Google: Ten Gold Rules," *Newsweek*, November 28, 2005, http://www.msnbc.msn.com/id/10296177/site/newsweek.

2. http://www.hitwise.com/datacenter/searchengineanalysis.php.

3. Ben Elgin, "So Much Fanfare, So Few Hits," http://www.businessweek.com /magazine/content/06_28/b3992051.htm?chan=search.

4. Unless noted otherwise, this comment and all others attributed to Google personnel are drawn from interviews conducted by the author.

5. Alan Deutschman, "Can Google Stay Google?"

Chapter 7

1. Barry Marshall, ed., *Helicobacter Pioneers* (Carlton South, Victoria, Australia: Blackwell Science Asia, 2002), 151–202.

2. Quoted in Madeline Drexler, "A Nobel Prize for Ingenuity," *International Herald Tribune*, October 8–9, 2005.

3. John Lynne, "Forging the Western Army in Seventeenth Century France," in *The Dynamics of Military Revolution, 1300–2050*, ed. MacGregor Knox and Williamson Murray (Cambridge: Cambridge University Press, 2001), 36–40.

4. Roy Jacques, *Manufacturing the Employee* (London: Sage, 1966), 40.

5. Ibid., 25.

6. Personal interview with the author.

7. Jacques, 166.

8. Ricardo Semler, *The Seven-Day Weekend* (New York: Portfolio, 2003), 8.

9. Ibid., 40.

10. Brad Wieners, "Ricardo Semler: Set Them Free," *CIO Insight*, April, 2004. http://www.cioinsight.com/article2/0,1540,1569009,00.asp.

11. Semler, *The Seven-Day Weekend*, 40.

12. Ibid., 9.

Chapter 8

1. Austin Bunn, "Welcome to Planet Pixar," *Wired*, June 2004; http://www .wired.com/archive/12.06/pixar.html.

2. Wang Zhuoqiong, "Tuskless Elephants Evolving Thanks to Poaching," *China Daily*, July 16, 2005. http://www2.chinadaily.com/english/doc/2005-07/16/content_400623.html.

3. In recent years, many writers have drawn parallels between biology and business. I believe they have often got the analogy wrong. In the conventional view, busi-

nesses are regarded as living organisms competing within a larger ecosystem, such as the U.S. economy. The problem, though, is that organisms don't adapt—populations adapt. Organisms are simply the means through which genes propagate themselves over time. By this logic, companies are incapable of evolving. Thus today's corporate dinosaurs will soon be replaced by tomorrow's homo sapiens. It's a mistake, though, to view a large company, such as IBM, Nokia, or Canon, as a single organism. These companies are ecosystems, diverse habitats, if you will. They encompass tens of thousands of employees, thousands of products and services, hundreds of vendors and business partners, dozens of investment projects, and a handful or more of independent business units. Rather than viewing IBM as a humpback whale, it is more appropriate to regard it as the Great Barrier Reef, home to 2,000 species of fish, 4,000 species of mollusks, and 350 types of coral. By this logic, Nokia isn't a single hibiscus plant, it's Maui. Canon isn't a solitary frigatebird, it's the Galapagos Islands. If large companies often appear to behave like unitary, nonadaptable organisms, it's only because managers have failed to nurture and exploit the potential for variety that exists inside every large organization.

4. Steve Jurvetson, personal interview with the author.

5. James Surowiecki, *The Wisdom of Crowds* (New York: Doubleday, 2004).

6. PricewaterhouseCoopers/National Venture Capital Association, *Money Tree Report*. http://www.pwcmoneytree.com/displays/notice-B.html.

7. Jennifer Egan, "Love in the Time of No Time," *New York Times*, November 23, 2003, Section 6.

8. It might be argued that this discount is justified by the fact that investing in the tried and true is usually a safer bet than pumping money into the new and untested. But this argument wrongly equates "newness" with "riskiness." Risk is a function of uncertainty, multiplied by the size of one's financial exposure. Newness is a function of the extent to which an idea defies precedent and convention. Novelty implies nothing about risk. The Starbucks debit card, which allows regular customers to purchase their daily fix of caffeine without fumbling through their pockets for the necessary cash, was undoubtedly an innovation for the quick-serve restaurant industry. Yet it's not at all clear that it was risky. The card provides a solid customer benefit and relies on well-proven technology. Indeed, the card was an immediate hit. Within 30 days of the card's launch, convenience-minded customers had provided Starbucks with a $32 million cash float. A persistent failure to distinguish between new ideas and risky ideas reinforces the tendency to overinvest in the past.

9. Monty G. Marshall and Keith Jaggers, *Polity IV Country Reports 2003* (College Park, MD: The Center for International Development and Conflict Management, and the Integrated Network for Societal Conflict Research, University of Maryland, 2005), http://www.cidcm.umd.edu/inscr/polity/report.html.

10. Morton H. Halperin, Joseph T. Siegle, and Michael H. Weinstein, *The Democracy Advantage: How Democracies Promote Prosperity and Peace*, New York: Routledge, 2005.

11. Joseph T. Siegle, Michael T. Weinstein, and Morton H. Halperin, "Why Democracies Excel," *Foreign Affair* 83, no. 5 (September–October 2004): 60, 62.

12. Michael Weinstein, in remarks made to the Carnegie Council's "Authors in the Afternoon" series, New York, March 17, 2005. http://www.cceia.org/resources/tran scripts/5129.html.

13. Francis Fukuyama, personal conversation, April 4, 2006.

14. Maria Bartiromo, "Bob Nardelli Explains Himself," *BusinessWeek Online*, July 24, 2006. http://www.businessweek.com/@@CIPxGmcQhG1l5wEA/premium/content /06_30/b3994094.htm?chan=search.

15. Rodney Stark and Roger Finke, *Acts of Faith: Explaining the Human Side of Religion* (Berkeley, CA: University of California Press, 2000), 91–92.

16. See, for example, Christopher G. Ellison, "Religious Involvement and Subjective Well-Being," *Journal for the Scientific Study of Religion* 34:1 (March 1991): 80–99; and, Christopher G. Ellison, "Religion, the Life Stress Paradigm, and the Study of Depression," in *Religion in Aging and Health: Theoretical Foundations and Methodological Frontiers*, ed. Jeffrey S. Levin (Newbury Park, CA: Sage, 1993), 78–121.

17. Bill George, *Authentic Leadership: Rediscovering the Secrets to Creating Lasting Value* (San Francisco: Jossey-Bass, 2003), 66.

18. Ibid., p. 68.

19. Richard Florida, *The Rise of the Creative Class* (New York: Basic Books, 2004), 235–248.

20. Jane Jacobs, *The Death and Life of Great American Cities* (1961; rpt. New York: Vintage Books, 1992), 143–238.

21. Florida, p. 262.

22. David Rocks and Moon Ihlwan, "Samsung Rocks," *BusinessWeek*, December 6, 2004, p. 88.

23. Jacobs, *The Death and Life of Great American Cities*, 448.

24. Ibid., 150–151.

25. Ibid., 188.

26. Robert Park, E. Burgess, and R. McKenzie, *The City* (Chicago: University of Chicago Press, 1925), 41.

Chapter 9

1. Mary Parker Follett, *Creative Experience* (London: Longmans, Green, 1924).

2. Jon Ashworth, "Executives Admit 24% of Decisions Are Wrong," *The Times* (London), August 16, 2004.

3. Michael L. A. Hayward and Donald C. Hambrick, "Explaining the Premiums Paid for Large Acquisitions: Evidence of CEO Hubris," *Administrative Science Quarterly* 42, no. 1 (March 1997): 103–127. The researchers used three factors as proxies for CEO hubris: the degree to which the company had recently outperformed its peers, the amount of media praise that had been recently lavished on the CEO, and the gap between the CEO's salary and that of his or her most highly compensated colleagues. On average, as the hubris index went up, so did the premium CEOs were willing to pay to clinch a deal. And the higher the premium paid, the bigger the decline in the acquirer's share price over the falling year.

4. Steven Weber, *The Success of Open Source* (Cambridge, MA: Harvard University Press, 2004), 91.

5. Ibid., 121. The Valloppillil memo is available in its entirety at http://www.catb.org/~esr/halloween/halloween4.html.

6. Michale Fitzgerald, "How I Did It: Philip Rosedale, CEO, Linden Lab," *Inc. Magazine*, February 2007, http://www.inc.com/magazine/20070201/hidi-rosedale.html.

Chapter 10

1. For more on how General Electric is reorienting its management processes around the challenge of growth, see: Christopher A. Bartlett, "GE's Growth Strategy: The Immelt Initiative," Harvard Business School Case No. 9-206-087, November 3, 2006; and Thomas A. Stewart, "Growth as Process: An Interview with Jeffrey R. Immelt," *Harvard Business Review*, June 2006.

2. To learn more about P&G's open innovation process, see: Larry Huston, "Connect and Develop: Inside Procter and Gamble's New Model for Innovation, *Harvard Business Review*, March 2006.

3. A detailed account of Whirlpool's management innovations can be found in: Jan W. Rivkin, Dorothy Leonard, and Gary Hamel, "Change at Whirlpool (A), (B), (C)," Harvard Business School Case nos. 9-705-462, 9-705-463, and 9-705-464, April 9, 2005.

4. Portions of the section on IBM are based on material that first appeared in the following articles: Alan Deutschman, "Building a Better Skunk Works," *Fast Company*, March 2005; David A. Garvin and Lynne C. Levesque, "Emerging Business Opportunities at IBM (A), (B), and (C)," Harvard Business School, Case Nos. 9-304-075, 9-304-076, and 9-304-077, February 28, 2005; and David A. Garvin, "Emerging Business Opportunities at IBM (A), (B), (C)," Harvard Business School Teaching Note no. 5-305-023.

5. Unless noted otherwise, this comment and all others attributed to IBM personnel are drawn from interviews conducted by the author.

6. Unless noted otherwise, this comment and all others attributed to Best Buy personnel are drawn from interviews conducted by the author.

Chapter 11

1. See http://www.catb.org/~esr/halloween/halloween1.html.

2. David Weinberger, *Small Pieces Loosely Joined* (New York: Basic Books, 2002), 82.

3. Richard Florida, *The Rise of the Creative Class* (New York: Basic Books, 2004), 22.

Index

About the Authors

Gary Hamel is Visiting Professor of Strategic and International Management at the London Business School, where he has been on the faculty since 1983. He is cofounder of the Management Innovation Lab, a consortium of leading business thinkers and progressive companies working together to invent the future of management.

Hamel is one of the world's most renowned management experts. He has been hailed as "the world's reigning strategy guru," by *The Economist* and as "the world's leading expert on business strategy" by *Fortune* magazine. The *Financial Times* calls Hamel "a management innovator without peer."

As the originator of such well-known concepts as "strategic intent," "core competence," and "industry revolution," Hamel has changed the language and practice of management around the world.

Hamel's previous books, *Leading the Revolution* and *Competing for the Future*, have appeared on every management bestseller list and have been translated into more than twenty languages. Over the past twenty years, Hamel has authored fifteen articles for the *Harvard Business Review*, five of which have won the prestigious McKinsey prize for excellence. He has also written for the *Wall Street Journal*, *Fortune*, the *Financial Times*, and many other business publications around the world.

As one of the world's most sought-after corporate advisers and speakers, Hamel has worked with leading companies across the globe. He is a fellow of the World Economic Forum. Hamel can be contacted at gh@managementlab.org

Bill Breen is the founding senior editor and senior projects editor of *Fast Company*. Since its launch in November 1995, the magazine has won numerous awards (including two National Magazine Awards) and gained an avid following among business leaders and innovators. Breen contributes articles that dig into the magazine's core themes: leadership, strategy, innovation, and design. He speaks to business audiences throughout the country and has appeared on CNN, Fox, CBS, and National Public Radio. A graduate of Colorado College, Breen has an MA from University College Dublin. He lives with his wife, daughter, and son in Gloucester, Massachusetts.